burda

SEWING
MADE EASY

© 1990 by Verlag Aenne Burda GmbH & Co.
D-7600 Offenburg, West Germany

Editors: Liselotte Dürrschnabel (responsible),
Ulrike Eberlein, Hildegard Ühlin, Ingrid Vollmer.
Foreign Language Issues Editor: Ina Rajapaksha
Translation: Elke Hübner, Ilse Kopmann
Art Direction: Claus Will, Klaus Löffel (foreign language)
Cover design: Wolfgang Dichtel
Printing: Burda GmbH, D-7600 Offenburg,
West Germany
ISBN 3-88978-037-7

burda

SEWING
MADE EASY

At last! The comprehensive sewing book featuring the burda illustrated teaching system for successful sewing.

30 easy-sew styles with detailed instructions and patterns guaranteed to fit printed on 3 trace-off pattern sheets and 2 fold-out pattern sheets.

This interesting teaching manual includes a collection of chic styles selected from burda's special issues "Sewing made easy," with educational, illustrated instructions as well as excerpts from the burda sewing books "Sewing made easy" and "Perfect Homesewing."

Dear dressmaker-to-be! We should like to introduce to you burda's illustrated teaching system. This is a unique step-by-step approach towards the art of dressmaking. Unique because we've put all our experience in designing patterns and dressmaking into it. Even if you have hardly any dressmaking knowledge you'll be successful right from the start.

If you haven't ever sewn at all, a sauna towel or a facecloth will be a good starter project. It will make you familiar with your sewing machine. Our first four dressmaking projects – training projects, so to speak – will teach you all the details about how to cut out and sew a garment form a paper pattern. The very first one is a bathrobe. You'll find the pattern pieces on the enclosed fold-out pattern sheet. This is supposed to give you an eye for the individual pieces of a dressmaking pattern. With the second style, a polo shirt, you'll learn how to trace pattern pieces from the pattern sheet. Choose a woven fabric for your first shirt. And if the tab

fastening will not look perfect the first time, don't worry … and hide it under a leather triangle stitched in place at the end of the opening. Remember that practice makes perfect.

The sweaterknit versions of the style won't give you problems of this kind: they are simple, slip-on shirts. With such a training you'll master the next two practice projects without any difficulty. At this stage you're fit enough to tackle the "regular" styles and try your skill at some more sophisticated details.

Moreover, we give you lots of sewing know-how about adapting patterns, cutting out, trying on, calculating fabric amounts for pleated skirts, and so on.

Want to sew more garments with burda's teaching system? Our dressmaking magazine "Sewing made easy" comes out quarterly, bringing you the fashion trends of the season.

We wish you a good start as a home dressmaker and lots of sewing success!

The Editors

Table of contents

Contents at a glance

The dashing, double-breasted coatdress is the prototype of the New Classics. See page 46

See page 46

OUR COVERPAGE STYLE

THE FOLD-OUT PATTERN

Ideal for beginners and for pros in a hurry - a bathrobe for ladies, gents and children. See page 12

Our practice projects for an easy launch into homesewing. See page 13

Machine-stitched cutwork graces the neckline and sleeves of a simple, kimono-sleeved dress. Illustrated instructions show how it's done. See pages 42-44

Chic summer ensemble. Rippling, pleated hem tiers lend the figure-hugging sunback dress charming softness. We recommend adding a super simple, short-sleeved jacket for perfection. See page 38

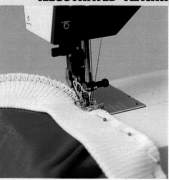

ILLUSTRATED TEACHING SYSTEM

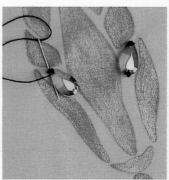

Petticoat dress, 50's style. See page 30

Everything you need to know about knit fabrics is located on pages 120/121

Appliquéing made easy with a fusing agent. See page 21

Snakeproof a t-shirt with textile paints. See page 73

6

The new blazer: long, fitted, elegant. See page 67

Quick and easy to sew: colorfully printed flared skirt. See page 60

Quite up-to-date: waist-length, wrapped blouse teamed with slim pants. See page 71

Sporty, elegant outfit. See page 59

Polo shirts, great partners for skirts. See page 53

Long, collarless jacket. See page 65

Batwing sleeved dress with elegant, ribbon trim. See page 50

LOVELY HOME DECORATIONS

You can easily create your own home decorations. Illustrated instructions show you how to make bedspreads and draperies, how to refurbish an old chair or an old lamp, how to make a spacesaving bag holder. See pages 136 to 140

For instructions on how to make a fabric-covered cosmetic tissue box see page 140

This heart-shaped mirror with its velvet and ruffled trim would make a lovely gift. See page 140 for instructions

7

Beginning projects

It is important that your very first sewing project be a success. Therefore, begin with something super simple like a sauna towel and mitt facecloth, for example, instructions for which are shown on page 11. Once you've become familiar with your sewing machine we recommend that you tackle a bathrobe as your first garment. The pattern is very simple and clearly arranged on both of the fold-out pattern sheets. See pages 12 - 15 for details. After finishing the bathrobe you are ready to have a go at the other practice projects in this book as well as the styles shown in the fashion section.

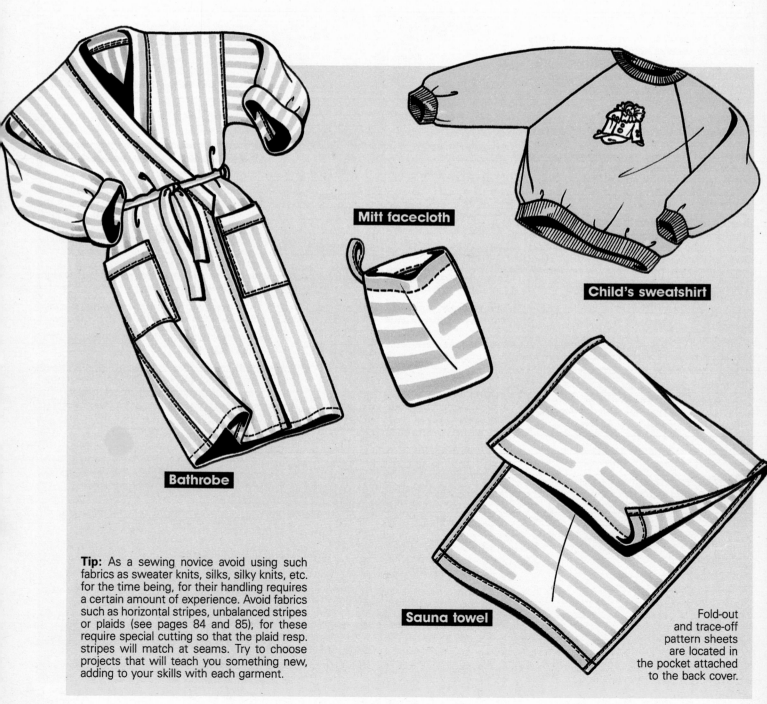

Mitt facecloth

Child's sweatshirt

Bathrobe

Sauna towel

Tip: As a sewing novice avoid using such fabrics as sweater knits, silks, silky knits, etc. for the time being, for their handling requires a certain amount of experience. Avoid fabrics such as horizontal stripes, unbalanced stripes or plaids (see pages 84 and 85), for these require special cutting so that the plaid resp. stripes will match at seams. Try to choose projects that will teach you something new, adding to your skills with each garment.

Fold-out and trace-off pattern sheets are located in the pocket attached to the back cover.

SEW A SAUNA TOWEL IN A FLASH

It is 80 cm (32") wide and 160 cm (63") long - see bottom ill. Both lengthwise edges are bound with bias tape, the ends, actually the selvages, are hemmed.

You will need:

0.80 m (⅞ yd) of 160 cm (63") wide terrycloth, either vertically striped as shown here, in a solid color or a bright print. As you like it. For binding edges you will need 3.20 m (3½ yds) of 3 cm (1¼") wide purchased bias tape, or pre-folded bias tape, usually 2 cm (⅞") wide.

Tip: Terrycloth for such a towel can often be purchased at a tremendous saving at remnant sales or shops.

Cutting out

Make sure that the long edges are exactly on the cross grain, or as close as possible. Pull a thread from selvage to selvage to determine exact cross grain and trim along this thread. These edges should be at an exact right angle to the selvages.

Tip: If you are purchasing your terrycloth from the bolt, i.e. NOT a remnant, then ask the sales person to cut exactly on the cross grain so that you won't have to fool around with it later on!

selvage
← 80 cm →
160 cm
lengthwise edge
selvage
(end)

Bind edges with flat bias tape …

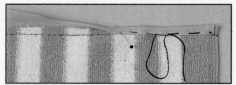

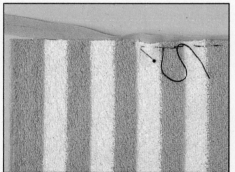

1 Stitch bias tape onto the **wrong** side of long edges with ¾ cm (⅜") seam allowance. Fold tape over its allowance and edge to the **right** side of towel, turn under its open edge, baste and stitch into place just outside (covering) the first stitching line.

… or with pre-folded tape

2 Pin the slightly wider half of pre-folded tape onto the **wrong** side of long edges so that edge lies in fold of tape. Baste tape into place.

… stitching from the right side

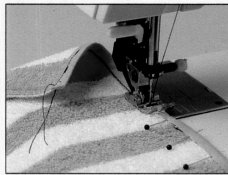

3 Fold slightly narrower half of tape over onto the **right** side of edge, pin into place. Edgestitch this half of tape into place, securing other half at the same time.

Hem ends last

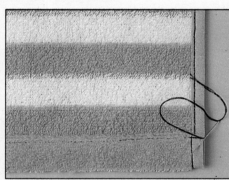

4 Press ends of towel 3 cm (1¼") to the **inside,** turn under selvage, machine stitch into place. Hand sew ends of hem allowances into place, making stitches as inconspicuous as possible.

MITT FACECLOTH

Simply pin and stitch - no basting necessary

Surely you have a terrycloth remnant about 25 cm (10") long and 30 cm (12") wide. For the hanger loop you'll need a 15 cm (6") piece of bias tape. Construction is quite simple. Before you begin sewing trim all edges exactly on the lengthwise resp. crosswise grain. The open end will be hemmed, the remaining open edges stitched together. The photos to the right will show you how it works.

Seam allowances are included in the dimensions stated.

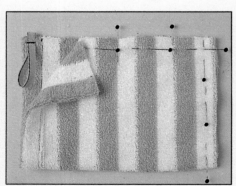

1 Press one of the 30 cm (12") long edges 3 cm (1¼") to the **inside,** turn under raw edge, pin and stitch into place. Press both long edges of bias tape toward the center. Then fold tape in half lengthwise, edges on the **inside,** press. Stitch along both long edges of tape.

2 Fold tape into a loop. Stitch loop onto the **right** side of hemmed edge at one corner as shown. Fold cloth in half, **right** sides together, so that hemmed edge is at one end. Stitch other end and open long edges closed with 1 cm (½") seam allowance. Overcast seam allowances together.

Our practice projects

We recommend that you sew up a striped bathrobe as your first practice project, for which we have put together detailed, illustrated instructions on pages 14 and 15. We demonstrate how to cut out easily and economically from balanced vertically striped fabric. By the way, you could make up chic housecoats in seersucker, piqué or cotton broadcloth from these patterns.

Tip: Tape pattern pieces together, edge-to-edge, and try on BEFORE cutting out fabric to check final length as well as pocket position. Mark any necessary corrections on pattern pieces. If you do this you can sew up the bathrobe without having to try it on for fitting.

1
34–40
42–44
46–48

1
44–46
48–50
52–54

1
104, 116, 128
140, 152

These sizes correspond:

Misses'		Men's
34-40	◄–►	44-46
42-44	◄–►	48-50
46-48	◄–►	52-54

Practice Project No. 2 was conceived to gently guide you into working with the pattern sheets that our publications are famous for as well as to familiarize you with our sewing instructions. Test-sew the polo closing with remnants of woven fabric. Once you've gotten the hang of it, tackle the knit fabric version. The sweatshirts are cut out from the same pattern pieces. By the time you complete both pant versions and the mini-skirt you'll be close to professional!

2, 3, 4
104, 116
128, 140

1 The ladies', gents' and children's bathrobes are all made the same way. There are length differences amongst the children's sizes, the bathrobes for the little ones (sizes 104 and 116) being ankle length and those for sizes 128, 140 and 152 being calf length, like the adult styles.

2 A shirt for boys and girls in three variations. View A is a polo shirt in printed cotton flannel with neck and wristbands made from tubular ribbed knit. When constructing the polo closing always keep in mind that the LEFT closing edge lies on top for a boy's version, the RIGHT closing edge lies on top for a girl's version. View B is made up in red sweatshirting with a purchased, iron-on appliqué motif. View C is made up in black sweatshirting and has an appliquéd clown motif made from fabric remnants and rickrack. Both sweatshirting versions have neck and wristbands made from tubular ribbed knit.

3 Pants with elasticized waist, a solid color version and a plaid version, both fabrics shown with contrasting wrong side. View A is the boy's version in plaid with front fly zip, View B the girl's version in a solid color and without zip. Note the interesting pockets with pleats held into place with studs.

4 A cute mini-skirt with the same pockets and elasticized waistband as the girl's pants, shown here in a doubleweave fabric with brushed wrong side.

Practice Project No. 1 is printed as a multi-size pattern on the fold-out pattern sheets found in the back of this book. We have chosen this form to simplify your start in the burda sewing system and to teach you how to handle patterns. And, you can see the difference between the sizes at a single glance. To determine which size you will need for this loose-fitting garment all you need to know is the bust (misses') resp. chest (men's) width - see pages 24 and 25. For children's sizes all you need to know is the height - see explanations on pages 16 and 17.

Practice Projects 2, 3 and 4 require exact measurement taking (see pages 16 and 17). Project No. 2, a polo shirt, teaches you how to work with our "roadmap" pattern sheets, i.e. how to find pieces and trace them off - see pages 18 and 19. Scale drawing of pattern pieces, cutting layouts and further instructions for each of our illustrated teaching projects are located in the supplement beginning on page 145. See pages 94 and 95 for a clear explanation of how to trace pattern outlines and markings onto fabric.

Children's sizes

Like organ pipes - all the same age but differing in height ...

... that's just the way kids are! For this reason you should as a rule never choose children's patterns according to age but only according to height. That's why we omit age references and mention height only, for it's really the only dependable "head to toe" measurement.

1

2

3

The handy chart below helps you get height into relationship with approximate age

86	92	98	104	110	116	122	128	134	140	146	152	158	164
1	2	3	4	5	6	7	8	9	10	11	12	13	14

The even age numbers correspond to the last digit of the height number (in centimeters).

For example:

If you were to sew up garments in size 116 for these three 6-year-olds you would run into problems with two of them, for these youngsters are 110 cm (43¼"), 116 cm (45¾") and 122 cm (48¼") tall. The differences found within the 10, 12 and 14 year age groups are even more crass. Ills. 2 and 3 show how to measure a child's height. If you are sewing "sight unseen" for someone, don't be embarrassed to ask for the child's height, for it's really the decisive factor for the successful completion of a garment. The average height for 2-year-olds is 92 cm (36¼"), for 4-year-olds 104 cm (41"), for 10-year-olds 140 cm (55"), and so on. But not every child grows 6 cm (2¼") a year. Some hardly grow at all one year and then "shoot up" the next, so you should always use the actual height as a size indication, never age.

Take measurements as follows:

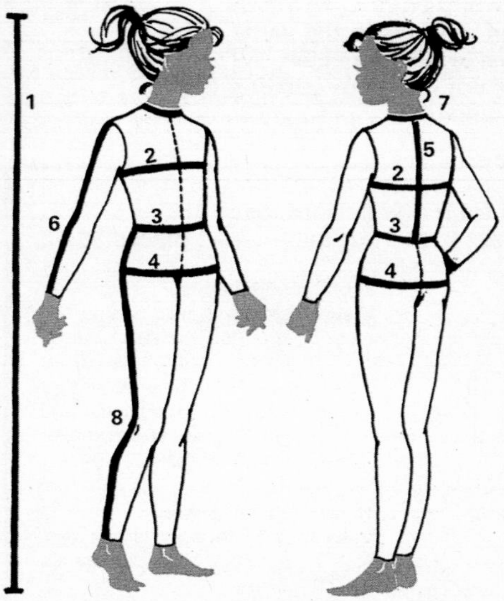

Date: Name:	Child's measurements	burda measurements	Difference
1. Height			
2. Chest			
3. Waist			
4. Hip			
5. Back length			
6. Sleeve length			
7. Neck			
8. Outside leg length			

How to determine the right pattern size

As we have already stressed, height is the most important measurement for choosing children's patterns. However, compare the child's other measurements with the burda measurement chart as well. In the table above list the child's measurements next to the burda measurements for the size nearest to the child's height. However, it may come about that the style you choose is not in the size needed. In this case you'd better choose another style, for drastic size alterations rarely go well.

To maintain the excellent burda fit, we recommend that you not alter a children's pattern more than 12 cm (4¾") in length or 8 cm (3") in width.

Side leg length is a measurement that depends upon the style of the garment and is therefore not listed in the measurement chart. But it is always included in the garment description located in the supplement. Check pant length before cutting out by holding the pattern piece for pant front to the child's body at the waist.

All burda chart measurements are body measurements. Each burda pattern contains the chart measurements plus the appropriate amount of ease allowance for the style of the garment in question. So, you're always getting the same size, regardless if you're sewing up a shirt, a skirt or a pair of pants.

How to alter children's patterns

Figure the differences between the child's measurements and the burda measurements and list these in the table above in the far righthand column. Let's suppose that you want to sew a shirt and pants for a "chubby" child that is 104 cm (41") tall. Upon comparing measurements you discover that you'll have to add 8 cm (3") width to a pattern in size 104. As a rule the pieces in a burda pattern represent one-half the garment (the only exception being asymmetrical styles). Therefore you must add one-half of the width needed, in this case 4 cm (1⅝"), to the pattern pieces shown here, distributing the width at the points shown.

Here's how to alter a shirt ...

Cut pattern pieces for front and back apart along the vertical line, cut pattern piece for raglan sleeve apart along the upper horizontal line. Enlarge pattern pieces by spreading them 1 cm (½") apart at these lines and taping strips of paper under these edges. Add 1 cm (½") wide paper strips to side seam edge of both front and back as well as to underarm seam edges of sleeves. Thus you have enlarged the front 4 cm (1⅝"), the back 4 cm (1⅝") and the sleeve 2 cm (⅞"). Should you have to enlarge the neck edge by 1 cm (½"), then cut sleeve pattern piece apart along the vertical line and spread apart ½ cm (¼"), taping a strip of paper underneath these edges.

... a pair of pants ...

Cut pant pattern pieces apart along the vertical lines and add 1 cm (½") between these edges. Add 1 cm (½") to side seam edges, on hip yoke and pocket pouch pieces as well.

... a skirt ...

Cut pattern pieces apart vertically as well and add 1 cm (½") between these edges. Add 1 cm (½") to side seam edges, on hip yoke and pocket pouch pieces as well.

Important for lengthening or shortening

If you want to lengthen a pattern from a size 104 to size 110, for example, add ½ cm (¼") at upper horizontal lines (on front, back and sleeve pieces for a shirt, on front and back pant pieces between waist and crotch, on front and back skirt panels just below hip). You should not alter more than 1 cm (½") at upper line, but you can change by 2 to 3 cm (⅞" to 1¼") at lower horizontal line (for skirts at hem edge). Although you have 6 cm (2¼") garment length difference between sizes, this makes up only ⅓ to ½ of the total height.

Raglan-sleeved shirt

By arranging shirt pattern pieces as shown, i.e. with the raglan sleeve perpendicular to front and back, it is easier to see that by adding at the upper horizontal line in sleeve you actually are widening the shoulders of the garment. You can't enlarge the body of the garment and not enlarge the shoulders as well.

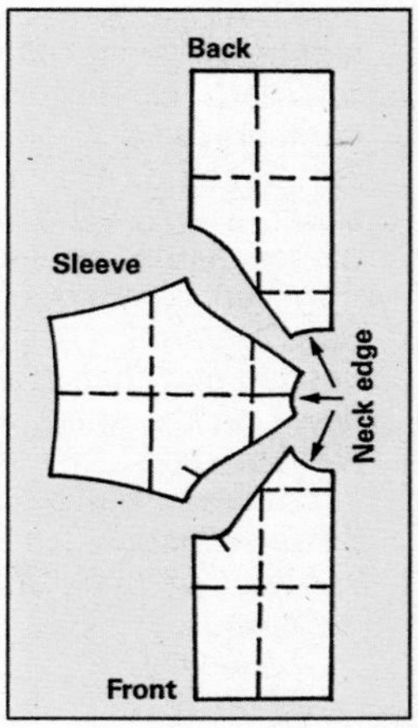

Pants

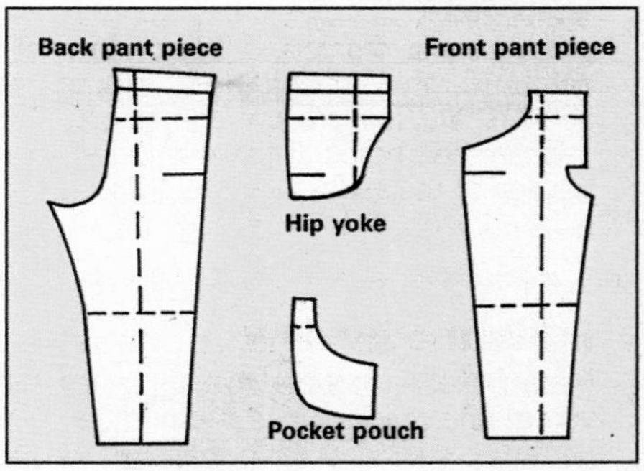

Skirt

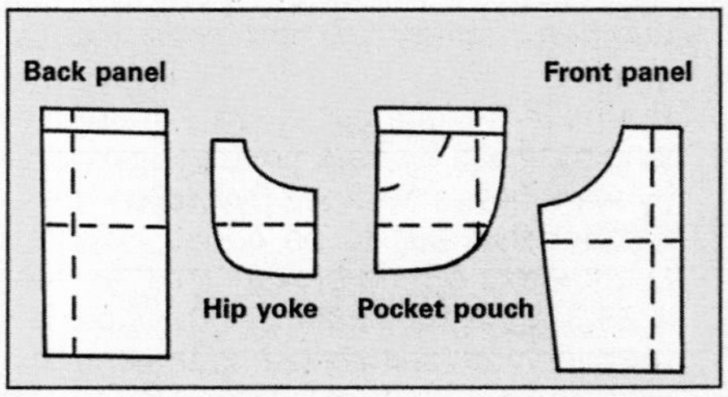

The pattern pieces shown below are those for our practice projects 2, 3 and 4, a shirt with raglan sleeves, pants and skirt with hip yoke pockets. The patterns for these garments are printed in sizes 104, 116, 128 and 140 on the trace-off pattern sheets.

The broken vertical and horizontal lines mark the points at which you alter width resp. length of pattern pieces.

If you wish to lengthen or widen garment, or both, cut pattern pieces apart at these points, spread apart and tape strips of paper under these edges. If you have to reduce length or width, fold pattern pieces at these points in the required amount.

Girls' sizes

height	cm in	86 33¼	92 36¼	98 38½	104 41	110 43¼	116 45¾	122 48¼	128 50½	134 52½	140 55	146 57½	152 59¾	158 62	164 64½	170 67	176 69½
chest	cm	55	56	57	58	59	60	62	64	66	68	72	76	80	84	88	92
	in	21¾	22	22½	23	23¼	23½	24½	25½	26	26¾	28¼	30	31½	33	34½	36¼
waist	cm	52	53	54	55	56	57	58	59	60	61	63	65	67	69	71	73
	in	20½	21	21¼	21¾	22	22½	23	23¼	23½	24	24¾	25¼	26½	27	28	28¾
hip	cm	56	58	60	62	64	66	68	70	72	74	78	82	86	90	94	98
	in	22	23	23½	24½	25¼	26	26¾	27½	28¼	29¼	30¾	32¼	33¾	35½	37	38½
back length	cm	22	23	24	25	26.5	27.5	29	30	31.5	32.5	34	36	38	39.5	41.5	43.5
	in	8⅝	9	9½	9⅞	10½	10⅞	11⅜	11⅞	12⅜	12¾	13⅜	14⅛	15	15½	16¾	17⅛
sleeve length	cm	28.5	31	33.5	36	38.5	41	43.5	46	48.5	51	53	55	57	59	61	63
	in	11¼	12¼	13⅛	14⅛	15⅛	16⅛	17⅛	18⅛	19	20	20⅞	21¾	22½	23¼	24	24¾
neck	cm	25	25.5	26.5	27.5	28	29	29.5	30.5	31.5	32	33	33.5	34.5	35.5	36	37
	in	9	10	10	10	11	11	11	12	12	12	13	13	13	14	14	14

Boys' sizes

height	cm in	86 33¼	92 36¼	98 38½	104 41	110 43¼	116 45¾	122 48¼	128 50½	134 52½	140 55	146 57½	152 59¾	158 62	164 64½	170 67	176 69½
chest	cm	55	56	57	58	59	60	63	66	69	72	75	78	81	84	87	90
	in	21¾	22	22½	23	23¼	23½	24¾	26	27¼	28¼	29½	30¾	32	33	34¼	35½
waist	cm	52	53	54	55	56	57	58	60	62	64	66	68	70	72	74	78
	in	20¼	21	21¼	21¾	22	22½	23	23½	24½	25¼	26	26¾	27½	28¼	29¼	30¾
hip	cm	56	58	60	62	64	66	68	70	72	75	78	81	84	87	90	94
	in	22	23	23½	24½	25¼	26	26¾	27½	28¼	29½	30¾	32	33	34¼	35½	37
back length	cm	22	23	24	25	26.5	27.5	29	30	31.5	33	35	37	39	41	43	45
	in	8⅝	9	9½	9⅞	10½	10⅞	11⅜	11⅞	12⅜	13	13¾	14½	15⅜	16⅛	17	17¾
sleeve length	cm	28.5	31	33.5	36	38.5	41	43.5	46	48.5	51	53	55	57	59	61.5	64
	in	11¼	12¼	13⅛	14⅛	15⅛	16⅛	17⅛	18⅛	19	20	20⅞	21¾	22½	23¼	24¼	25⅛
neck	cm	25	25.5	26.5	27.5	28	29	29.5	30.5	31.5	32	33	33.5	34.5	35.5	36.5	37.5
	in	9⅞	10	10½	10⅞	11	11⅜	11⅝	12	12⅜	12⅝	13	13⅛	13½	14	14⅜	14¾

Polo closings: practice makes perfect

Our practice project no. 2, View A, is made up in colorfully printed woven fabric. Neckband and wristbands are made from tubular ribbed knit fabric. Inspite of the knit neckband a polo closing is necessary when making this shirt up in a woven fabric but can be omitted when using a knit, as shown in Views B and C to the right.

Style 2
View B
Page 13

Easier to sew - the version without polo closing with iron-on appliqué

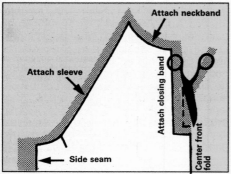

Trim pattern piece for front along band attachment line from neck edge down to marker line end of closing. Then pin pattern piece onto fabric and cut out with the required allowances, adding ¾ cm (⅜") to closing edges.

3 Press seam allowances into bands. Turn bands **right** side out, fold along foldline. Turn under open long edge of inner band layers, baste into place over attachment seam, press. From the **right** side edgestitch along all band edges, securing inner layer of each.

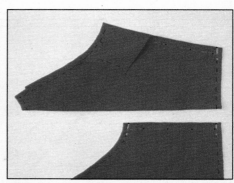

6 Pin and stitch side seams and underarm seams in sleeves with long-set, narrow zigzag stitching. Insert pins perpendicular to seamline and leave them in while stitching to prevent fabric layers from slipping out of line.

1 Stitch closing bands to front closing edges along attachment lines, **right** sides together. Fold bands along their foldline, **right** sides together. Stitch upper end of each.

4 Pin right band onto left band, center-on-center. Stitch lower band ends to front from corner to corner, **right** sides together.

7 Pin sleeves to armholes, **right** sides together, matching seam numbers as well as marked seamlines. Underarm and side seams should match as well. Baste and stitch sleeves into place. Overcast seam allowances together.

2 Clip front allowance in close to last stitch at each lower corner, taking care NOT to catch in band allowance.

5 Press band ends down into front. Topstitch lower end of closing as shown (a crossed square), securing band ends. Hammer small snaps into closing bands following directions in the packet. Pierce small holes into bands first with a large darning needle or an awl.

8 Fold neckband in half lengthwise, **wrong** sides together, and press, stretching open edges somewhat with the iron. Stitch ends of band **right** sides together, forming a ring.

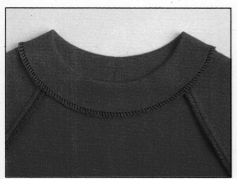

9 Pin open edges of neckband onto the **right** side of neck edge so that neckband seam lies at center back.

A clown steals the show

Construct this shirt in the same manner as for View B. Rummage through your remnant box for fabric scraps of the same type and weight for the appliqué. Neck ruffle and hat are trimmed with rickrack, eyes are hand embroidered. Heart-shaped buttons decorate the clown's waistcoat. It's much easier if you finish the appliqué before sewing sweatshirt together.

10 Stitch neckband into place with your overlocker (serger) or with an overlock stitch setting, overcasting seam allowances together at the same time. Press seam allowances down into shirt.

Tip for beginners: construct the clown appliqué onto a fabric remnant. Trim fabric back to appliqué edges. Iron appliqué onto sweatshirt front using a fusing agent, then zigzag stitch outer edges into place.

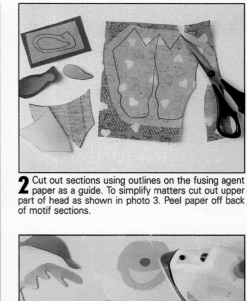

2 Cut out sections using outlines on the fusing agent paper as a guide. To simplify matters cut out upper part of head as shown in photo 3. Peel paper off back of motif sections.

11 Stitch ends of each wristband **right** sides together, forming a ring. Fold wristbands in half lengthwise, **wrong** sides together. Pin open edges of wristbands to the **right** side of lower sleeve edges, matching seams. Overlock stitch wristbands into place, stretching them as you stitch.

3 Iron sections into place, **wrong (coated)** side down, and overlapping sections 1 mm. Iron again from the **wrong** side of front using a damp presscloth.

12 Place appliqué motif COATED SIDE DOWN onto front where desired and iron into place. Iron again from the **wrong** side of front.

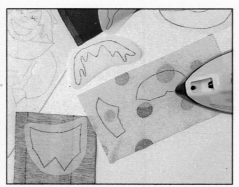

1 Trace the clown motif off the pattern sheet. Trace single sections, i.e. hat, hair, waistcoat, etc., onto paper of fusing agent. Iron fusing agent coated side down onto the **wrong** side of desired fabric remnants.

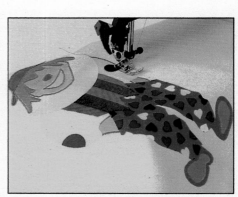

4 Zigzag stitch all edges of all motif sections into place with close-set, tiny zigzag stitching.

Style 3
Pants, View B
Page 13

Roll up lower leg edges to the length desired

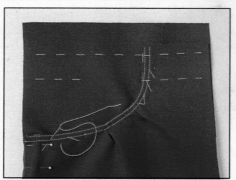

4 Fold pouch pieces over to the **inside.** Baste, press, edgestitch and topstitch ¾ cm (⅜") along seamed (pocket opening) edges. Baste front pant pieces onto the **right** side of the corresponding hip yoke so that pocket opening edge lies on placement line marked on hip yoke.

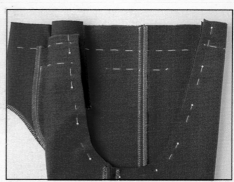

8 Fold legs lengthwise, **right** sides together. Stitch inside leg seams. Overcast and press open seam allowances. Insert one leg into other, **right** sides together, matching side as well as inside leg seams. Stitch crotch seam twice from upper front around to upper back edge.

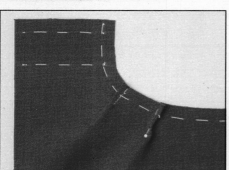

1 On front pant pieces fold tucks into pocket opening edges, x-onto-o, **right** sides together. Pin and stitch tuck lines together down to tuck mark. Press tucks toward center front.

5 Baste and stitch pouch pieces to hip yokes from side edge around to lowermost line for waist casing. See ill. 6.

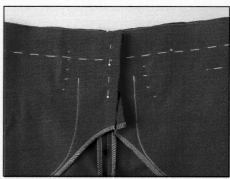

9 Overcast crotch seam allowances, press open in front and back down to curve. Stitch hip yokes **right** sides together at center front. Overcast and press open seam allowances.

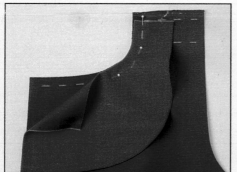

2 Pin pouch pieces to front pant pieces along pocket opening edges, **right** sides together. Upper edge of pouch piece should lie on facing line on upper pant edge.

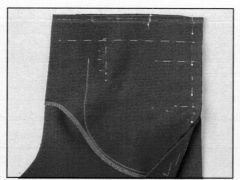

6 Baste pockets into place at side seam edges, matching marked seamlines. Baste and stitch front pant pieces to back pieces **right** sides together at side seams.

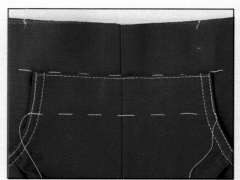

10 Fold the allowance on upper edge of front pants to the **inside,** press, edgestitch onto hip yoke. Continue and edgestitch pocket opening edges into place down to lowermost casing line.

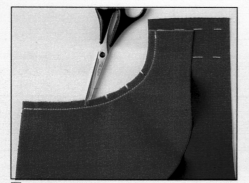

3 Stitch pouch pieces into place along opening edges. Trim seam allowances, clip at curves.

7 Overcast side seam allowances together and press into back pants. From the **right** side edgestitch and topstitch back pieces ¾ cm (⅜") along side seams, securing the allowances.

11 Press the extended facing on upper pant edge to the **inside,** turn under its open edge, baste into place over lowermost casing line from pocket opening edge around the back to other pocket opening edge.

12 Stitch facing into place along both casing lines from one pocket opening edge around the back to the other pocket edge. Measure and cut 2 sections of elastic to fit, insert into casings. Pin elastic ends into place at casing ends.

Style 3
Pants, View A
Page 13

Style 4
Skirt
Page 13

The boy's version has a front fly zipper

The pockets on this little skirt are constructed exactly like those for style 3

13 Beginning and ending at upper edge of pants, edgestitch again along pocket opening edges, securing elastic ends. Topstitch front pants along lowermost casing line, securing facing on inside.

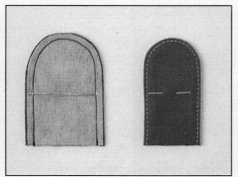

16 Iron fusible interfacing (vilene or pellon) onto the **wrong** side of one tab piece. Stitch tab pieces **right** sides together along outer edges, leaving straight end open. Turn tab **right** side out. Baste, press and edgestitch along its seamed edges.

1 Stitch center front seam from upper edge down to slit mark. Overcast and press open seam and slit allowances. From the **right** side edgestitch and topstitch ¾ cm (⅜") on each side of center seam down to slit, securing the allowances.

14 Tip: Prevent elastic from twisting by stitching across casings at side seams and center back, at the center of each hip yoke if desired.

17 Baste tab onto the **right** side of extended facing on upper edge of left front pant piece so that line marked on tab lies on center front line and rounded end of tab lies toward pocket opening.

2 Stitch tucks at pocket opening edges. Stitch pouch pieces to pocket opening edges, **right** sides together. Upper end of pouch pieces should lie on facing line on upper skirt edge. Complete hip yoke pockets as in style 3.

15 Hammer studs into tucks at pocket opening edges following the instructions in the packet.

18 Edgestitch right half of zipper under right placket edge so that edge lies very close to teeth. Close zipper. Pin placket closed, center-on-center. Baste and stitch left half of zipper under left placket edge along the marked topstitching line.

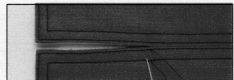

3 Stitch side seams, overcast and press open seam allowances. Press hem allowance to the **inside,** then press front slit allowances to the **inside** over hem allowance. Beginning and ending at upper end of front slit, edgestitch and topstitch along slit and hem edges, securing allowances.

Everything you need to know about pattern sizes

To determine the proper pattern size for yourself or whomever you might be sewing for you must carefully take measurements first. This is explained in detail for men and women on the following page, for children on pages 16/17.

Ladies' sizes
Here there are three basic groups:

Misses' or standard sizes
Height 168 cm (5'6"), European sizes 34, 36, 38, 40, etc., corresponding sizes 8, 10, 12, 14, etc.

Half-sizes
Height 160 cm (5'3"), European sizes 17, 18, 19, 20 etc., corresponding sizes 8½, 10½, 12½, 14½, etc.

Tall/extra length sizes
Height 176 cm (5'9"), European sizes 68, 72, 76, 80 etc., corresponding sizes tall/extra length 8, 10, 12, 14, etc.

The main difference between these three groups is the height. The width measurements (bust, waist, hip, etc) are fairly much the same for all three groups.

The width is always the same for								
standard sizes	**34**	**36**	**38**	**40**	**42**	**44**	**46**	**48**
half-sizes	68	72	76	80	84	88	92	96
tall sizes	17	18	19	20	21	22	23	24

Take another look at these size groups in the arrangement above and you'll notice the European size numbers for the tall group are doubled those in the misses' group and the numbers for the half-size group are half those for the misses' group.

For example: if you are 176 cm (5'9") tall and have a bust width 88 cm (34½"), then your ideal size is 76, even though you have the same bust size as a size 38. If you are 160 cm (5'3") tall then your ideal size is half-size 19.

Being as most magazines containing patterns as well as most pattern catalogues and even this book (lack of space) contain only misses's sizes, then those with a tall or half-size should learn how to alter a misses' pattern. See pages 26/27 for detailed instructions for pattern alterations, showing you the easiest method for enlarging and reducing patterns. You'll see that it's not so difficult after all.

Choose patterns for dresses, blouses, jackets, coats and shirts according to your bust width, patterns for skirts and pants according to hip width.

By the way ...
Pattern sizing is not always identical with ready-to-wear sizing. The garment industry and pattern publishing companies in West Germany all work with the same measurement charts, but there are still considerable deviations due to differing ease amounts. Certainly you have had the experience of fitting into a size 40 (14) from one ready-to-wear company and into a size 38 (12) or 42 (16) from another. Therefore it is of utmost importance that you compare your measurements with the burda measurement chart exactly. All burda chart measurements are taken directly on the body. Of one thing you can be sure: each burda pattern contains the chart measurements plus the ease allowance required for the style of garment in question. You are always getting the same size, even if you're making up a full-cut coat, a figure-fitted dress or a plain shirt.

Even if your measurements correspond exactly to those of a certain pattern size it can happen that minor alterations will have to be made. In school we learned very early that two bodies that have the same height and width measurements can be totally different. One can be wide and flat, for example, and the other slim but round. Thus there are innumberable, less dramatic deviations from the so-called normal figure that cannot be expressed with measurements. Fitting alterations of this type should be made when trying on the garment in question.

On pages 96 through 101 you will find a detailed explanation of how to baste a garment together for fitting as well as how to make necessary alterations.

The latest group surveys have shown that no less than 81 different sizes would be necessary to provide all women with the proper size! One thing is clear: patterns that fit all women equally well do not exist. Our endeavour will be, in the future as well, to construct patterns that fit as many women as possible - and fit very well. The fit of our burda patterns is world famous. This reputation is obligatory for us. An obligation that we take very seriously and in which we also invest a great deal.

All burda chart measurements are body measurements, i.e. just like those that you take on your own body.

See pages 16/17 for complete information regarding children's sizes.

Take ladies' measurements as follows:

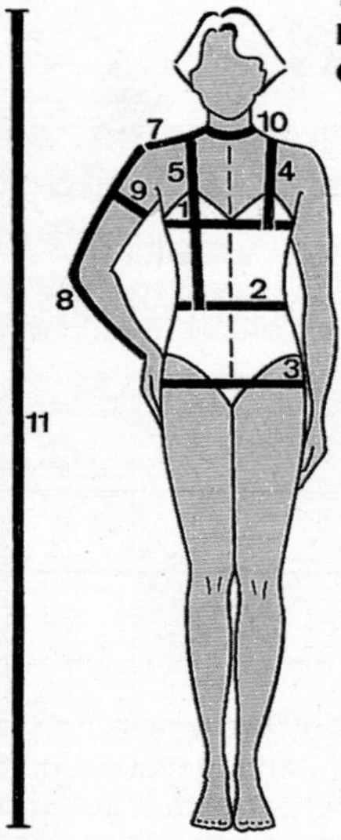

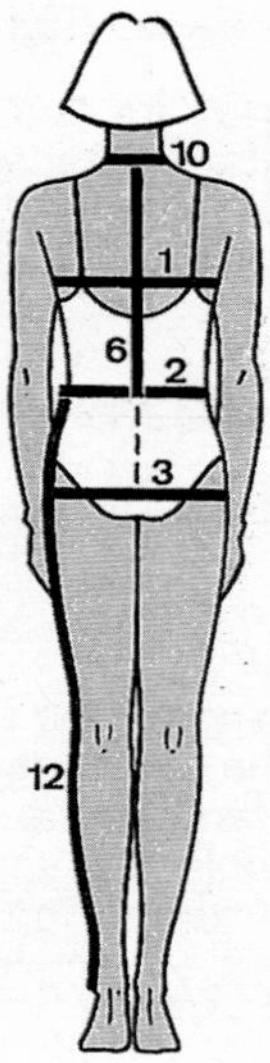

These diagrams show you where to take measurements.

Bust, hip and upper arm width should always be taken at the fullest point. We show side leg length here but not on the measurement chart because it varies according to the style and lower leg width of the pants in question. This length is stated in the description for the style printed in the supplement.

How to determine the right pattern size

As a rule one chooses patterns for dresses, blouses and jackets according to the bust width, for skirts and pants according to hip width. Compare your bust and hip width with the burda measurement charts. List your measurements in the table below next to the measurements for the burda size coming nearest to your bust resp. hip width. If you are shorter or taller than 168 cm (5'6"), see pp. 26/27. List the difference, if any, between your measurements and the burda chart in the far right column of the table with a plus (+) or a minus (-) sign so that you'll later know whether to enlarge or reduce your pattern and where.

Date: Name:	Your measurements	burda measurements	Difference
1. Bust			
2. Waist			
3. Hip			
4. Bust depth			
5. Front waist length			
6. Back length			
7. Shoulder width			
8. Sleeve length			
9. Upper arm width			
10. Neck			
11. Height			
12. Outside leg length			

All burda chart measurements are direct body measurements. Every burda pattern contains these measurements plus the ease allowance required for the style of the garment in question. So, you're always getting the same size, be you sewing up a full-cut jacket, a slim-fit dress or a plain shirt.

Check pants length by holding the paper pattern pieces against your body before cutting out.

What are combined sizes?

There are patterns in this book that apply to one size only, e.g. size 36 (10), 38 (12), 40 (14), etc. and there are combined sizes, e.g. size 36-38 (10-12). This type of pattern will fit both sizes 36 and 38 (10 and 12). This type of sizing is found for casually cut garments only that are not figure-fitted and do not have normally set in sleeves. If you want to sew up a dress, for example, and have a size 36 (10) bust and size 38 (12) hips, you wouldn't have to alter a combined size 36-38 (10-12) pattern because it would be wide enough for size 38 (12) hips.

Women's sizes (height 168 cm / 5'6")

burda size corresponding size		34 8	36 10	38 12	40 14	42 16	44 18	46 20	48 22
bust	cm	80	84	88	92	96	100	104	110
	in	31½	33	34½	36¼	37¾	39¼	41	43¼
waist	cm	64	66	70	74	78	82	86	92
	in	25¼	26	27½	29¼	30¾	32¼	33¾	36¼
hip	cm	88	90	94	98	102	106	110	115
	in	34½	35½	37	38½	40¼	41¾	43¼	45¼
bust depth	cm	25	26	27	28	29	30	31	32
	in	9⅞	10¼	10⅝	11	11⅜	11⅞	12¼	12⅝
front waist length	cm	42.5	43.5	44.5	45.5	46.5	47.5	48.5	49.5
	in	16¾	17⅛	17½	18	18¼	18¾	19	19½
back length	cm	40	40.5	41	41.5	42	42.5	43	43.5
	in	15¾	16	16⅛	16⅜	16½	16¾	17	17⅛
shoulder width	cm	12	12.5	12.5	13	13	13.5	13.5	14
	in	4¾	5	5	5⅛	5⅛	5¼	5¼	5½
sleeve length	cm	60	60	60	60	60	61	61	61
	in	23⅝	23⅝	23⅝	23⅝	23⅝	24	24	24
upper arm width	cm	26	27	28	29	30	31	32	34
	in	10¼	10⅝	11	11⅜	11⅞	12¼	12⅝	13⅜
neck	cm	34	35	36	37	38	39	40	41
	in	13⅜	13¾	14⅛	14⅝	15	15⅜	15¾	16⅛

Women's tall sizes (height 176 cm / 5'9")

burda size:		72	76	80	84	88
bust	cm	84	88	92	96	100
	in	33	34½	36¼	37¾	39¼
waist	cm	66	70	74	78	82
	in	26	27½	29¼	30¾	32¼
hip	cm	90	94	98	102	106
	in	35½	37	38½	40¼	41¾
bust depth	cm	27	28	29	30	31
	in	10⅝	11	11⅜	11⅞	12¼
front waist length	cm	45.5	46.5	47.5	48.5	49.5
	in	18	18¼	18¾	19	19½
back length	cm	42.5	43	43.5	44	44.5
	in	16¾	17	17⅛	17⅜	17½
shoulder width	cm	12.5	12.5	13	13.5	13.5
	in	5	5	5⅛	5¼	5¼
sleeve length	cm	62	62	62	62	63
	in	24⅜	24⅜	24⅜	24⅜	24¾
upper arm width	cm	27	28	29	30	31
	in	10⅝	11	11⅜	11⅞	12¼
neck	cm	35	36	37	38	39
	in	13¾	14⅛	14⅝	15	15⅜

Women's half sizes (short fitting, height 160 cm / 5'3")

burda size: corresponding size		18 10½	19 12½	20 14½	21 16½	22 18½	23 20½	24 22½
bust	cm	84	88	92	96	100	104	110
	in	33	34½	36¼	37¾	39¼	41	43¼
waist	cm	66	70	74	78	82	86	92
	in	26	27½	29¼	30¾	32¼	33¾	36¼
hip	cm	90	94	98	102	106	110	115
	in	35½	37	38½	40¼	41¾	43¼	45¼
bust depth	cm	25	26	27	28	29	30	31
	in	9⅞	10¼	10⅝	11	11⅜	11⅞	12¼
front waist length	cm	41.5	42.5	43.5	44.5	45.5	46.5	47.5
	in	16⅜	16¾	17⅛	17½	18	18¼	18¾
back length	cm	38.5	39	39.5	40	40.5	41	41.5
	in	15⅛	15⅜	15½	15¾	16	16⅛	16⅜
shoulder width	cm	12.5	12.5	13	13	13.5	13.5	14
	in	5	5	5⅛	5⅛	5¼	5¼	5½
sleeve length	cm	58	58	58	58	59	59	59
	in	22⅞	22⅞	22⅞	22⅞	23¼	23¼	23¼
upper arm width	cm	27	28	29	30	31	32	34
	in	10⅝	11	11⅜	11⅞	12¼	12⅝	13⅜
neck	cm	35	36	37	38	39	40	41
	in	13¾	14⅛	14⅝	15	15⅜	15¾	16⅛

Take men's measurements as follows:

Mens sizing

Here we have two groups:

Standard European sizes 46, 48, 50, 52, etc., corresponding sizes 36, 38, 40, 42, etc.

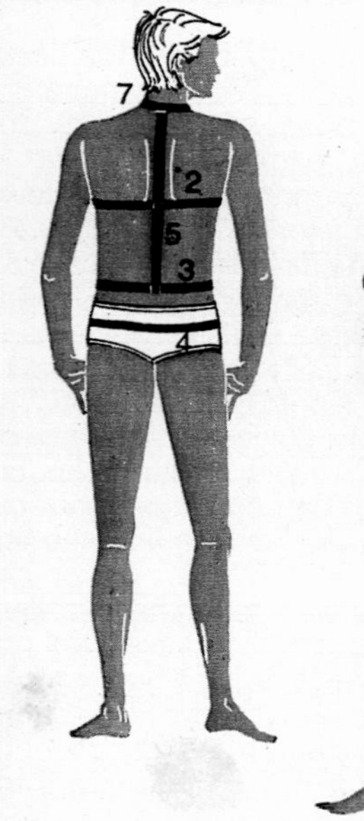

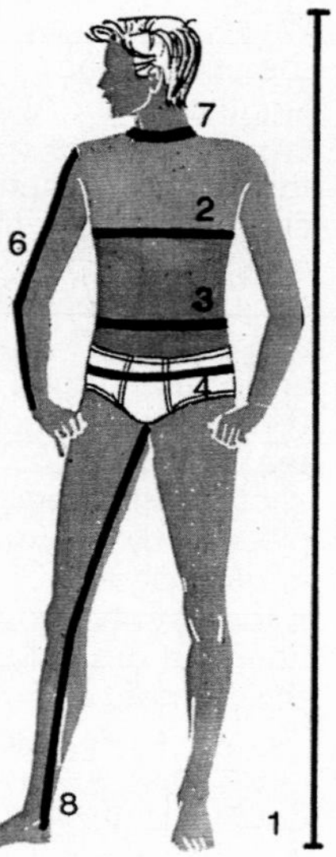

Tall European sizes 90, 94, 98, 102, etc., corresponding sizes 36 tall, 38 tall, 40 tall, 42 tall, etc.

Tall sizes are not only longer but also slimmer. The size numbers 90, 94, etc. designate the chest width in centimeters. The normal size numbers 46, 48, etc. designate half the chest width, i.e. size 46 has a chest width of 92 cm (36¼"), size 48 a width of 96 cm (37¾").

If you haven't already done so, take the time now to read our general instructions for determining the correct pattern size (see above).

Patterns for casual shirts, sweatshirts, jackets, and coats are chosen according to chest width, trousers according to waist width and dress shirts (with buttoned collar or collar with stand) according to neck width.

Date: Name:	Your measurements	burda measurements	Difference
1. Height			
2. Chest			
3. Waist			
4. Hip			
5. Back length			
6. Sleeve length			
7. Neck			
8. Inside leg length			

Men's standard sizes

burda size		44	46	48	50	52	54	56
height	cm	170 to 174			175 to 178			
	in	67 to 68½			69 to 70			
chest	cm	88	92	96	100	104	106	112
	in	34½	36¼	37¾	39¼	41	42½	44
waist	cm	78	82	86	90	94	98	102
	in	30¾	32¼	33¾	35½	37	38½	40¼
hip	cm	92	96	100	104	108	112	116
	in	36¼	37¾	39¼	41	42½	44	45¾
back length	cm	44	45	46	47	48	49	50
	in	17⅜	17¾	18⅛	18½	18⅞	19¼	19¾
neck	cm	37	38	39	40	41	42	43
	in	14⅝	15	15⅜	15¾	16⅛	16½	17
sleeve length	cm	63	63	63	64	64	64	64
	in	24¾	24¾	24¾	25⅛	25⅛	25⅛	25⅛
inside leg length	cm	80	80	80	81	81	81	81
	in	31½	31½	31½	31⅞	31⅞	31⅞	31⅞

Men's tall sizes

burda size		90	94	98	102	106
height	cm	180 to 184		185 to 188		
	in	71 to 72½		72¾ to 74		
chest	cm	90	94	98	102	106
	in	35½	37	38½	40⅛	41¾
waist	cm	78	82	86	90	94
	in	30¾	32¼	33¾	35½	37
hip	cm	94	98	102	106	110
	in	37	38½	40⅛	41¾	43¼
back length	cm	48	49	50	51	52
	in	18⅞	19¼	19¾	20	20½
neck	cm	38	39	40	41	42
	in	15	15⅜	15¾	16⅛	16½
sleeve length	cm	65	65	66	66	66
	in	25½	25½	26	26	26
inside leg length	cm	83	83	84	84	84
	in	32⅝	32⅝	33	33	33

1 Stitch bust darts, catching in seam tape or stretched out bias tape. Knot threads at dart point and clip. Press dart allowance downward and tape upward.

2 Overcast neck and armhole allowances, fold to the **inside.** Overcast edges by hand with whipstitch. Then topstitch with twin ballpoint needles from the **right** side of garment along whipstitching.

3 Gather upper edge of skirt to match lower edge of bodice. Pin skirt to bodice, **right** sides together. Catch in seam tape or stretched out bias tape on the skirt side when basting sections together. Then stitch.

Sewn in a snap!

Mixed prints in jersey - light, breezy, easy to sew!

5

5
36, 38
40, 42
44, 46

5 Looking for a quickie pattern? We have created one just for you. A simple tank-top bodice attached to a gathered skirt is sewn in no time at all. The scalloped neck and armhole edges are attained by overcasting edges with whipstitch (see ill. 2 in the illustrated instructions to the left).

Summer dresses in retro-look

7 Cheerful summer prints, bright stripes, tiny checks or crinkled solids are all suitable for this feminine summer dress with its sweetheart neckline and unusually shaped shoulder yoke. Flattering vertical seaming emphasizes your curves. The versatility of this pattern is amazing: make a smart overblouse by cutting out down to 10 cm (4") below the waist mark. Make a matching gored skirt from the same pattern pieces, folding them at waist mark.

Illustrated teaching instructions are located on page 35.

7
36, 38
40, 42
44, 46

A simple shift made exclusive

11
36 — 38
40 — 42
44 — 46

11 Most fashionable - the latest slender shape transposed into the simplest of patterns! Machine stitched cutwork embroidery on neckline and sleeve edges lends this simple white dress an exclusiveness all its own. Center back slit guarantees walking ease. Embroidery motifs are printed on pattern sheet. We suggest that you iron on interfacing before embroidering - it facilitates things wonderfully. See page 45 for a "quick" version of this style. Illustrated teaching instructions located on page 44.

Style 11
View A
Pages 42/43

There are neither hems nor facings on the embroidered edges.

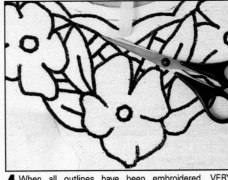

4 When all outlines have been embroidered, VERY CAREFULLY trim interfacing back to stitching. Remove all interfacing.

Style 11
View B
Page 45

A chic contrast: neck, pocket and sleeve edges finished with braid.

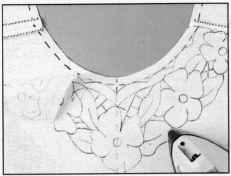

1 Stitch center back and shoulder seams, press open seam allowances. Trace embroidery motifs onto the **uncoated** side of fusible interfacing. Iron (use steam) interfacing COATED SIDE DOWN onto the **wrong** side of neck edges.

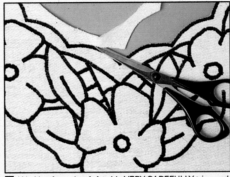

5 Working from the **right** side VERY CAREFULLY trim neck edge back to embroidered scalloping. Use sharply pointed scissors and take care NOT to cut embroidery threads.

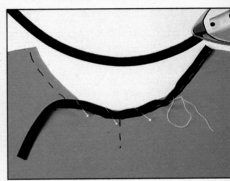

8 Pre-shape braid with a steam iron to match neck edge. Baste braid onto the **wrong** side of neck allowance so that its shorter edge lies on neck seamline.

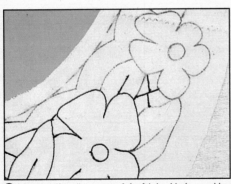

2 Mark motif outlines onto **right** fabric side by machine stitching along the lines with a normal, straight stitch setting. Backstitch ends of all lines.

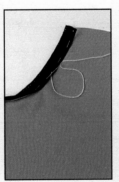

6 Then VERY CAREFULLY cut out the fabric from the shaded motif sections. Again, work with sharply pointed scissors, getting into all corners.

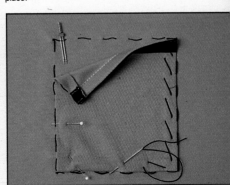

9 Working from the **wrong** side edgestitch shorter edge of braid into place along neck seamline. Fold braid and allowance to the **right** side of dress, baste into place (braid covers allowance), press. Edgestitch long edge of braid into place.

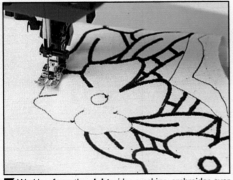

3 Working from the **right** side, machine embroider over these lines with the satin stitch setting. Should your machine not have such a setting, then close-set, wide zigzag stitching is required. Experiment on a fabric scrap first! Pull thread ends to the underside and knot securely.

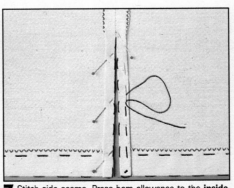

7 Stitch side seams. Press hem allowance to the **inside**, baste into place. Turn under edges of back slit allowances, baste into place, press. Topstitch hem and slit allowances into place.

10 Pocket: bind upper edge with braid in the same manner. Press side and lower edge allowances to the **inside**. Pin and stitch pocket into place where marked stitching very close to edges with twin ballpoint needles.

44

A quick
finish
with braid

11

Chic citywear

should appear modern and self-confident, should be versatile and most of all multi-purpose

12

12
36, 38
40, 42
44, 46

12 Introducing the prototype for the New Classics: a sporty, double-breasted coatdress that can be worn belted, if desired. Eyecatching details are sharply pointed lapels, cap sleeves and easy-sew pockets. Flattering section seams guarantee a figure-fitted look and yet can camouflage figure problems at the same time. The tunic-length hemline on pattern applies to the brown version that you can wear alternately with a straight skirt in a matching brown shade or with a lightcolored version with a full-circle tier attached just below the hips.

13 The straight skirt is easy to sew. Darts shape the waist. The same pattern is used for the lightcolored version.

5 This easy-sew shirt is made in soft jersey. See illustrated teaching instructions on pages 28, 48 and 69

13
36, 38
40, 42
44, 46

16

16	
36 — 38	
40 — 42	
44 — 46	

New:
country & western duds

16

56

17
36, 38
40, 42
44, 46

16 Two blouses from the same pattern, both with beautifully shaped yoke, metal collar corners and tiny, hammer-in snaps.
17 The hem ruffle on the gingham petticoat shapes the hem edge of this 6-gored skirt with high-rise waist, i.e. no waistband. Both practical and striking: metal zippers in front section seams for easy donning. Illustrated teaching instructions located on page 55

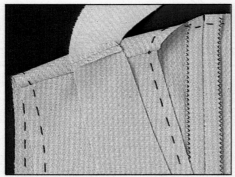

1 Stitch darts, center back seam, shoulder and side seams. Stitch (interfaced) back facing to front facings **right** sides together at shoulder seams. Press open all seam allowances.

5 Turn sleeve hem allowances to the **inside,** press, blindstitch into place. Press vent facing to the **inside.** Stitch upper ends of vent underlap and facing together.

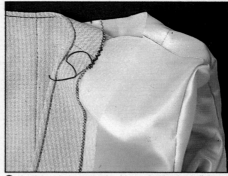

9 Hand sew facing onto shoulder pads. Hand sew lining to armhole edges (see p. 77, ill. 20). Slip lining sleeve into sleeve, **wrong** sides together.

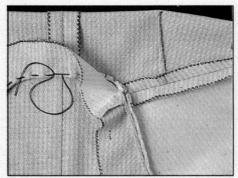

2 Complete hem. Stitch facing to closing and neck edges, **right** sides together, matching shoulder seams. Clip seam allowances at curves. Turn facing to the **inside,** baste and press seamed edges.

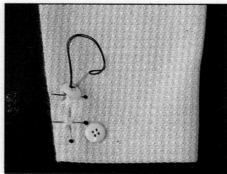

6 Hand sew vent facing onto hem allowance (ill. 5). Mark button position with pins. Sew buttons into place, catching in vent underlap.

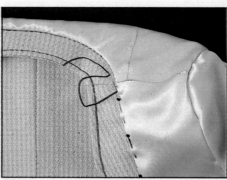

10 Turn under neck and front edges of lining, pin and hand sew onto facing down to 5 cm (2") from hem edge. Make stitches as inconspicuous as possible.

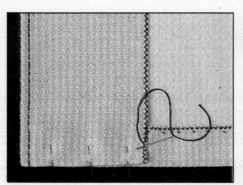

3 Turn up lower ends of facings even with hem edge, pin into place. Topstitch ¾ cm (⅜") along closing and neck edges. Hand sew facing onto hem allowance.

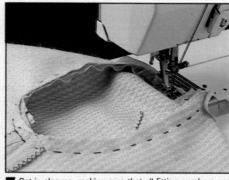

7 Set in sleeves, making sure that all fitting numbers and marker lines match and catching in a 13 cm (5") long bias strip at upper edge of armhole.

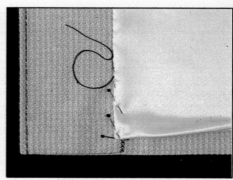

11 Slip lower lining edge upward, slipstitch onto upper edge of jacket hem allowance. Then finish sewing lining onto facings. A fold will be formed at lower lining edge.

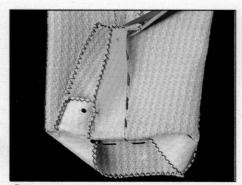

4 Clip seam allowance on under sleeve piece in close to seam at corner above vent. Turn sleeve hem allowance to the **outside** and stitch its ends to vent underlap and facing.

8 Hand sew shoulder pads to sleeve attachment and shoulder seam allowances so that their straight edge extends approx. 1 cm (½") into sleeve cap. Hand sew fleece strip into place on sleeve side of attachment seam (see ill. 11 on p. 62).

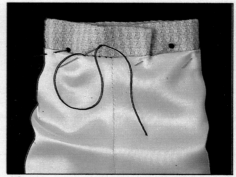

12 Slip lower edge of sleeve lining upward, slipstitch onto upper edge of sleeve hem allowance. Then slip lining downward, forming a fold in lower edge.

Long, slim jackets are in

22
36, 38
40, 42
44, 46

22 This classically styled, collarless jacket with its flawless, 2-seam sleeves is the perfect partner for a straight skirt or slim dress and can be easily worn under a full-cut winter coat. Illustrated teaching instructions located on pages 59 and 64

19

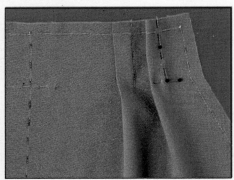

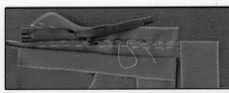

1 **Wrap blouse:** stitch shoulder seams, catching in seam tape or stretched out bias tape. Clip seam allowance on fronts in close to last stitch at corner.

1 **Pants:** fold and stitch waist tucks x-onto-o, **right** sides together, press toward center front. From the **right** side topstitch ½ cm (¼") along tuck seams, securing allowances, then stitch diagonally in to end of tuck.

5 Baste and edgestitch left half of zipper under left placket edge so that edge lies close to teeth and catching in underlap as you stitch. Stitch right half of zipper to right placket facing only.

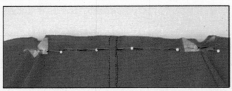

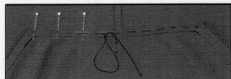

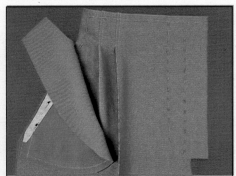

2 Stitch fronts **right** sides together at center seam in extended collar. Stitch extended collar to back neck edge from corner to corner, **right** sides together. Press seam allowances upward, turn under their edges, baste into place.

2 Pin and stitch pouch pieces to front pant pieces at pocket opening edges, **right** sides together. Fold pouch pieces over to the **inside**. Baste, press and topstitch ½ cm (¼") along seamed (opening) edges.

6 Insert one leg into the other, **right** sides together, matching side as well as inside leg seams. Stitch back crotch seam. Press open seam allowances in back down to curve. Fold waist facing to the **inside**.

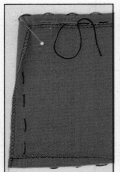

3 Baste the allowance on all outer edges of blouse to the **inside.** From the **right** side topstitch edges 1 cm (½") with twin ballpoint needles, securing allowances but retaining elasticity of fabric.

3 Baste pant fronts onto the **right** side of the corresponding hip yoke so that pocket opening edge of each lies on placement line marked on hip yoke. Stitch pouch pieces to hip yokes. Baste hip yokes into place along center front and upper edge of pants.

7 Hand sew waist facing onto placket underlap. Hand sew right placket facing onto waist facing as shown.

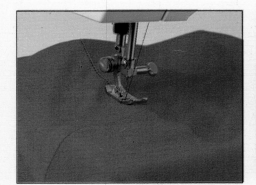

4 Set in sleeves, making sure all fitting marks and numbers match. Press seam allowances into body of blouse, edgestitch into place from the **right** side of blouse.

4 Turn right placket facing to the **outside** and pin into place at upper edge. Stitch waist facing sections **right** sides together. Stitch facing to upper edge of pants, **right** sides together.

8 Topstitch along upper edge of pants where marked, securing waist facing. Stitch belt carriers onto pants where marked.

24 Team a chic belt with these pants with tucked and faced waist.
25 Rediscover your figure. This wrapped blouse flatteringly emphasizes your curves and can be worn equally well with pants, full or straight skirts.

Wrap blouse

JERSEY IS A MUST!

25
36—38
40—42
44—46

24
36, 38
40, 42
44, 46

25

Casual shirts,
CLEVERLY DECORATED

26 All six shirts shown were sewn from the same pattern and are narrow at the hips, have a boat neckline and offshoulder, dolman sleeves that taper to the wrist. Here are six suggestions for individualizing your shirt by very simple means. The instructions on page 73 show you how to iron on sequins or paint palms or an exotic snake. The appliqués and rhinestones shown were purchased.

26

36—38
40—42
44—46

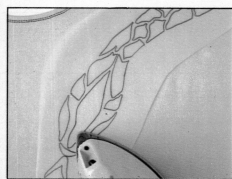

4 Place wax paper onto the **right** side of fabric so that the motif lies on fabric. Iron over paper, transferring motif onto fabric.

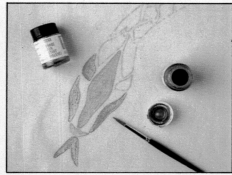

5 Paint motif with metallic textile paints. Use a finely pointed brush for the outlines. Apply paint generously.

Interesting decorative details

Sheets with iron-on metallic dots can be purchased in notions/haberdashery departments. Cut out sections in the shapes desired and arrange on front of shirt (see View B on page 72). Iron dots into place. These dots will withstand handwashing as will the textile paints used for the snake as well as the felt pens used for the palm motif. Use burda's blue iron-on transfer pencil and wax paper for marking motifs onto shirt (see ills. 3 and 4), or purchase an iron-on transfer.

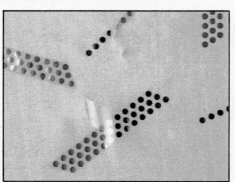

2 Allow dots to cool completely. Test to see if dots have completely fused before carefully peeling away paper.

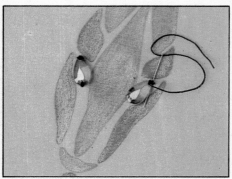

6 Allow motif to dry thoroughly. Remove interfacing from underside by applying steam and peeling off. Iron over motif from the **wrong** side. Sew on eyes.

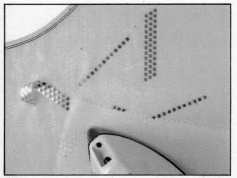

1 Place metallic dot sections onto fabric so that the paper lies on top. Iron on dots with a medium iron setting and using a press cloth.

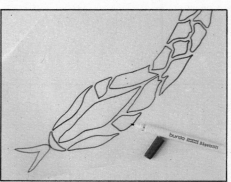

3 Trace the snake motif off the pattern sheet onto wax paper with burda's blue transfer pencil. Iron interfacing (with steam) onto the **wrong** side of area that is to be painted.

7 Transfer palm motif as in ills. 3 and 4. Color in motif with felt pens, allow to dry thoroughly, then iron from the **wrong** side.

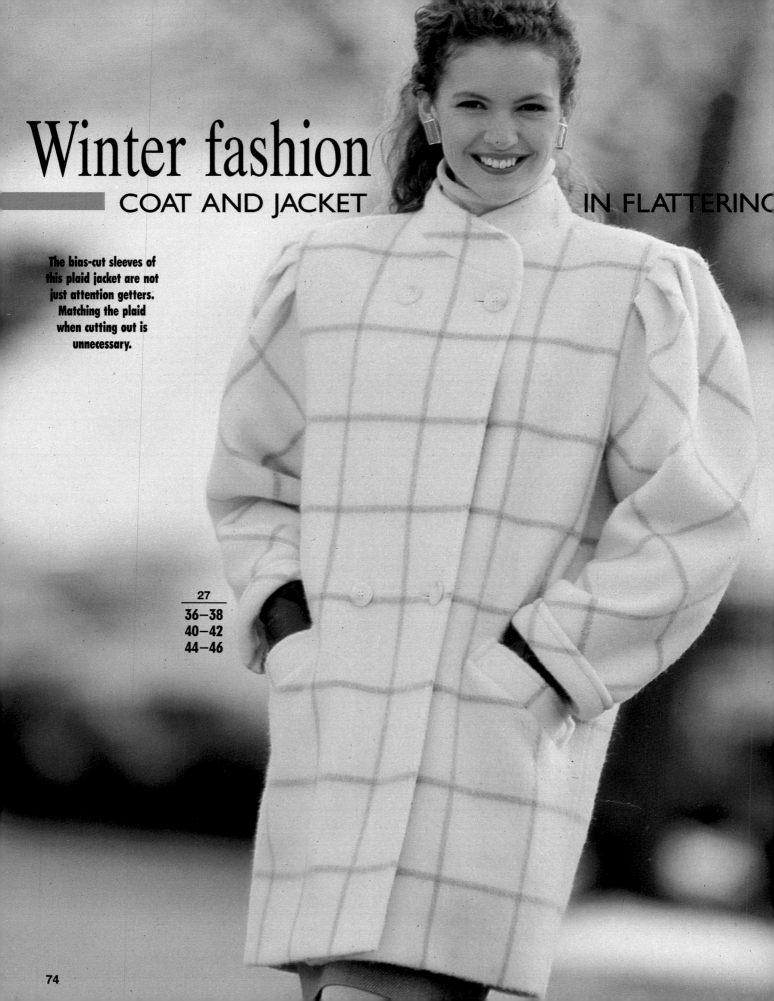

Winter fashion
COAT AND JACKET
IN FLATTERING

The bias-cut sleeves of this plaid jacket are not just attention getters. Matching the plaid when cutting out is unnecessary.

27
36—38
40—42
44—46

REAM AND BEIGE

27: Attractive: perfectly placed buttons and comfortable standing collar. Generously proportioned sleeves furnish plenty of space for a bulky sweater.

Tweed, poplin, fake fur and synthetic leathers are also suitable for this style.

Illustrated teaching instructions located on pages 76/77.

What you should know about fabric types and designs

A design can be printed onto, woven or knitted into a fabric and must be taken into consideration when cutting out. The next 4 pages explain what you need do know about designs and fabric types.

Uneven, unbalanced or directional designs

If all the flower stems in a floral print point in the same direction, then this print is directional (ill. 5). In an unbalanced stripe the width and color of stripes does not repeat evenly but differs (ill. 6). The stripe width and color can be different on all four sides of an uneven plaid (ill. 7). In all three cases extreme care must be taken when cutting out. All pattern pieces must be placed onto fabric so that they point in the same direction, so that all flower stems point toward hem edge, for example.

Border fabrics

These fabrics have a design printed or woven along one selvage (ill. 8) and constitute a great exception when cutting out. Pattern pieces are usually pinned onto these fabrics on the cross grain. Make sure that the style you choose has a straight hem edge. Pin pattern pieces onto fabric so that their lower edge lies on border design.

Even or balanced designs

These designs do not dictate a direction when cutting out. This could be a floral design, for example, in which the stems point both up and down or in all directions (ill. 1), or a graphic design with no recognizable direction (ill. 2). Even plaids consisting of repeated, four-sided areas in which the pattern and color of the design are complete (ill. 3) also belong to this group, as do balanced vertical and horizontal stripes, designs in which stripe width and color arrangement are repeated evenly in a lengthwise resp. crosswise direction (ill. 4). Even or balanced designs are the easiest and most economical of the designed fabric group to cut out.

Panel prints

These are fabrics with a large design, or panel, that is printed repeatedly onto the fabric (ill. 9). A panel can be long or wide enough for a large scarf, a skirt, a streetlength dress or even an evening gown.

Napped fabrics

To this group belong such fabrics as velvet, corduroy, velour, terry velour, wool fleece, pile fabric, fake fur, loden and some terrycloth types, i.e. fabrics that have hairs or loops on one side. Stroke along one selvage of such a fabric with your fingertips. If the hairs lie flat and the fabric feels smooth, then you are stroking "with the nap." If hairs stand up and the fabric feels rough then you are "against the nap." The illustration below shows velvet "with the nap" in

velvet ▲   ▼ corduroy

the upper half, "against the nap" in the lower half. Nap direction arrows are printed onto pattern pieces for garments where a napped fabric is required.

Important: velvet, fine corduroy, terry velour and velour should always be cut out "against the nap" to give the fabric a richer, deeper color. Against the nap means that you can run your hand from

▼ wool fleece

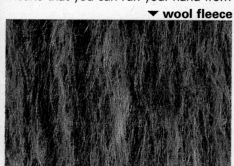

hem edge up to shoulder to flatten the fabric hairs. Fabrics with short or flatlying hairs such as panné velvet, widewaled corduroy, looped terrycloth with a clear loop direction, pile fabric, fake fur, wool fleece, loden and many other wool fabrics are cut out "with the nap," i.e. you can run your hand from shoulder to hem edge to flatten fabric hairs. The cardinal rule for cutting out napped fabrics, however, regardless of whether you're cutting out with or against the nap, is that all pattern pieces be placed on the fabric so that they point in the same direction. The terrycloth shown above is vertically striped and the loop direction is crosswise. The only thing you

would have to pay attention to when cutting out in this case would be the stripe direction.

Other fabric types

Seersucker: a cotton or cotton blend fabric with puckered, lengthwise stripes, lending the surface of the fabric a crinkled effect. The puckered stripes in genuine seersucker (ills. 10 and 11) are attained by different tension settings on the warp (lengthwise) threads. The looser set threads are the raised striped. Cheap imitations are made by applying caustic soda (potash) to the fabric.

Crinkled fabrics: have been made to look wrinkled. There are heavier crinkled cottons (ill. 12) that are used for coats, jackets, etc. in which the wrinkles run lengthwise only, and there are crinkled silks and synthetics with very pronounced wrinkles that run both lengthwise and crosswise.

Piqué: a fabric with raised, "blistered" designs (stripes, diamonds, etc.) on the right side (ill. 13).

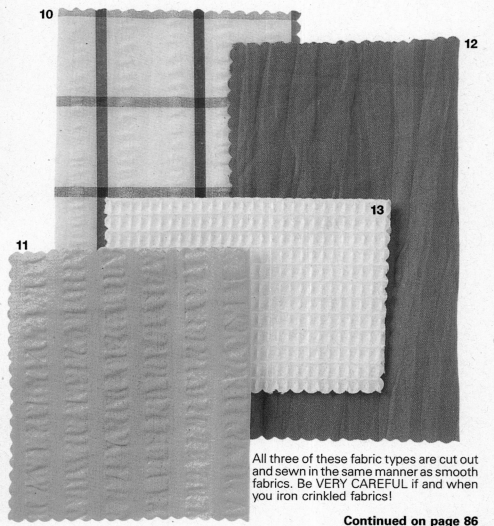

All three of these fabric types are cut out and sewn in the same manner as smooth fabrics. Be VERY CAREFUL if and when you iron crinkled fabrics!

Continued on page 86

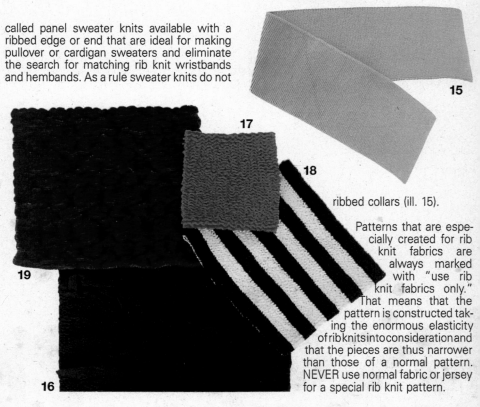

stretch as much as rib knits, so you can use normal patterns with them or those specified especially for sweater knits. Cut out sweater knits with noticeable knit direction as you would a directional or napped fabric.

Rib knits: alternating knit and purl stitches in the same row (ills. 10, 11) lend this type of knit enormous elasticity. It is used mainly for neck and wristbands, for straight, tight skirts with elasticized waist or for clingy dresses. Horizontal seams are problematic, shoulder seams for example. It is absolutely necessary to catch in seam tape or stretched-out bias tape when stitching these seams to prevent them from stretching out of shape. Hems should be stitched with twin ballpoint needles. Neck, wrist and hembands made from rib knit are usually folded, i.e. doubled layered, and are stretched as they are stitched into place. Recently rib knits have come onto the market that can be cut apart horizontally by drawing out a horizontal thread (ill. 12). This type can be used in a single layer as can purchased ribbed bands (ills. 13 and 14) and

Knits

The general term used for both weft and warp knit fabrics. The difference between weft and warp knitting is not recognizable at first glance. Weft knits are done on machines that imitate hand knitting, knitting individual stitches in rows that are connected to each other. Warp knitting is much more complicated with several stitches being knitted at the same time. Here is a list of the most important knit fabrics available:

Jersey: Available in a wide variety of single or double knits in solid colors (ill. 1), prints (ill. 2), with printed or knitted in metallic highlights (ill. 26), jacquard patterns, etc. Color coordinated printed and striped jerseys are available with which you can make great outfits. See ills. 3-5 for an example of coordinated striped jerseys.

Sweatshirting: An absorbent fabric with a brushed wrong side and smooth right side (ill. 6). Usually in cotton but also available in blends. Some sweatshirts are made of a double knit jersey with a textured or crinkled right side (ill. 7).

Sweater knits: are made to look like handknits (ills. 8 and 9) and can be used for dresses, jackets, pullovers, etc. There are so-

called panel sweater knits available with a ribbed edge or end that are ideal for making pullover or cardigan sweaters and eliminate the search for matching rib knit wristbands and hembands. As a rule sweater knits do not

ribbed collars (ill. 15).

Patterns that are especially created for rib knit fabrics are always marked with "use rib knit fabrics only." That means that the pattern is constructed taking the enormous elasticity of rib knits into consideration and that the pieces are thus narrower than those of a normal pattern. NEVER use normal fabric or jersey for a special rib knit pattern.

Cloqué jersey: a type of jersey that stretches both lengthwise and crosswise (ills. 16-18) and that is usually available in tubes, called tubular knits. These tubes are great for making summer tops or tight sunback dresses. You just hem the upper and lower edges and slip on the garment. If this fabric is being used for a garment with set-in sleeves, the pattern should be one suitable for very stretchable knits. Patterns for normal fabrics are not recommended for cloqué jersey, nor for cloqué velvet (ill. 19).

Noble classics

Baby houndstooth: a finer version of houndstooth check, a four-pointed star check in a twill weave (ill. 20). The check is so fine that you can cut out this fabric as you would a non-directional print.

Houndstooth check: sometimes called dogtooth check. Also a fourpointed star check with extensions on the points that connect the checks (ill. 21)

Glen check: one of a number of check patterns originating in Scotland. Usually a smaller check pattern with a larger, superimposed plaid added (ill. 22). There are even, uneven and multicolored glen checks, so take care when cutting out that the horizontal bars in the plaid match at vertical seams of your garment.

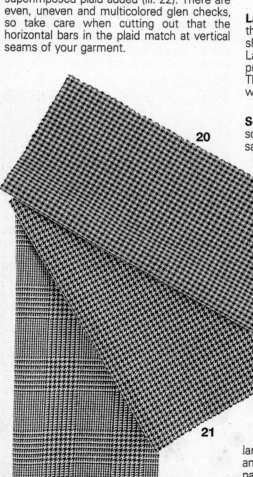

Dressy metallics

Lamé: a fineweave fabric made from metallic threads, usually non-oxidizing. Illustration 23 shows lamé with a flocked velvet pattern. Lamé made with real metal threads is produced only in France and Italy and oxidizes. Thus it must be stored away from light, wrapped in chlorine free paper.

Sequinned fabrics: available in many forms, sometimes woven, sometimes knit. Our sample in ill. 24 is woven and has stitched on ribbons and sequins attached by a continuous thread. See page 123 for detailed instructions on how to cut and handle this type of fabric.

Net lace: a transparent fabric consisting of a net or tulle base that is machine embroidered with a pattern in chain and satin stitch (ill. 25). It is similar to real lace but without the holes.

Metallic print jersey: a very decorative, soft fabric (ill. 26). Take the type of print (i.e. directional or non-directional) into consideration when cutting out. The one we show is non-directional.

Jacquard and dobby weaves: fabrics with woven-in designs, can be solid or multicolored. Jacquard patterns are larger (ill. 27) and require special machines and techniques to produce. Dobby weave patterns are geometric and require a special attachment to a normal loom.

Fake furs, imitation leathers

There is a tremendous selection that can be purchased by the meter/yard. Normal patterns can be used together with these fabrics. Always cut out **fake fur** WITH the nap. Choose a garment with as few seams as possible, regardless if using a knit type (ill. 28) or a woven type (ill. 29). The same rule applies to deep pile fabrics (ill. 30). There is a wide range of quality amongst the **leather imitations,** so always ask about care instructions before purchasing and keep in mind that smooth ("nappa") leather imitations (ill. 31) don't soil as easily as suede or chamois imitations (ill. 32). See page 125 for detailed instructions on handling these fabrics.

Preparations for fitting

Accurate cutting and marking pays off at the first fitting

Proper preparation is essential

The garment should be basted together for fitting with seams only lightly pressed. Normal, set-in sleeves should be pinned into armholes for the first fitting. Before separating pieces cut from doubled fabric layers, make sure that you have marked all construction markings, center front, center back, etc. onto BOTH fabric layers. If you have not used tailor's tacking, then thread-trace neck and armhole seamlines onto the right fabric side. Do this for all pocket opening or placement lines, buttonholes, hemlines, pleat lines, etc. Apply interfacing where required before fitting. Zippers should be carefully basted into place, not just pinned.

Mini stickers - ideal pattern markers

Mark similarly shaped pieces, side front and side back for example, or the wrong side of a fabric whose right and wrong sides hardly differ with small stickers. Seam numbers can also be marked in this manner. Apply stickers to the **wrong** fabric side. They can easily be peeled off later on and are available in most stationery shops.

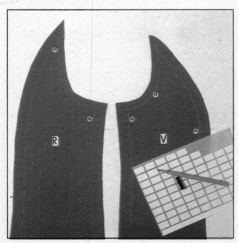

Which interfacing for which fabric?

One generally differentiates between fusible and sew-in interfacings that are available in different weights and types.

The easiest to use are the fusible types that are ironed onto the wrong side of the outer fabric. You thus avoid the basting and padstitching required for the sewn-in interfacings used in classical tailoring.

The weight of your interfacing depends upon the weight and type of outer fabric used and upon whether you want the garment to be soft and supple or crisply tailored. Chose a thin type for blouses and dresses, for example vilene (pellon) H200 resp. vilene 327 or vilene (pellon) F220 resp. vilene 304. Use extremely soft and lightweight vilene (pellon) H180 on fineweave, silky or transparent fabrics. For a casual, unfitted jacket always use a soft interfacing (vilene/pellon G 405 resp. vilene 315), but for suits and coats a stiffer fusible type (vilene/pellon H315 resp. vilene 316) or sew-in wool or horsehair interfacing. For belts, cuffs and crafts we recommend stiff interfacing vilene/pellon H250 resp. vilene 305, for waistbands on pants and skirt Vilene Fold-a-band firm resp. Vilene Fuse and Fold resp. Pellon Waist Shaper.

Important:

when purchasing interfacing bear in mind whether the planned garment is to be washed or drycleaned.

Both fusible and sew-in vilene/pellon is washable and drycleanable. The F220 resp. 304 and H250 resp. 305 types can be hot washed up to 95 degrees centigrade. Both types have a shiny coated side and are ironed on with a dry iron. The types H180, H200 resp. 327, H315 resp. 316 and G405 resp. 315 are washable up to 40 degrees centigrade. H200 resp. 327 and H180 are ironed on with a dry iron, H315 resp. 316 and G405 resp. 315 require steam. See the diagram to the right. Care symbols and ironing instructions are printed in blue on the edges of these interfacings.

How to cut out interfacing

Non-woven interfacings do not have a straight grain and can be cut out in all directions, the quickest and most economical method being important.

Woven interfacings such as organza, wool and horsehair must be cut out on the grain for closing and neck edges, on the bias for collars.

Fusible interfacings

ALWAYS TEST FIRST before ironing interfacing onto your garment pieces. This is especially important for thin fabrics. Should the interfacing show through or mar the right side of your garment, then apply it to the facings or switch to a lighter, finer interfacing type.

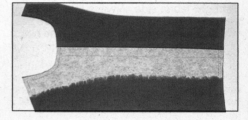

Avoid ridges on the right fabric side

by fraying the outer edges of interfacing before ironing it into place.

Front reinforcement with fusible interfacing

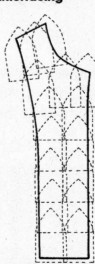

For a suit jacket, for example, place vilene/pellon G405 resp. vilene 315 coated side down onto the **wrong** side of front. Seamlines and markings have been traced onto the uncoated side of interfacing. Place a damp cloth over interfacing. Set your iron between the wool and cotton settings and press down onto the damp cloth, holding about 12 seconds. DO NOT SLIDE iron!

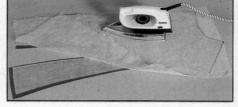

Pick up and put down, holding for 12

seconds each time, until you have worked up and down the entire front as shown in the diagram. If you have a steam iron, then turn off the steam. The steam made with the damp cloth is more evenly distributed than that from the slots of a steam iron.

Important: allow these interfaced pieces to cool for at least 30 minutes before handling them further.

Tip: If you wish to remove fused interfacing, re-heat briefly with your steam iron and pull it away from fabric.

Baste garment together for fitting
Darts

Begin at the dart point and with a knot in thread ends. Stitch from side edge in to point, clipping off basting thread knot just before reaching point.
Never stitch on basting threads. Try

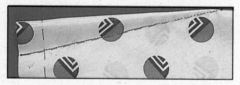

stitching 1 mm to one side of them. They're easier to remove that way!

Side and section seams
Make sure that right sides are together. Place the layers flat on a table for basting. If you hold them rounded over one hand or leg, the lower layer will automatically come up shorter than the upper layer.

Shoulder seams
Don't forget to ease in back shoulder edges as indicated on pattern. Always baste and stitch shoulder seams from the wrong side of back.

Attach yokes

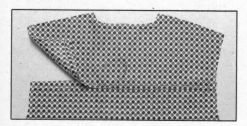

Baste the allowance on lower

(attachment) edge of yoke to the **inside,** press. Baste the **wrong** side of yoke onto the **right** side of corresponding piece so that its basted edge lies on marked seamline.

Stripes and plaids
require special attention when basting, for they should match at all vertical and horizontal seams. Pre-requisite is of course exact cutting out (see pages 92/

93). If the stripes or plaid is visible on the wrong fabric side then you can easily baste from the wrong side. Pin layers together, matching stripes resp. plaid exactly and inserting pins perpendicular to seamline. Baste. Leave pins in seam and stitch over them later on.

Tip: Even if you have used shorter basting stitches, the fabric layers can slip out of line during stitching. Therefore, it is a good idea to insert pins perpendicular to the seamline to prevent slipping. You can easily stitch over these pins without fear of breaking your needle.

What you should know about sleeves
Today's fashion contains many types of sleeves. Therefore, it is important that you take a careful look at the sleeves when choosing your pattern. If you prefer a style with wider shoulders, sleeves are often attached off-shoulder on these styles and have a slightly curved upper edge rather than a classic sleeve cap. Dolman sleeves are a good example of this. Obviously these casual shapes cannot be compared with the classic, slender sleeve that we show on page 98, and you should never try to alter the sleeves of such a casual pattern to resemble a classic sleeve. It just won't work!
The longer and narrower the sleeve cap, the smoother the fall of the sleeve. Flatter sleeve caps tend to crease diagonally at the attachment seam,

something that is usually accepted due to the comfortable cut. If you are a stickler for classic, perfectly fitting sleeves then you should carefully study the pattern overviews which often show you the true shape of a sleeve more clearly than the view illustration.

If sleeves have to be eased in
For best results run a row of machine

basting 3 mm (⅛") on each side of the marked seamline between the easing dots (●). Pull up the bobbin threads at both ends of this stitching slightly to ease.

Baste the underarm seam in right sleeve first and pin this sleeve into place for your first fitting. Any alterations made can be immediately marked onto the open left sleeve.

There's a certain order for basting a skirt together, for example...
Begin with the darts, then close all seams, leaving the zipper placket open in center back or left side seam. Then baste zipper into place. Baste waistband interfacing, open edged, to the upper edge of skirt for fitting.

... or a blouse
Baste interfacing to the **wrong** side of closing edges or iron onto facings. Fold extended facings to the **inside** along facing line, baste fold edges. Baste darts and all section seams. Cut out collar from interfacing and pin to neck edge for fitting. Pin right sleeve into place.

... or a dress with waist seam
Baste skirt panels to the corresponding bodice piece at waist seam. Then baste side seams of entire dress from upper edge of bodice to lower edge of skirt. Width adjustments are thus easier to execute. Take care not to catch in waist seam allowances when basting.

Interesting details

On the following pages we will show you different types of slits and plackets, how to set in v-shaped insets resp. bands. Buttonhole and welt pockets as well as flapped welt pockets are explained in detail in our illustrated teaching instructions.

Striking: a simple slit with buttonloops and decorative topstitching

Buttonloop closings are also suitable for long, close-fitting sleeves, located either in the underarm seam or where a vertical dart normally would be.

Here's how:

Mark the slit lines (ill. 1). Cut between these lines (ill. 2). Make tubing for button loops: fold bias strip in half lengthwise, **right** sides together. Stitch ½ cm (¼") from fold, stretching as you stitch so that the seam won't break when turning. Do not cut off threads too short at one end of strip. Knot a darning needle securely to these threads. Slip the needle, eye first, back through strip, turning it **right** side out and thus making tubing for loops (ill. 3). The length of loops depends upon the size of your buttons. For best results experiment first by folding strip into loops and slipping button through. Baste loops onto the **right** side of right slit edge so that their ends lie over the edge (ill. 4 and 5). Stitch neck facings to slit facing, **right** sides together (ill. 6). Stitch shoulder seams in garment and, if required, center back seam below back zipper placket. Overcast and press open seam allowances. Turn placket allowances to the **outside** and pin into place at neck edge. Pin facing to neck edge, **right** sides together, matching shoulder seams (ill. 7). Working from the **wrong** side of garment, stitch facing into place along neck and slit edges. Slash facing between slit stitching lines (ill. 8). Turn facing to the **inside.** Mark topstitching lines with lines of basting (ill. 9). If using thicker thread for decorative topstitching,

wind this onto your bobbin and topstitch from the **wrong** side of the garment (ill. 10). Ill. 11 shows the finished closing.

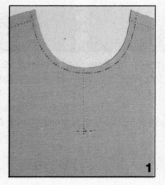

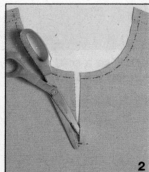

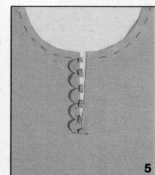

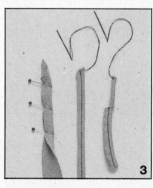

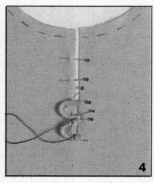

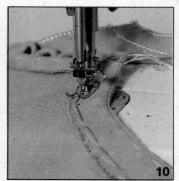

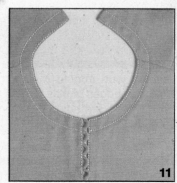

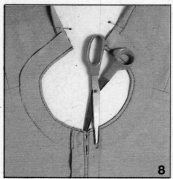

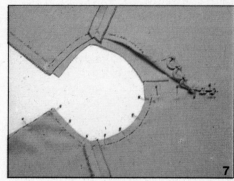

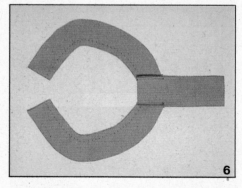

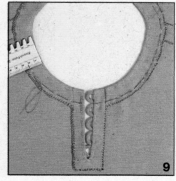

All these details can be applied to the pattern of your choice. We also list interesting things to know about handling sweater knits, jersey, velvet, terry velour, sequinned fabric and leather. Pleats, tucks, pintucks and commercial pleating are also included. You can add an exclusive touch to your garments with decorative trims, topstitching, smocking, appliqués, lace inserts and motifs. And we haven't left out tips for lining, either. Attractive home decorations come last but not least, including oodles of super suggestions for bedspreads, draperies, etc.

Sleeve slits

There are many types of openings used at lower sleeve edges and just as many ways of finishing them. Here are the 2 most commonly used types.

Slashed opening

Cut out facings for openings, each 3 cm (1¼") wide and about 2 cm (⅞") longer than the slit lines. Make sure you match any stripes or plaids! Pin facing into place over slit lines, **right** sides together, centering it over the lines. Stitch along slit lines with close-set stitches, taking 2 stitches across end of slit. Carefully slash sleeve and facing between these stitching lines. Tip: a dab of clear nail polish will prevent the end of slit from pulling open. Turn facing to the **inside,** press slit edges. Turn under facing edges, pin, baste and edgestitch into place. Important: when cutting out, interfacing and constructing cuffs make sure that you have a righthand and a lefthand cuff and that any stripes or plaids match. Attach cuffs as in ills. 2 - 4.

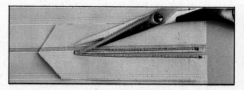
1 Pin slit facing onto sleeve over slit lines, **right** sides together. Stitch into place from **wrong** side of sleeve along slit lines. Slash between stitching lines. Turn facing to the **inside,** turn under its raw edges, pin and edgestitch into place (ill. 2).

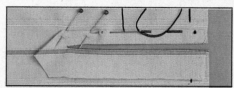

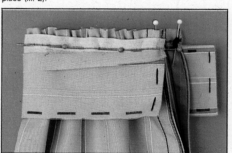
3 Turn cuffs **right** side out, baste and press seamed edges. Pin interfaced cuff halves to lower sleeve edges, **right** sides together.

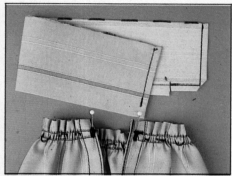
2 Gather lower sleeve edges to match cuffs. Fold cuffs in half lengthwise, **right** sides together. Stitch both ends and underlap of each. Trim seam allowances, trim corners diagonally, clip in close to last stitch at underlap.

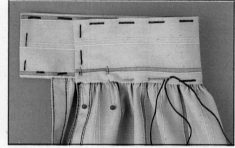
4 Important! Before stitching make sure that cuff underlap lies at slit edge nearest underarm seam in sleeve. Stitch cuffs into place. Press allowances into cuffs. Baste inner layers into place over attachment seam. Edgestitch along all cuff edges, securing inner layer of each.

Practice makes perfect plackets

Cut a 3 cm (1¼") wide strip on the grain, 2 cm (⅞") longer than double the length of placket. Complete placket as in ills. 5 - 7. Fold binding on placket edge furthest away from underarm seam to the **inside** and baste into place. Again, cuff underlap should lie at slit edge nearest underarm seam in sleeve.

5 Slash lower sleeve edge between placket lines. Spread edges apart. Fold binding strip in half lengthwise, **wrong** sides together, press. Pin folded strip onto the **wrong** side of sleeve so that its open edges lie on placket edges.

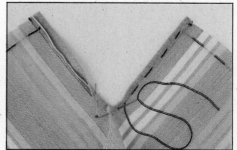
6 Stitch binding strip into place, at upper end of placket with only 1 mm seam allowance. Fold binding strip in half lengthwise. Fold outer half to the **outside** of sleeve, baste into place over attachment seam.

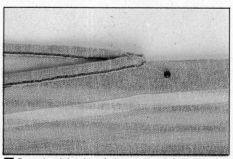
7 From the **right** side of sleeve edgestitch binding strip into place. From the **wrong** side of sleeve stitch diagonally across binding at upper end of placket.

Polo closings - timeless classics

The attractive dress to the left illustrates how you can customize a very simple style by adding chic details such as a polo closing, side slit and notched sleeves, all accented with contrasting fabric. You can work a polo closing into any dress, shirt or blouse, regardless if the neckline is round, scooped or, as in this case, slightly scooped. Contrasting bands are most striking on a slender, straight dress with short, cut-in-one sleeves. We have added a 30 cm (12") long slit in left side seam. If you do not plan to use contrasting fabric, don't worry about slit and hem facings. Just add 4.5 cm (1¾") allowance to hem and slit edges

Prepare pattern as follows:

Mark the desired length of closing, usually between 15 and 25 cm (6" and 10") from neck edge, onto the center of front pattern piece. The bands in the closing shown above are 3.6 cm (1½") wide. In this case you would draw in a line 1.8 cm (¾") from and parallel to center front. Trim pattern piece along this line down to line marking end of closing, then trim out end. These edges will be the attachment edges for the closing bands. Now draw in 3.6 cm (1½") wide facings onto pattern pieces along hem, slit, neck and lower sleeve edges. Using this as a guide, make extra pattern pieces for these facings. Cut out hem facing with a right side seam.

Cut out dress as follows:

Cut out front and back each once on the fold. Don't forget to add 1 cm (½") allowance to front closing edges (see ills. 1 and 2).

Cut out closing bands ...

For RIGHT band one piece in dress fabric and one in contrasting fabric, each 3.6 cm (1½") wide and 3 cm (1¼") longer than closing. For LEFT band a 7.2 cm (2⅞") wide piece in contrasting fabric, also 3 cm (1¼") longer than closing. Cut out all bands with 1 cm (½") allowance on all edges.

1 Baste and stitch neck facing to neck edge, **right** sides together. Trim and clip seam allowances. Turn facing to the **inside**.

2 Baste seamed (neck) edge. Turn under inner edge of facing, baste into place along the marked line (3.6 cm - 1½" wide).

3 Stitch right band to right closing edge from neck edge down to horizontal marking, **right** sides together. Stitch the other band to left closing edge in the same manner.

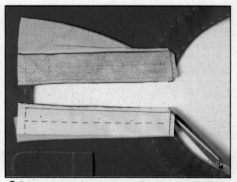

4 Fold bands in half lengthwise, **right** sides together. Stitch upper end of each from fold over to attachment seam. Trim seam allowances back to ½ cm (¼") width, trim corners diagonally.

Cut out shaped facings ...

Cut out all shaped facings in contrasting fabric with 1 cm (½") allowance on all edges.

Construct in this order:

Iron interfacing onto the **wrong** side of neck and sleeve facings, onto **wrong** side of RIGHT band in dress fabric, of one half of left, contrasting band. Stitch neck facings together at shoulder seams. Stitch front to back at shoulder seams from neck edge over to 3.6 cm (1½") from lower sleeve edge. Attach neck facing and turn to the **inside** as in ills. 1 and 2.

Polo closing:

Stitch pieces for RIGHT band **right** sides together at long edges. Stitch dress fabric band to the right closing edge, contrasting band to left closing edge, **right** sides together (ill. 3). Fold bands in half lengthwise, **right** sides together, and stitch upper end of each from fold over to attachment seam (ill. 4). Clip seam allowance of front in close to last stitch at each lower corner of closing (ill. 5). Turn bands **right** side out, fold along foldline, turn under inner layer of each and baste into place over outer layer attachment seam (ill. 6). Edgestitch along both long edges and upper end of each band, securing inner layer. Pin right band onto left band, center-on-center. Stitch front allowance at lower end of closing to band ends from corner to corner, **right** sides together (ill. 7). From the **right** side topstitch lower end of right band with a crossed square as shown in ill. 8.

Shaped sleeve, hem and slit facings:

Stitch side seams in dress as well as hem facing, stitch underarm seam in sleeve facings. Pin sleeve facings to lower sleeve edges, **right** sides together. Beginning and ending exactly at end of shoulder seam, stitch facing to sleeve slit and lower sleeve edges (ill. 9). Turn facings to the **inside,** turn under inner edge, baste into place. Edgestitch along all facing edges (ill. 10). Attach hem and slit facing in the same manner, beginning and ending exactly at lower end of left side seam. Turn facing to the **inside,** turn under inner edge (finished facing width 3.6 cm - 1½"), baste into place. Edgestitch along all facing edges (ill. 11 and 12).

Important

The proper stitch setting is of utmost importance for immaculate topstitching. For clarity we have shown all topstitching in contrasting thread. You should always use thread matching your fabric in needle and bobbin, e.g. upper thread in the same color as contrasting fabric and bobbin thread in the color of your dress fabric, or vice versa. When using two colors of thread in this manner, experiment first on scraps of your fabric to check the tension.

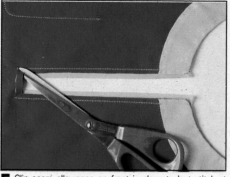

5 Clip seam allowance on front in close to last stitch at both lower corners of closing.

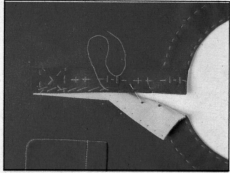

6 Turn bands **right** side out. Turn under inner layer of each, baste into place over attachment seam. Edgestitch along both long edges of bands, along both long edges of neck facing as well.

7 Stitch front allowance to lower band ends from corner to corner, **right** sides together.

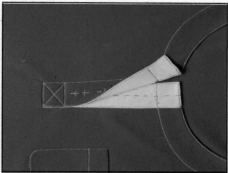

8 Trim lower band ends even with front allowance, press downward. Topstitch lower end of right band as shown.

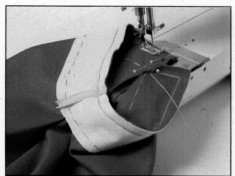

9 Begin and end sleeve facing attachment seam exactly at end of shoulder seam, stitching from the **right** side of sleeve.

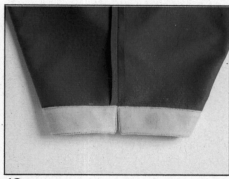

10 Trim seam allowances, trim corners diagonally. Turn facings to the **inside,** turn under open edges, baste and edgestitch into place.

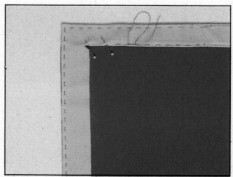

11 Stitch hem and side slit facing into place, **right** sides together. Turn facing to the **inside,** turn under open edge, baste into place (finished width 3.6 cm - 1½"). Stitch into place.

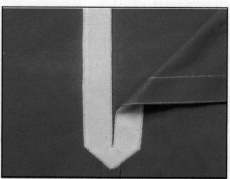

12 Begin and end edgestitching for slit facing exactly at side seam.

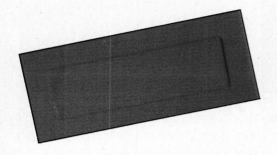

Welt pocket

This type of pocket can be worked vertically, horizontally or diagonally. For best results, however, try on in front of a mirror first, adjusting position to better suit your figure if necessary

For one pocket you will need:
Welt cut out from garment fabric
2 pouch pieces cut out from lining
Fusible interfacing for welt and for reinforcing pocket opening

Preparation and construction
Thread trace pocket opening line and welt placement lines onto **right** fabric side (ill. 1). Cut out a 7 cm (2¼") wide interfacing strip that is 4 cm (1⅝") longer than opening line. Iron this onto the **wrong** side over opening and welt lines (ill. 2). Iron interfacing onto the **wrong** side of one half of welt. Fold welt in half lengthwise, **right** sides together. Stitch both ends. Turn welt **right** side out, baste and press its seamed and fold edges. Baste welt, interfaced layer down, onto the **right** side along attachment line (ill. 3). Baste a pouch piece into place over welt, baste other pouch piece onto the **right** side of garment above welt so that straight edges touch over pocket opening line (ills. 4 and 5). Stitch pocket pieces into place with ¾ cm (⅜") seam allowance. Lower stitching line ends at welt ends, upper stitching line should be ½ cm (¼") shorter at both ends (ill. 6). Working from the **wrong** side, slash between these stitching lines (ill. 7). Clip diagonally to each last stitch, forming small triangles at opening ends (ill. 8). Pull pouch pieces through opening to the **inside.** Press welt up over opening, pin into place along placement lines (ill. 9). Fold opening end triangles to the **inside.** Working with front on top and folded back as shown in ill. 10, stitch pouch pieces together. Begin and end directly above opening end triangles and stitch across base of each. Overcast pouch allowances together (ill. 11). Slipstitch welt ends into place, making stitches as inconspicuous as possible (ill. 12).

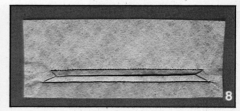

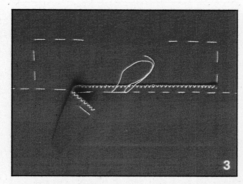

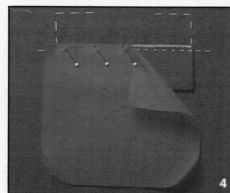

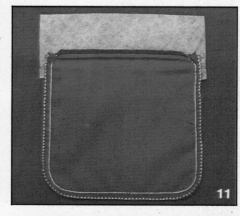

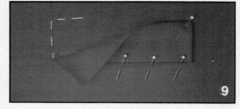

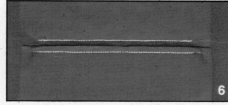

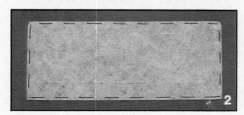

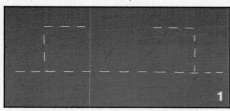

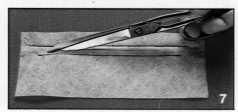

Welt pocket with flap

This type of pocket can be worked in horizontally or diagonally. Flap shape can of course be varied. Try cutting out flaps on the bias in plaid fabric for an attractive contrast

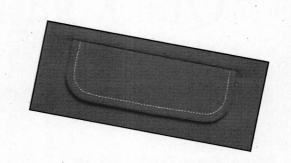

Tip: Construct these pockets into the appropriate garment section before constructing garment. It is thus easier to work with, i.e. you have less bulk on your machine.

For one pocket you will need:

2 flap pieces cut out from garment fabric
2 welt strips cut on the grain from garment fabric, 6 cm (2¼") wide and 4 cm (1⅝") longer than opening line
2 pouch pieces cut from lining
Fusible interfacing for flap and for reinforcing pocket opening

Preparation and construction

Iron interfacing onto the **wrong** side of one flap piece. Stitch flap pieces **right** sides together along both ends and one long edge. Turn flap **right** side out. Baste, press and edgestitch along seamed edges. Thread trace flap placement and pocket opening lines onto the **right** fabric side (ill. 1). Cut out a 5 cm (2") wide interfacing strip, 4 cm (1⅝") longer than pocket opening line. Iron this onto the **wrong** side over opening line (ill. 2). If working with a very thin fabric, cut out pouch pieces from this fabric rather than from lining. In this case you will not need the welt strips.
Stitch welt strips to straight (upper) edge of lining pouch pieces, **right** sides together. Press open seam allowances (ill. 3). Baste flap, interfaced layer down, onto the **right** side so that its finished edges lie above opening line. Baste a welt strip + pouch piece into place over flap, **right** sides together. Baste other welt strip + pouch piece into place, **right** sides together, so that welt strips just touch over opening line (ill. 3). Stitch pocket pieces into place. Upper stitching line should be in flap length, lower stitching line should be ½ cm (¼") shorter at both ends than upper one (ill. 4). Working from the **wrong** side slash along opening line. Clip diagonally to each last stitch, forming small triangles at opening ends (ill. 5). Take care NOT to cut or clip pocket pieces! Pull pouch pieces through opening to the **inside**. Press open seam allowances on lower welt strip attachment seam. Fold lower welt so that its fold lies on flap attachment seam and fills opening (ill. 6). Baste. From the **right** side take back stitches through lower welt attachment seam groove, securing its inner layer. Press flap down over opening, pin into place (ill. 7). Working with front on top and folded back as shown, stitch pouch pieces together. Begin and end directly above opening end triangles and stitch across the base of each (ill. 8). Overcast pouch allowances together (ill. 9).

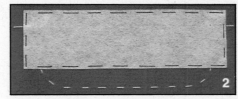

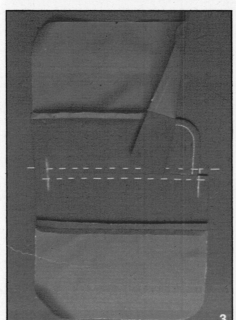

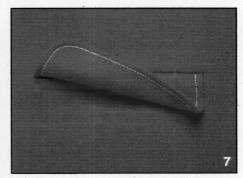

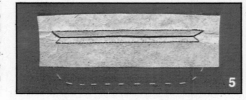

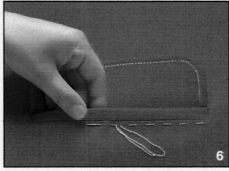

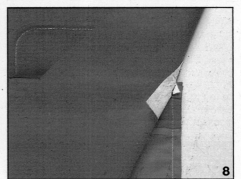

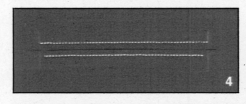

Important construction tips for...

Velvet

All types of velvet have a "nap" direction, i.e. the pile or hairs run in the same direction, parallel to the selvages. Generally speaking there are two types of velvet, one with unpressed pile, the other with pressed pile or patterns (e.g. panne velvet, velours frappé).

Velvet is always cut out "against" the nap. The same applies to corduroy.

The everlasting exceptions to this rule are panne and printed velvets with a directional pattern, forcing you to cut out "with" the nap for the sake of the pattern.

Determining nap direction

Run your fingers along the selvage of your velvet. If the pile or hairs all lie flat, then you are stroking "with" the nap; should they stand up, then you are stroking "against" the nap. Nap direction arrows are printed onto patterns foreseen for velvet garments and point in nap direction, i.e. with the nap. See cutting layout to the right. By cutting out against the nap, velvet garments have a richer, deeper color as illustrated below.

Cutting out

All pattern pieces are placed onto velvet so that the nap direction arrows all run in the same direction, be it with or against the nap.

In other words, the lower edge of all pieces lie in the same direction. Cutting out "against" the nap means that the pile lies flat when stroking from lower to upper edge of garment.

Pinning, basting, stitching

To prevent two layers of velvet from slipping out of line or bunching during stitching - and this almost invariably happens - proceed as follows. For short pile types insert pins across

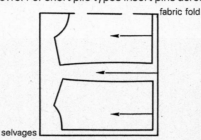

the seamline at close intervals and stitch across them as shown below, eliminating basting. For deep pile velvets take a row of hand basting stitches on each side of the marked seamline with silk thread. Stitch exactly between these rows of basting, stitching in nap direction whenever possible (see illustrations above). A teflon-soled presser foot facilitates matters greatly! Be very careful when removing the basting

threads. You could damage the pile by pulling them out all at once, so clip at intervals and carefully remove the sections.

Pressing

For optimal results use a steam iron combined with a needleboard, a flat board with metal needles mounted in it that prevent the pile

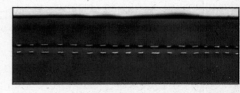

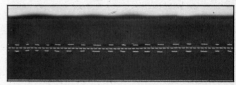

from being pressed flat. Velvet is placed pile down onto needleboard so that the hairs can "hang" between the needles during pressing. If this is not available substitute a thick terry towel or another piece of velvet placed pile side up onto ironing board. Gently glide your iron across the backside of velvet. Do not apply pressure!

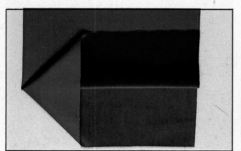

Terry velour

This is a stretchable knit fabric with cut and brushed pile on one side that feels much like velvet. Like velvet, it is optically most effective when cut out against the nap. Stitch vertical seams in the same manner as for knits (see pages 120/121), either with long-set zigzag stitch or with overlock stitch. Bear in mind, though, that overlock stitching is difficult and tedious to remove. Finish any closing slits with woven bias tape for best results, for it reinforces the slit edges and is thinner than a self-fabric facing (ill. 1). Prevent shoulder seams from stretching by catching in a stretched piece of bias tape or a bias strip cut from woven fabric (ill. 2). Catch in a 20 cm (8") long strip of stretched bias tape when

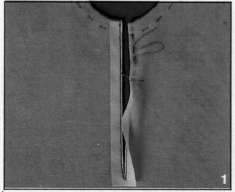

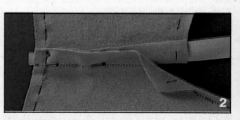

stitching sleeves into place to prevent these seams from pulling out of shape (ill. 3). Hand sew blind hems with catch stitch in the same manner as for knits. Press in the same manner as velvet.

Moiré

Moiré is a taffeta or ribbed fabric with a finish of wavy lines that looks much like watermarks. This typical finish is produced by pulling 2 dampened lengths of fabric under pressure between two rollers. This "genuine" moiré does not contain any pattern repeats, as found in the types produced with engraved rollers. You should not wash moiré. Beware of viscose rayon moiré, for its pattern often does not withstand drycleaning. Acetate moiré retains the pattern well, for acetate fibers do not expand when moistened. Also, be very careful with dressmaker's carbon on moiré, for it is usually not removable, not even by drycleaning.

Cutting out, sewing

Examine your moiré to see if its wavy lines form a directional pattern. If not, you can cut out economically, i.e. pin on pattern pieces in both directions as long as they are on the straight grain. However, do not cut out moiré on the cross grain unless stated in the pattern cutting instructions. Sew up moiré as you would any normal, woven fabric.

Pressing

Once creases are pressed into moiré they are very difficult to remove. Therefore, do not press seams and hems for first fitting, or finger press only. Press only after seams have been adjusted and finally stitched. Use a medium-warm iron without steam, which would mar the moiré pattern. Test press on a scrap of your moiré first!

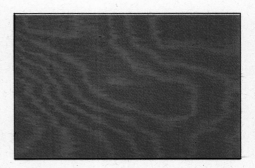

Sequinned fabric

Sequinned fabric is available in a number of forms. The stretchable knit type is usually 28 cm (11") wide and is used mainly for strapless tops. It stretches lengthwise, so wrapped around the body it fits beautifully. The selvages serve as upper and lower top edges.

This type of top is sewn in a snap, for it consists of a single piece of stretch sequinned fabric and has only one seam. For size 36 you will need a piece 78 cm (30¾") long and 28 cm (11") wide, for each larger size add 4 cm (1⅝") in length. Wrap this piece of fabric, **wrong** side out, around your body and pin the seam at left side, making the top as snug as desired (ill. 1). After stitching this seam trim seam allowances back narrowly and bind with satin ribbon (ill. 2). Shape top at righthand side by constructing a dart that is 2 cm (⅞") wide at its widest point. Hand sew dart allowance into place at upper edge (ill. 3). Woven, non-stretch, sequinned fabrics are usually 70 to 90 cm (28" to 36") wide and are used for blazers, dresses, tops as well as for straight skirts.

Cutting out

Depending upon the way they are fastened to the fabric, sequins can come off easily once the fabric is cut, so always cut out with at least 2 cm (⅞") allowance on all seams. It is a good idea to secure the ends of any threads to the allowances with clear nail polish. DO NOT trace onto sequinned fabrics! Rather, make any markings with tailor's tacks (ill. 4).

Sewing

Don't worry! Sequins won't break your machine's needle! Go ahead and stitch over them. If you are not lining your sequinned garment, then bind seam allowances together with satin ribbon. Make facings from interfaced lining or other smooth fabric in a color matching your sequinned fabric (ill. 5 and 6). Avoid wearing sequins next to your skin!

Pressing

Always use a press cloth on sequinned fabrics, NEVER use steam and DON'T use a high setting, for you will melt the sequins. Always test press on a scrap of your fabric first. Dart points are easier to press if you insert a straight pin at point first (ill. 7).

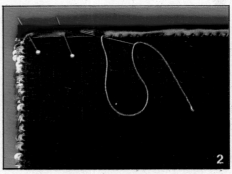

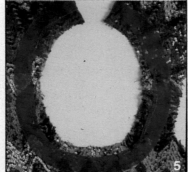

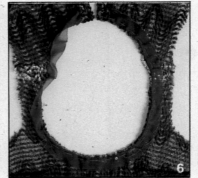

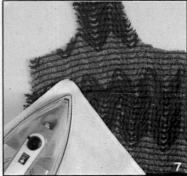

How to work with leather...

Leather is one of nature's products, so there will be thinner areas in every skin, or hide, sometimes even small holes or slits. If you intend to make up a sophisticated garment or outfit in leather, we recommend that you purchase one skin more than required to make sure that you have enough good sections of leather. Always take along the complete pattern for the garment planned when purchasing leather. The thinner, leftover sections of leather can be saved and used later for patchwork, appliqués, belts, etc.

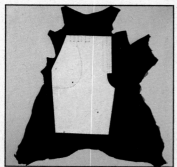

There's no avoiding a horizontal section seam in leather pants. An upper front pant piece will usually require an entire skin, as shown here.

Front and back hip yokes and upper back pieces should also be cut out in the lengthwise direction as shown.

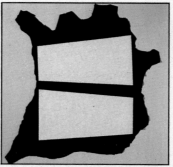

Lower front and back leg pieces can be cut out in the crosswise direction as shown, economizing the amount of leather needed. 6 skins = 1 pair of long pants.

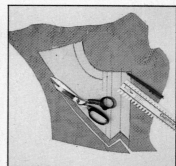

Mark seamlines and markings onto the wrong side of leather with pencil or ballpoint pen.

When choosing your color bear in mind that the dye will come out of suede dyed with intense colors. If you make a pair of pants in wine red suede, for example, you must reckon with chance of red dye rubbing onto other garments worn with the pants.

Appliqués made from intensely dyed suede and applied to lightcolored fabrics are very decorative but not advisable. Drycleaning firms usually won't accept garments with this type of decoration, for the leather usually "bleeds" onto the fabric around it. If you really want to make an appliqué of this type, then choose one of the numerous imitation leathers or synthetic suedes available.

When purchasing leather always take along the entire pattern for the garment planned. If leather is not available in your area, see our dealer/stockist list for firms from which you can order leather. Always send your pattern along with your leather order, making sure that you specify how many times each piece is to be cut out. Better yet, make a second pattern piece for those pieces that are to be cut out twice and clearly mark them as right front pant piece, left front pant piece, etc.

Leather is sold by the square foot (30 x 30 cm = 12 x 12"). Being as the skins vary greatly in size and shape (see illustrations above) we also state how many skins you will need for a certain garment, giving the minimum length and width required for each skin. The illustrations above show the pieces for one-half of a pair of pants cut from 3 skins of suede. Being as all these pieces must be cut out twice, you will need 6 skins for the entire pair of pants.

The minimum lengths and widths that we state in our requirements do not correspond to the square feet that the leather merchant has figured for a skin, being as he has taken all curves and extensions of the skin into consideration in his calculations.

● You usually cut out and mark leather from the **wrong** side, so make sure that pattern pieces are placed printed side down onto leather, especially for asymmetrical garments. The printed side of pattern piece corresponds to the **right** side of garment! Tape pattern pieces onto leather. Mark seamlines and allowance lines with pencil or ballpoint pen. If you wish to trace, then use a tracing wheel with a smooth edge, but be careful!

● When cutting out always bear in bind that leather stretches more crosswise than it does lengthwise, so don't economize by cutting out the left front lengthwise and the right front crosswise, for example. You'll notice the difference in stretch while sewing, at the very latest the first time you wear your leather garment!

● Cut out all pieces of a suede garment in the same direction, i.e. "with the nap," the nap direction running from the upper to lower edge of garment.

● Do not pin or baste leather, and avoid having to open any stitched seams, for the holes made by the needle are permanent! Make up the garment planned in muslin or cheap fabric first to check the fit! Hold leather pieces together with paper clips instead of basting.

● A rotary cutter is ideal for cutting out leather and leather imitations. Always cut from a single layer of leather. Straight edges are quickly and accurately cut when using a ruler or sewing gauge as a guide, as shown above.

● Use a size 80 = 12 or 90 = 14 needle for stitching most leathers. Should this not suffice try out a jeans needle, which is a bit more pointed. Use a special, wedge point needle on thicker leathers and with a longer stitch setting. This type of needle could damage thin, delicate leather, so test sew first. (European needle size = U.S. needle size).

● Always press leather on the **wrong** side with a dry iron and under a press cloth or brown paper. Test press on a scrap of your leather first to check iron setting!

● Help prevent the dye from rubbing off richly colored suede by spraying the **right** side of the garment with hairspray. Test spray first on a scrap of your leather!

...and leather imitations

This striking cardigan suit is an example of just what you can do with synthetic suede. Scalloped edges and perforations lend it couture character. It's worth the patience required for the work and the acquisition of a pair of punching pliers and some pinking shears. Our publications continuously offer patterns for similar styles in normal fabric that can be easily adapted for leather look-alikes. Pre-requisites are simple shape and uncomplicated construction

There are tremendous quality differences among imitation leathers, so take a look at the care instructions before purchasing and note them once you have made your purchase.

● If you are working with a napped material, then cut out "with" the nap, pinning all pattern pieces onto the material so that they point in the same direction and so that the nap runs from the upper to lower edge of the garment.

● Use a very thin needle for basting.

● Use a size 90 = 14 needle in your machine. A special leather needle is not necessary. (European needle size = U.S. needle size).

● If you are not lining the garment, finish seams with the flat-felled method, both functional and chic.

● You can usually press with steam, but always from the **wrong** side. Use a press cloth if pressing from the **right** side.

● If you plan to launder your garment yourself, follow care instructions. Use a delicate detergent that does not contain any brighteners. Machine washing with the delicate cycle at 30 degrees centigrade (cool wash) will do no harm, but do not spin! Place garment on a hanger and allow to drip dry, keeping out of direct sunlight.

A few tricks

● Holes made by straight pins and basting stitches close up when steam is applied.

● Should your machine be one of the few that does not transport imitation leather easily, try a presser foot with a teflon-coated sole or a so-called roller foot, available at most sewing machine stores. Or, place strips of tissue paper underneath fabric that are caught in when stitching and torn away later.

● "All purpose" sewing threads are ideal and are available in a wide range of colors produced by several companies.

● Avoid unsightly ridges on the **right** side of seams by placing strips of brown paper between the allowance and garment during pressing.

Handle thin leathers and leather imitations like fabric

In fact, some things are easier
Being as these materials do not fray, it is not necessary to seam facings into place. These edges are "open" and are cut without allowances.

Facings
Pin facing to the corresponding edge, **wrong** sides together, matching edges. From the **right** side of garment edgestitch and topstitch ¾ cm (⅜") along edge, securing facing.

Interfacing
We recommend that you use special fusible interfacing for leather and imitation leather which fuses firmly at the silk or wool iron setting.

Buttonholes
After facing has been applied, machine stitch a rectangle around buttonhole marking, ½ cm (¼") above and below line. Slash along buttonhole marking, clip diagonally to each corner at end nearest closing edge (see ill. to the left).
Hems For sporty garments press hem allowance to the **inside,** edgestitch and topstitch ¾ cm (⅜") into place.

Collars
Collar layers are worked open-edged, with allowance on the attachment edge only. Stitch the **right** side of collar layers to **inside** and **outside** of neck edge. Press layers up over their attachment seam so that they lie **wrong** sides together. Trim their outer edges evenly. Edgestitch and topstitch ¾ cm (⅜") along outer edges, stitching collar layers together.

Patch pockets
Again, cut out pockets and upper edge facings without allowances. Place facings onto upper pocket edges, **wrong** sides together. Stitch into place from the **right** side of pockets. Then stitch pockets into place.

Shaped bands
These are cut out without allowance and are edgestitched into place along both their long edges (see ill. below). Carefully baste bands into place, matching their edges exactly to garment edges.

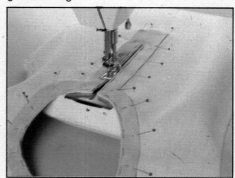

Lace luxury

Lovely lace insertions ....

The trick is to stitch lace on first and then trim away fabric underneath

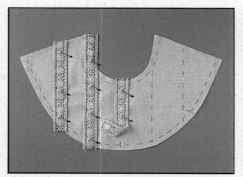

1 Thread trace lace placement lines onto the **right** fabric side, parallel to center front and spaced equally apart. Pin lace onto the **right** fabric side where marked.

2 Edgestitch both long edges of lace into place, backstitching seam ends.

3 From the **wrong** fabric side slash along the center of fabric beneath lace. Press this fabric away from lace as shown.

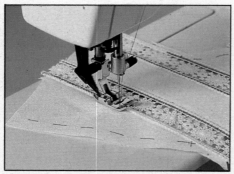

4 From the **right** fabric side overcast both long edges of lace with close-set, tiny zigzag stitching.

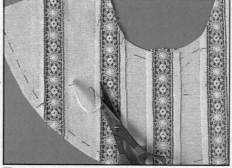

5 On the **wrong** fabric side very carefully trim excess fabric back close to this zigzag stitching.

6 The final touch: baste the allowance on lower edge of garment or garment section to the **inside.** Baste lace edging underneath this edge and secure when machine hemming or when attaching the garment section.

Trim a v-neckline with lace

Thread trace placement lines for lace onto the **right** side of the faced v-neckline. Place lace **right** side down onto neckline exactly along these lines. Fold lace **right** sides together to a point at center front, forming a dart (ill. 1). Pin this dart, then mark seamline with basting. Remove lace from fabric and stitch dart, the point of which should be very narrow. Stitch with a very short straight stitch setting. Trim allowances back to ¼ cm (⅛") width and overcast together. Baste the **wrong** side of lace onto the **right** side of neck edge along placement lines. Edgestitch first the upper edge of lace into place, then the lower edge. Overcast both edges of lace with close-set, tiny zigzag stitching (ill. 2). From the **wrong** side of garment carefully trim away fabric lying beneath the lace, the lower edge of facing as well (ill. 3). Attach back neck facing after shoulder seams are finished, turn to the **inside,** topstitch into place (ill. 4).

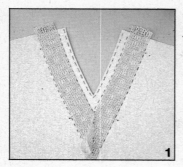

1

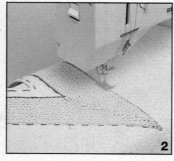

2

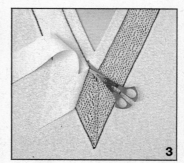

3

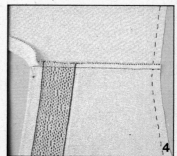

4

Add lace appliqués

A very flattering decoration for a rounded neckline

Mirror image lace appliqué motifs can be purchased in pairs and zigzag stitched onto the neck edge of a dress, blouse or nightgown for a striking effect

1 Mark center front with basting. Carefully pin lace motifs onto garment, positioning them exactly.

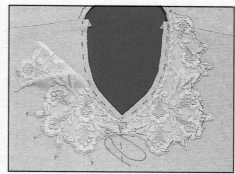

2 The right motif should slightly overlap left motif at center front. Baste both motifs into place, taking small basting stitches.

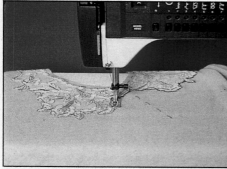

3 Use a sewing thread the same color as your lace. Overcast outer edges of both motifs into place with close-set, tiny zigzag stitching.

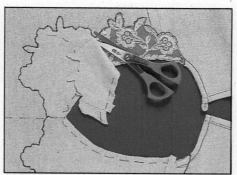

4 Remove basting threads. Very carefully trim the fabric beneath the lace back close to zigzag stitching.

5 Hand sew right motif onto left motif at center front.

This dress in delicate point d'esprit is perfect proof of the chic effect achieved with a simple shape and straight, fitted sleeves. Wrist ruffles are trimmed with lace edging

Special seam finishing for sheer fabrics

Transparent fabrics require inconspicuous seams. Therefore, seam allowances are narrowly trimmed and overcast together

Being as most tulle and lace fabrics do not fringe or ravel, you can stitch the lace edging directly onto the unfinished edge of wrist ruffle (ill. 1), using a short, straight stitch setting. Elbow darts and seams are also stitched with a short, straight stitch setting. Overcast allowances together, stitching 3 mm (⅛") from seam. Very carefully trim allowances back close to this stitching (ill. 2). Wrist ruffle attachment seams should also be as inconspicuous as possible (ill. 3). Remove gathering and marking threads after attaching ruffles. Trim seam allowances back to 3 mm (⅛") width and overcast together.

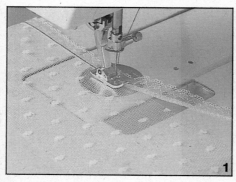

1

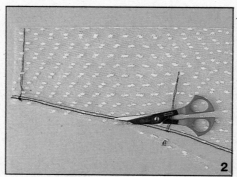

2

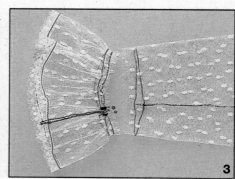

3

Sewing machine magic

Details often make the difference, often lend a garment an unmistakably personal note. Here are a few more examples of fantastic effects achieved with a modern sewing machine, imagination and that certain touch

Striking: stitching over a cord

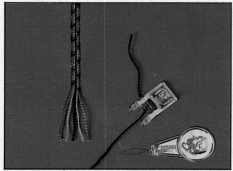 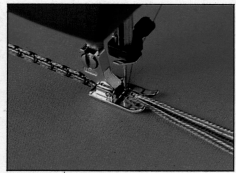 

1 The ideal tool is a special, multi-cord presser foot manufactured by Husqvarna that has 5 holes in it. Using a needle threader, thread pearl/crochet cotton through these holes before attaching presser foot. These 5 cording threads are then stitched into place with a decorative stitch.

2 This presser foot enables you to apply scalloped or wavy lines of stitching, always keeping the 5 threads exactly in line and guaranteeing that all are caught in during stitching. Test sew first!

3 You can achieve this effect without this special presser foot, in a straight line only, however. Glue the cording threads onto fabric with Gütermann's glue stick, positioning as desired. Then carefully machine embroider over them.

Create your own borders

Left ill.: attach grosgrain ribbon with decorative machine stitches. Secure the edges with scalloping stitch. Right ill.: edgestitch 2 strips of braid into place along both long edges. Attach rickrack between braid with scalloping stitch.

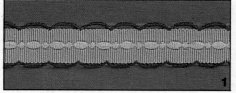 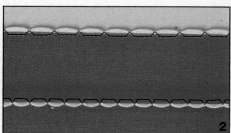

A lovely edging

Place pre-folded bias tape under hemfold so that its fold edge extends ¼ cm (⅛") beyond hemfold. Set your machine on the blind hem stitch setting and stitch along hem edge in the opposite direction as you normally would, i.e. with the fabric to the RIGHT of the needle as shown. The hem stitch will catch in the fold edge of bias tape and gather it, creating a lovely scalloped finish. Stitch length can be varied as shown.

Cutwork embroidery done the easy way

You can easily create lovely patterns such as this yourself

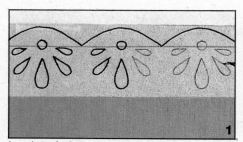

Iron interfacing onto the **wrong** side of edge to be embroidered. Remember to use steam when applying interfacing! Draw outlines for cutwork onto interfacing with a pencil. Machine stitch along these lines with a short, straight stitch setting, thus marking them onto the right fabric side. From the **right** side

machine embroider over these lines with satin stitch (close-set zigzag stitch). Using sharply pointed scissors, VERY CAREFULLY trim out the fabric inside the embroidered outlines, taking care not to damage the stitching. Then remove interfacing by applying steam and then pulling away. This WILL NOT work if you applied interfacing with a dry iron!

Machine-worked picots

Picot finished edges on a collar or neckline lend a garment a couture look. Try using metallic threads as shown below, that are available in a variety of colors. Fold a strip of paper into triple layers and place underneath the garment edge so that it extends 4 cm (1⅝") beyond edge. Use a clear plastic presser foot on your machine. Place paper and fabric onto machine, lining up the fabric edge with the left inside edge of the presser foot.

Use pearl/crochet cotton as cording thread, placing it underneath the presser foot. Set your machine for scalloping stitch (determining stitch length beforehand) and machine embroider over the cording thread with metallic thread, catching in the edge of fabric at the end of each scallop. Try working several rows of picots as shown below for a lacy effect.

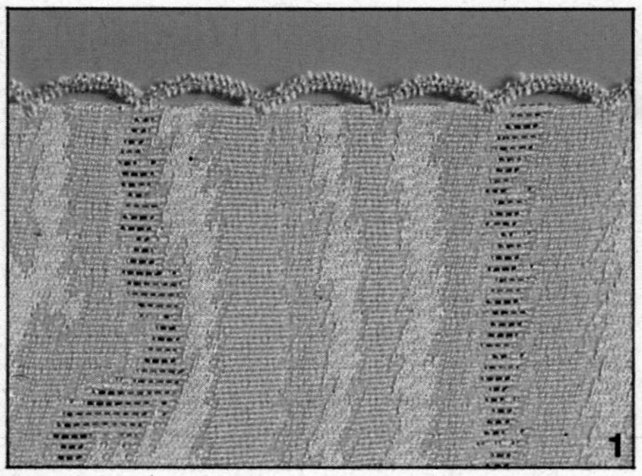

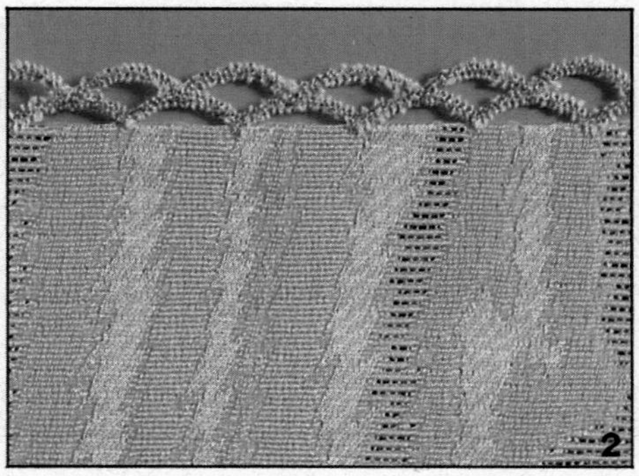

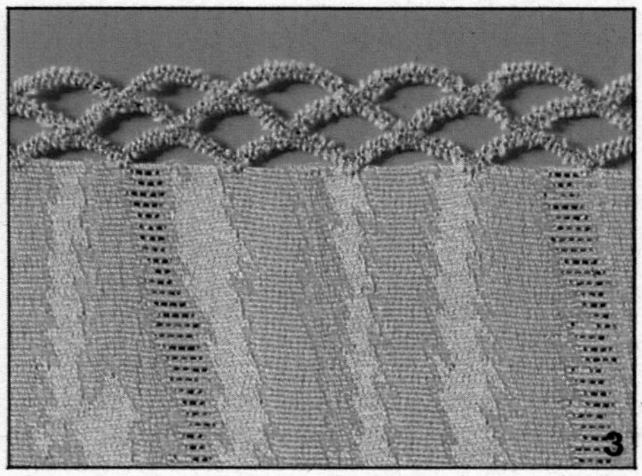

Impeccable topstitching: The sign of a serious sewer

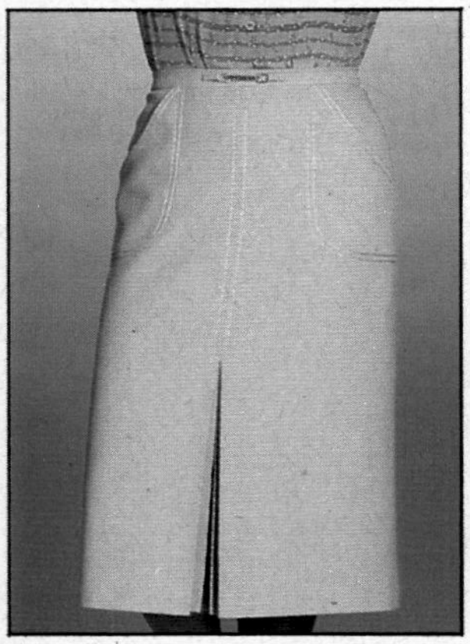

A number of special topstitching threads are available that will help you achieve beautifully embellished seams

The secret of success: these topstitching threads cannot be used in the machine needle. Rather, they are wound onto the bobbin and you topstitch from the **wrong** side resp. the **inside** of the garment. Before tackling the real thing, however, practice on scraps of your fabric first. Depending upon the fabric type, you may have to adjust the bobbin tension. If you are topstitching without an edge or a seam as a guide, then ALWAYS thread trace the topstitching line on the **inside** of garment. A good example is the skirt shown to the left. The center front seam is covered on the inside by the pleat underlay. Therefore, it is necessary to thread trace the topstitching lines. On a pocket opening edge, however, you can work without thread tracing. Just edgestitch along the edge and topstitch again in presser foot width from edge.

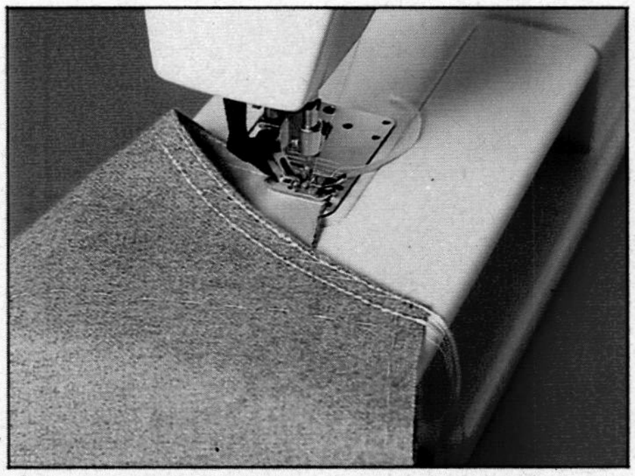

1 Being as you are stitching from the **wrong** side, make sure that the bobbin tension is set correctly so that the stitches on the **right** side are even (test stitch first!).

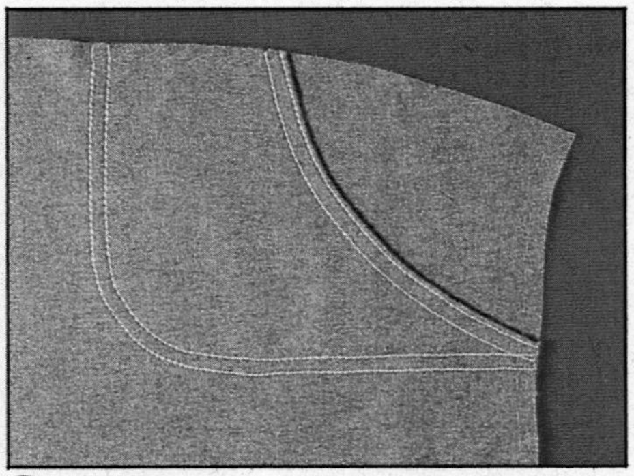

2 If the lower edge of a hip yoke pocket is shorter than the hip yoke and is to be formed by topstitching, then thread trace these lines onto hip yoke.

Zigzag stitching done with special topstitching thread is also very decorative, as shown in ill. 1. When topstitching lapel edges with this thread it will be necessary to stop stitching just at lapel fold, turn over edge and continue topstitching for closing edge from the facing side. Begin this stitching exactly in the last stitch at lapel fold (ill. 2 at the lower right).

Other methods of decorative topstitching for those machines that cannot handle the bobbin method

Double topstitch with buttonhole twist. Use buttonhole twist in needle and normal sewing thread in the bobbin, a size 90 = 14 needle and 4 (the longest) straight stitch setting. For a raised effect topstitch a second time exactly in the first row of stitching, matching stitches exactly. Achieve the same effect more quickly by threading 2 strands of buttonhole twist through a size 100 = 16 needle. If your machine cannot handle buttonhole twist in the needle, try threading a size 80 = 12 needle with two strands of normal sewing thread. (European needle size = U.S. needle size).

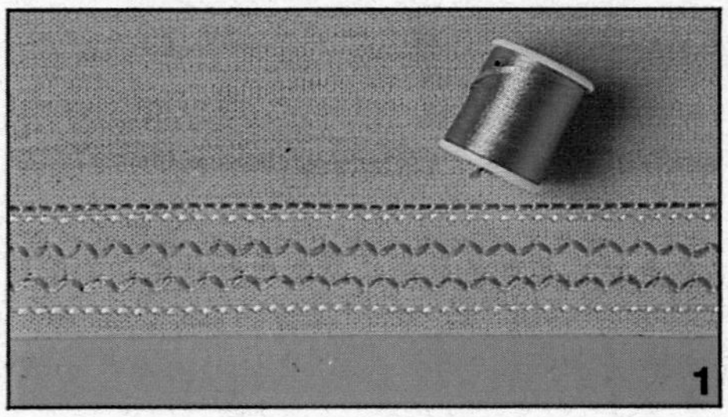

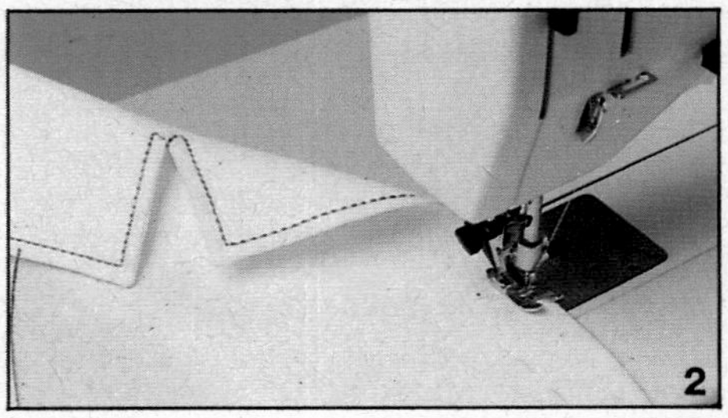

Appliquéing

These projects were selected to demonstrate just how easy it is to lend a garment drama with relatively simple materials and little effort. Create your own motifs! You'll discover just how much fun you can have!

Choose your favorite colors for your favorite dress

Iron interfacing onto the **wrong** side of your contrasting (appliqué) fabric. Draw triangles

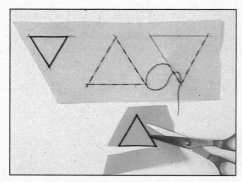

onto interfacing. Thread trace along these lines, marking them onto the **right** fabric side. From the **right** side machine satin stitch (close-set zigzag stitch) along these lines. Cut out triangles just outside this stitching. Iron a

fusing agent onto the **wrong** side of triangles. Peel paper off fusing agent. Place triangles, fusing agent down, onto the **right** side of garment and press into place. Then press from the **wrong** side under a damp press cloth.

Special fusing agent simplifies matters greatly

Appliqué a lovely cascade of dots

Use different fabric remnants for dots, choosing fabrics of the same weight and type, however. Iron interfacing onto the **wrong** side of this fabric. Draw dots onto the interfacing. Thread trace dots onto the **right** fabric side. From the **right** side machine satin stitch (close-set zigzag stitch) along dot outlines. Cut out dots just outside this stitching. Iron fusing agent onto the **wrong** side of dots. Peel off paper. Pin dots, fusing agent down, onto the **right** side of garment and press into place by applying iron briefly. Then secure by pressing from the **wrong** side under a damp press cloth. Remember! If working with pile fabric such as terrycloth, terry velour or velvet, use a press cloth of the same fabric type when pressing from the right side. When pressing from the **wrong** side place this press cloth

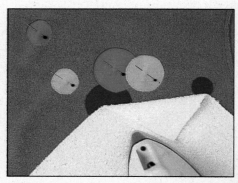

pile side up onto your ironing board. The pile or looped side of press cloth and garment should always lie together during pressing, thus preventing the pile or loops from being pressed flat. Pass iron gently over fabric.

Decorate a back with oriental charm

The "finishing touch" for your garment can be purchased

Machine embroidered, sew-on and iron-on initials and oriental letters are available at well-appointed notions/haberdashery stores. The iron-on ones are simple: just arrange their position and press! Combine initials for monograms. Also available are iron-on metal studs and stud motifs that look super on sporty garments made in denim as well as rhinestone motifs and borders that add glamour to a dressy style. There are multitudes of amusing motifs for childrenswear to choose from, almost all of which are simply ironed on. Bear in mind that fusible appliqués require a smooth fabric underneath. Pile fabrics such as velvet or terry velour are not suitable, nor are they suitable

as appliqué motifs. Pin appliqué onto garment and try on to check the position. Then iron into place.

Create your own fashion mood with an appliqué

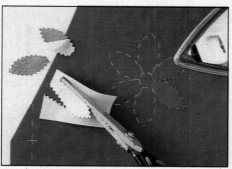

Make a 6-petal flower from imitation leather. Iron fusing agent onto the **wrong** side of material. Mark the motif outlines onto fusing agent paper. Cut out petals with pinking shears. Peel paper off fusing agent. Arrange the motif sections, fusing agent down, onto the **right** side of fabric, press and edgestitch into place.

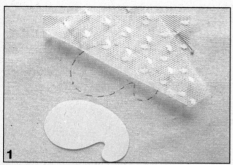

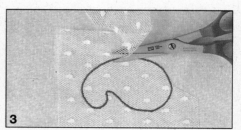

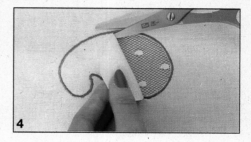

Eyecatchers: transparent tulle appliqués

This type of appliqué is particularly suitable for lingerie, summer dresses and even fine knit sweaters. Thread trace the motif outline(s) onto the **right** fabric side. Place tulle onto the **wrong** side of fabric over motif outline (ill. 1). From the **right** side machine satin stitch (close-set zigzag stitch) along motif outline, catching in tulle on the underside (ill. 2). From the **wrong** side very carefully trim excess tulle back to this stitching (ill. 3). From the **right** side very carefully trim away the fabric within the motif outline(s), trimming closely to zigzag stitching (ill. 4).

Tip: if silky fabrics slip around during stitching, baste a piece of tissue paper into place underneath tulle. This can easily be torn away after stitching.

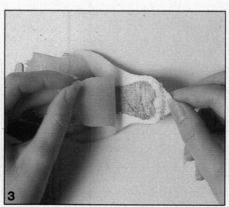

Appliqué motifs made from print fabrics

Iron fusing agent onto the **wrong** side of fabric over the motif that you wish to use as an appliqué (ill. 1). Cut out motif (ill. 2). Peel paper off fusing agent (ill. 3). Turn over motif and place its **wrong** side onto the right side of garment. Press into place under a damp press cloth (ill. 4). Fusing agent is available in packets of strips in most notions/haberdashery stores, by the meter/yard in better fabric stores.

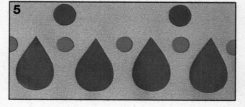

Fusing agent can also be used for leather appliqués (ill. 5) and for appliqués made from transparent fabric such as organza (ill. 6).

Lining, yes or no?

You will sometimes run across a pattern that does not call for lining, and you feel that the garment should be lined. In this case lining is neither forbidden nor is it a must. The decision of whether or not to line this garment is up to you, depends upon your individual taste and needs as well as upon the fabric you plan to use. Obviously a wool coat lined with a silky lining will hang better and be easier to slip in and out of, especially when worn over a wool dress, than an unlined one. On the other hand, though, nowadays unlined garments are gaining popularity, for they are lightweight, easier to care for and easier to sew.

What you should know before making your decision

Dresses: surely you have experienced how an unlined dress will "cling" to your stockings, or how a lined jersey dress loses its easy wearing qualities, because of the lining. The quick solution for both problems is to wear a half-slip underneath such dresses. If sewn up in a neutral color you can wear it underneath numerous garments. This jiffy half-slip is sewn in a flash without a pattern (see instructions in the center column). Attach the half-slip to the **wrong** side of a one-piece dress with elasticized waist. Its upper edge should match the width of dress at waist level. Stitch into place with 2 lines of stitching and slip in elastic between these lines. **Straight or slightly flared skirts and pantskirts** fall better if they are lined. The lining is cut out from the skirt resp. pantskirt pattern, pinning any pleats into pattern pieces before pinning them onto lining. Construct lining in this case with side seam slits for freedom of movement. For **fully pleated skirts** cut out the lining from the pattern for a straight or slightly flared skirt, again with side seam slits. **Ruffled or tiered skirts** are seldom lined. If you insist upon lining such a skirt, then we recommend a separate skirt made from lining fabric, i.e. a type of half-slip.

The jiffy half-slip

As mentioned above, the ideal undergarment for dresses is a slim half-slip made in anti-static knit lining that is available in a number of colors. This fabric is 140 cm (55") wide, so you will need a piece in the length of your skirt plus 5 cm (2") allowance. Draw the half-slip directly onto the fabric following our directions in the center column. There is a left side seam, a righthand dart and elasticized waist.

Cutting out

Fold lining in half lengthwise, **right** sides together. Fold again lengthwise so that the distance from first and second folds is ¼ of your hip measurement (Diagram 1). The second fold on lefthand edge is actually 2 folds that will become center front and center back of your half-slip. At upper edge of first fold begin drawing the seamline for a dart 3 cm (1¼") from fold and tapering out to fold 18 cm (7") from upper edge. Along this line and first fold mark 1.5 cm (⅝") seam allowance. Cut out half-slip along this allowance line. Beginning at second fold, i.e. center front/center back, trim upper edge 2 cm (⅞") deeper. Taper out to dart resp. side seam (diagram 2). At first fold resp. side edge trim 2 cm (⅞") off hem edge, tapering toward center as shown. These tricks guarantee a perfect fit.

Now start sewing

Stitch left side seam with 1.5 cm (⅝") seam allowance, stitching with long-set

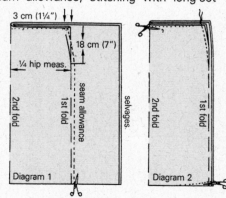

3 cm (1¼")
18 cm (7")
¼ hip meas.
2nd fold
1st fold
seam allowance
selvages
2nd fold
1st fold
Diagram 1
Diagram 2

zigzag stitch. Stitch dart in right side. Press hem and waist edges ½ cm (¼") to the **inside.** Then press waist edge 1.5 cm (⅝"), hem edge 2.5 cm (1") to the **inside** and machine stitch into place. Insert elastic into waist edge and your half-slip is finished!

How to line straight skirts

Stitch seams and darts in lining, leaving zipper placket open where marked. Bear in mind that a skirt with a zipper in the left side seam will require lining with a zipper placket in the RIGHT side seam. You should

also leave 10 to 15 cm (4" to 6") long slits open in lower end of side seams. Overcast and press open seam allowances. Pin lining into skirt, **wrong** sides together, matching darts and seams. Hand sew lining onto zipper tapes, baste into place along upper skirt edge, matching marked seamlines. Attach waistband. Lining should be 2 cm (⅞") shorter than skirt and should be machine hemmed.

A trick from the sewing industry: side seams in waistband facilitate alterations

The advantage to this construction is that you don't have to remove waistband for taking in or letting out the waist edge of a skirt. Pre-requisite is a center back seam with zipper. This type of waistband requires a bit more work, for it consists of 3 different pieces, but should be taken into consideration by women with fluctuating weight and figures. The diagram at the upper left on page 135 clearly illustrates just how easy alterations can be made on lined skirts with this type of waistband.

Here's how it works

Cut out waistband 12 cm (4¾") longer than the pattern piece or the length stated in the cutting instructions. Iron waistband interfacing onto the **wrong** side of waistband. Stitch center back seam in skirt and insert zipper. Attach one edge of waistband to upper edge of each back panel: the righthand section should have 1 cm (½") allowance at placket edge and approx. 3 cm (1¼") allowance at side seam edge (or the same amount as the skirt); the lefthand section should have 2 to 3 cm (⅞" to 1¼") underlap at placket edge and approx. 3 cm (1¼") side seam allowance. Ease each panel ½ cm (¼") if fabric allows (some stiff fabrics do not ease well). Stitch the remainder of waistband to upper edge of front panel, again easing in panel 1 cm (½"). Front waistband section should also have 3 cm (1¼") side seam allowances.

Stitch the corresponding lining panels to the other long edge of waistband sections, **right** sides together. Press seam allowances into waistband sections as shown below. Now stitch side seams in lining, waistband and skirt, beginning at lower edge of skirt and ending at lower edge of lining. Press open seam allowances. Fold waistband along its foldline, **wrong** sides together,

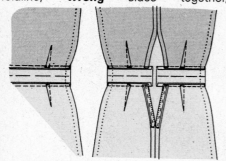

automatically folding lining down into skirt. From the **right** side of skirt stitch exactly in waistband attachment seam groove, securing inner waistband layer. This is the only horizontal seam that must be opened for altering width.

Attaching lining at vent

When cutting out lining for a skirt with vent, vent facing and underlap are left off lining. Cut out lining with 1 cm (½") allowance on vented seam. Stitch this seam in lining down to vent mark. Pin lining into skirt, matching vented seams exactly. Turn under lining 1 cm (½") along vent underlap and pin into place. Cut across other lining panel about 1 cm (½") below vent mark, clip diagonally up into corner to underlap edge (ill. 1 below) and trim out in underlap width down to lower edge. Turn under this edge 1 cm (½") and hand sew onto vent facing

(see ill. 2 below). Lining is machine hemmed and is 2 cm (⅞") shorter than skirt.

Lining coats and jackets

Transfer any alterations you have made in the garment onto the pattern pieces before

cutting out lining. Cut out front lining pieces minus facing width. For movement pleat in center back cut out with 3 cm (1¼") allowance on center back seam or with 2 cm (⅞") extra at center back fold. Another trick: sleeve lining won't pull if you cut it out with 2 cm (⅞") allowance along sleeve cap. Lining is attached to sleeves before they are set in!

Proceed as follows

Stitch front and back lining pieces together, press open seam allowances. Pin lining into garment, turn under its edges 1 cm (½"), pin onto facings, upper collar and hem allowance. Secure lining, open edged, to

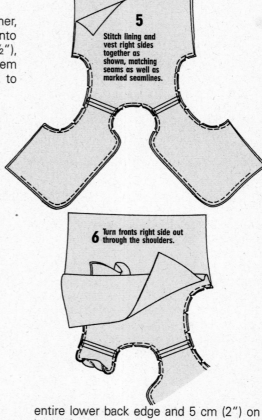

1 Stitch center back seam in lining with 1 cm (½") allowance. To make movement pleat stitch again for 5 cm (2") at upper and lower edge with 3 cm (1¼") seam allowance. Backstitch seam ends. If cut out on the fold stitch 2 cm (⅞") from fold. Press pleat to one side.

2 Slip lining sleeve over fabric sleeve, wrong sides together, matching seams. Turn under lower edge of lining 1 cm (½"), slipstitch onto upper edge of sleeve hem allowance.

3 Lining fronts are cut out minus facing width plus 1 cm (½") seam allowance. Shoulder edge of lining back will be longer than that on lining fronts.

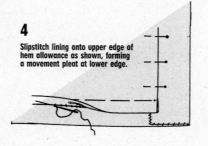

4 Slipstitch lining onto upper edge of hem allowance as shown, forming a movement pleat at lower edge.

sleeve attachment seam allowances with back stitches. Fold sleeve lining over this and hand sew into place.

Lining a bolero vest

This method is also ideal for other types of unbuttoned vests. Facings are not needed, you actually "face" the vest edges with the lining. The trick is to leave side seams, the

5 Stitch lining and vest right sides together as shown, matching seams as well as marked seamlines.

6 Turn fronts right side out through the shoulders.

entire lower back edge and 5 cm (2") on lower front edges open until after vest is turned.

Proceed as follows

Stitch shoulder seams in vest and lining, press open allowances. Pin lining and vest **right** sides together, matching seams as well as marked seamlines. Beginning and ending 5 cm (2") from side seam on lower front edges, stitch layers together along hem, closing and neck edges (ill. 5). Then stitch layers together along armhole edges. Trim seam allowances, clip curves. Turn each front **right** side out through shoulder (ill. 6). Press open seam allowances for 5 cm (2") at ends of armholes. Baste fabric fronts to fabric back **right** sides together at side seams, continue and baste lining side seams. Stitch side seams in vest and lining, matching armhole seams. Press open seam allowances. Turn in open lower edges of vent and lining, press, baste together. Edgestitch along all vest edges, stitching lower back edge closed.

A lovely bedspread

The bedspread shown on page 136 consists of a wave-quilted comforter, 18 cm (7″) wider than your mattress, with unquilted ruffles attached to long edges. The ruffles consist of doubled fabric layers, the fold constituting the hem edge. The corners at foot end of bedspread are held into place with a hook and

thread loop. Should there not be a comforter manufacturer in your area, send your fabric with exact dimensions and specifications to Mrs. Riether, who is listed in our dealer/stockist list. She will send upon upon request cost estimates for the batting, the jersey lining and the quilting work. Bear in mind that the volume of the batting will have to be compensated for, requiring at least 10 cm (4″) more fabric. If the bedspread is supposed to be 2.85 m (112½″) in length as shown in the diagram below, then you will need at least 2.95 m (116¼″) of fabric. The diagram is for the bedspread shown on page 136 that fits a bed 120 cm (47¼″) wide, 200 cm (79″) long

```
|←------------ 285 ------------→|
|←30+30→|←------ 210 ------→|←15→|
 ┌─────────────────────────────────┐
 │   ruffle attachment seam         │
 │ ┌─┬─┬──────────────────────┬─┐ ─┐
 │H│f│f│                      │h│H│ 138
 │e│o│o│   comforter          │e│e│
 │m│o│l│   section            │a│m│
 │ │t│d│                      │d│ │
 │ │e│l│                      │e│ │
 └─┴n┴i┴──────────────────────┴n┴─┘─┘
   │d│ loop  ruffle attachment seam  │21
   └─┴──────────────────────────────┘─
  hook   ruffle     fabric fold
```
(dimensions shown: 30, 30, 210, 15; 9 9; 138; 21)

and 46 cm (18¼″) high from the floor to upper edge of mattress. For a king or queen-sized bed you will have to stitch 2 panels of fabric together for the comforter section. If you want a floor-length bedspread, you'll have to lengthen side ruffles and foot end of comforter accordingly. The ruffles that we show are 21 cm (8¼″) high when finished and 2.10 m (83″) long after pleating. Being as they are worked in doubled fabric layers you will need 42 x 350 cm (16½″ x 138¼″) plus 1 cm (½″) allowance for each ruffle. Fold strips for ruffles in half lengthwise, **right** sides together. Stitch both ends of each. Turn **right** side out, baste and press edges. Then fold box pleats: outer pleat width is 4.5 cm (1⅞″), pleat extensions are 3 cm (1¼″) wide, distance between pleats 4.5 cm (1⅞″). Hold pleats into place by stitching along upper edge. The length of 3.50 m (138¼″) that we state consists of 2.10 m (83″) for ruffle attachment and 1.40 m (55¼″) for pleat extensions. See ills. 1 - 5 for further construction tips.

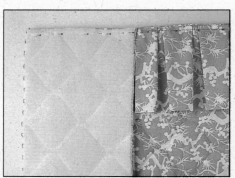

1 Pin ruffle to side edges of comforter section, **right** sides together. Turn hem allowance at foot end of comforter to the **right** side so that hem edge touches end of ruffle.

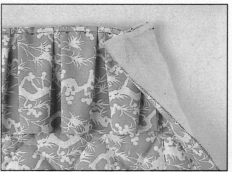

2 The other end of ruffle should lie on foldline at head end of comforter. Fold hem allowance on head end to the **outside** and pin into place over ruffle end. Stitch along both long edges of entire comforter, securing ruffles and ends of hem allowances. Overcast seam allowances together.

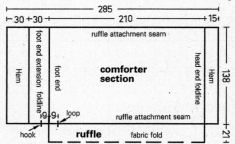

3 Turn hemmed ends **right** side out. Baste and press seamed and fold edges. Press ruffle attachment seam allowances into comforter section, edgestitch into place, taking care NOT to catch in hem allowance on foot end.

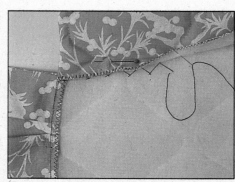

4 Secure hem allowances with blind catch stitch, taking stitches in comforter lining and batting. Stitches should NOT be visible from the right side of bedspread!

5 Sew a hook onto foot end of bedspread, 9 cm (3½″) from each corner. Construct a thread loop onto each ruffle attachment seam, 9 cm (3½″) from ruffle end. Hook foot end of comforter into place, forming corners.

Practical storage pouches

Ideal for storing handbags, boots, etc. that don't fit into your wardrobe closet. Our version can be hung on the side of a 2.30 m (91″) high wardrobe and is hardly noticeable when hung on the side nearest a wall. You will need 10 cm (4″) space between wardrobe and wall, however. Attach a hook onto the top of the wardrobe and attach a loop of cording to it through which you insert the hanger. You thus avoid damaging the wardrobe. Pouch width depends upon the width of the coathanger used. You will need sturdy fabric, preferably 140 cm (55″) wide, which you can economically cut out on the cross grain. Cut out strips from selvage to selvage in the width of your coathanger and without seam allowance. The backing layer should be as along as the height of your wardrobe minus coathanger height. The pouch layer should be longer, 10 cm (4″) longer for each pouch compartment plus allowance for attaching to coathanger. Stitch all fabric strips **right** sides together at ends with flat-felled seams. Bind both long edges of entire strip with bias tape. Arrange the number and size of pouch compartments according to your needs. Try your best to hide the joining seams for strips underneath folds of pouches, stitching in these seams for compartment seams whenever possible. Attach coathanger as in ill. 3.

1 Press both long edges of bias tape to the **inside** so that they meet at center of tape. Fold tape again lengthwise, **wrong** sides together, press. Slip tape over both long edges of fabric strip, edgestitch into place.

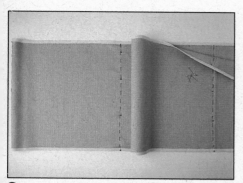

2 Arrange the number and size of pouch compartments according to your needs. Remember to figure 10 cm (4") more fabric for each compartment. Stitch across strip to make each compartment.

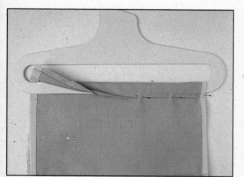

3 Stitch open ends of strip together, slip through coathanger, turn under, pin and edgestitch into place using a zipper presser foot.

The chair shown here is one of unusual shape that we chose to use for demonstrating a few techniques. You should first make a pattern for the chair you plan to cover. For good, fast results we recommend using the burda tracing set with clear plastic sheets that are easily pinned onto the chair without tearing.

Use the special pen for marking edges, outlines, etc. onto the plastic. Then cut out your pattern pieces. We have covered the seat and front side of the chairback with quilted fabric. If you are making the bedspread on page 136 as well, then have an extra section of fabric padded and quilted. Or quilt a piece of fabric yourself, remembering to cut out somewhat larger than your pattern piece.

The backside of the chairback is covered with a single fabric layer. A chairback in this shape makes a zipper in the cover mandatory. Insert as inconspicuously as possible into one of the side seams on the chairback (we put ours in the right seam). This zipper and the elasticized ruffle make removal for laundering simple.

Chair legs are hidden by a floorlength ruffle that is attached to the seatcover and lower edge of back cover. A strip of fabric is stitched onto inside along ruffle attachment seam that holds seatcover into place. Elastic is inserted into the lower (hemmed) edge of this strip and pulled up very taut. Sew elastic ends onto fabric strip ends. Join these ends together with hooks and eyes.

Give an old chair a new lease on life

It's hard to believe that the chairs shown below and to the right are one and the same. With a bit of imagination and some practice you can refurbish not only old chairs, but also hassocks, easychairs, chests, even old sofas.

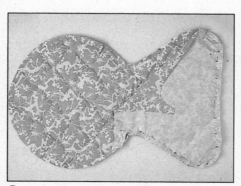

1 Make your pattern: place clear plastic sheet onto chair, mark the outlines of the seat and front side of chairback, then the backside. Cut out pattern pieces from plastic.

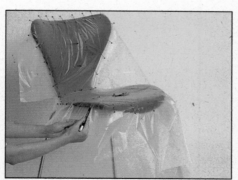

2 Cut out cover for seat and frontside of chairback from quilted fabric, for backside of chairback from a single layer of unquilted fabric. Stitch layers for chairback **right** sides together along outer edges, leaving zipper placket open.

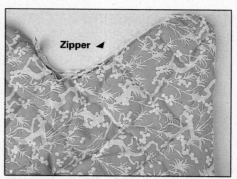

3 Turn cover for chairback **right** side out. Pin zipper under placket edges so that its teeth are covered (centered application). Machine stitch zipper into place using a zipper presser foot.

4 Fold pleats into upper edge of ruffle section (see instructions for bedspread). Ruffle should match outer edge of seatcover plus lower edge of backside cover and should have 5 cm (2") underlap. Turn in open long edges, stitch into place.

5 Stitch ruffle to outer edge of seatcover and lower edge of backside cover, **right** sides together. Clean finish upper edge of underlap. Turn in one long edge and both ends of fabric strip, stitch into place. Stitch other long edge of strip into place along ruffle attachment seamline.

6 Insert elastic into casing in lower edge of fabric strip. Machine hem ruffle.

Sweetheart mirror

Make a stencil in the shape you require - oval, round, square or heartshaped. Have a glazier cut out a mirror in this shape (he makes the mirror glass as well), or try a glass fitting company. It might cost a bit more to have a heartshaped mirror cut out because of its more complicated shape. A piece of hard or wallboard makes a suitable backing and should be cut out 1.5 cm (⅝") larger on all edges than the mirror. Bore a couple of holes into upper edge of backing board for hanger, then glue mirror onto board. See ills. 1 - 4 for further instructions.

You will need:

A piece of hard or wallboard; the mirror; cardboard; 5 cm (2") wide velvet ribbon to fit twice around edge of mirror and to make hanger loop; narrow embroidered band to fit once around edge of mirror and for circle on hanger loop; 2 purchased bows; 1 metal ring; glue; sewing thread.

1 Glue mirror onto the backing board. Cut out a 3 cm (1¼") wide frame from cardboard, the inner edge of which should exactly match mirror edge.

3 Stitch ends of velvet ribbon together, forming a ring. Take a row of hand running stitches (with doubled thread) along the center of ribbon. Pull up threads, gathering ribbon to fit over cardboard frame. Then hand sew embroidered band onto center of this ribbon over gathering threads.

2 Cut a section of velvet ribbon to make hanger. Slip ribbon through ring, fold in half. Sew ends into place through holes bored in backing board. Trim cardboard frame a bit narrower at the point that should fit over hanger. Glue frame into place.

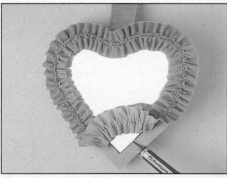

4 Glue velvet ribbon onto cardboard frame so that outer edges of frame are covered. Seam in velvet and ends of embroidered band should lie at center of upper edge. Hand sew bows into place.

Chic tissue box

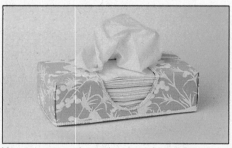

Use an empty tissue box as a base. Dress up little boxes in different shapes by covering them with fabric. These make ideal gifts.

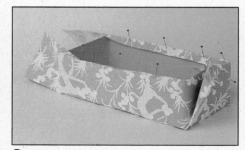

2 Wrap fabric around box, folding at ends as shown. Trim at lower edge, leaving 1 cm (½") allowance. Fold this allowance to the **inside,** pin and hand sew into place, taking stitches through the cardboard.

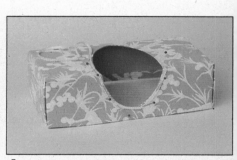

4 Cover stitches at lower and opening edges by hand sewing a pliable braid or embroidered band onto these edges.

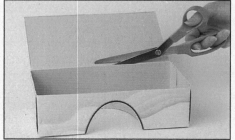

1 Cut away the bottom of the empty tissue box, cutting exactly in the folds. Carefully pull apart the lower end of corners and re-glue so that lower edge of box is somewhat larger, making it large enough to fit over a new tissue box.

3 Trim out fabric at opening, leaving 1 cm (½") allowance. Clip allowance at intervals around entire opening, fold to the **inside,** hand sew into place with tiny back stitches.

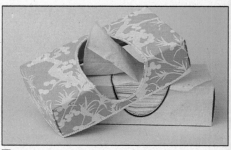

5 Now place your covered box over the full box of tissues.

140

Take something old, make something new

How to make a contoured sheet from a flat sheet

Contoured sheets are just great! No more straightening and smoothing out of rumpled up flat sheets! Just slip them onto the mattress. The beauty of it is that you can transform any flat sheet into a contour sheet - if its size allows. The four corners are quickly made. This custom-made sheet has the advantage that it does not stretch out of shape after repeated washing, nor is there any stretched out elastic to replace, as is often the case with stretch terry types. Plus, it is easier to fold and store

Here's how:

a) Take your mattress measurements - length, width and thickness. Let us assume that your mattress is 2.00 m (79") long and 1.00 m (39½") wide. Fold flatsheet in half lengthwise, pin open edges together. Mark your mattress length and half its width onto folded sheet, centering markings on sheet as shown, i.e. allowances on ends and long edge should be the same width.

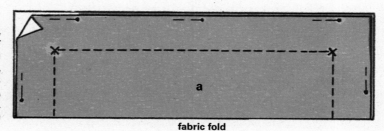

fabric fold

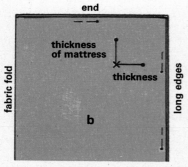

b) Beginning at the marking for each corner, draw 2 lines, one parallel to end, one parallel to long edge, both as long as the mattress is thick.

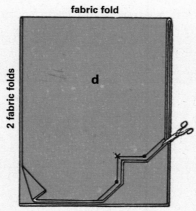

d) Fold sheet in half widthwise as shown, matching ends exactly. Using previously cut corner as a guide, cut out the other corner.

f) Here's what a finished corner should look like.

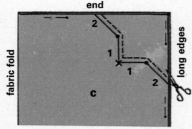

c) Place a ruler across corner of sheet so that it touches ends of both these lines. Draw a diagonal line from the end of these lines over to edges of sheet as shown. Trim corner along these lines with 1 cm (½") allowance.

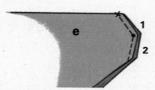

e) Open out flat sheet. Fold edges of each corner **right** sides together. Stitch together in the order indicated by the numbers 1 and 2, stitching with the "stretch stitch" setting. If your machine does not have this setting, then stitch with small straight stitch. Overcast seam allowances together with zigzag stitch.

TIP:

If you're really in a hurry, or if your flat sheet isn't large enough for constructing corners, simply pull each corner of sheet over mattress corner and tie into a knot. Untie knots before laundering!

Index

SEWING INSTRUCTIONS K 620

(Englisch)

Size tables for ladies and gentlemen on pages 24/25, for children on pages 16/17

STYLE 1

Bathrobes on page 16

here are patterns for ladies and gents:
ze 34-40 = Size 44/46
ze 42/44 = Size 48/50
ze 46/48 = Size 52/54

r children:
zes 104, 116, 128, 140 and 152

otal back length for adult version:
ze 34-40 = Size 44/46: 126 cm (49³/4")
ze 42/44 = Size 48/50: 127.5 cm (50¹/4")
ze 46/48 = Sizes 52/54: 129 cm (50¹/2")

otal back length for children's version:
ze 104: 79.5 cm (31¹/2")
ze 116: 90.5 cm (35³/4")
ze 128: 93.5 cm (37")
ze 140: 101 cm (39³/4")
ze 152: 110.5 cm (43¹/2")

Style 1
ee pages 13, 14 and 15 for important information pattern size information and for
etailed cutting and sewing instructions for beginning sewers.

abric requirements
dult version:
60 cm (63") wide, vertically striped terrycloth:
80 m (3¹/8 yds) for **all sizes**
hildren's version:
0 cm (36") wide printed terrycloth:
ze 104: 2.15 m (2³/8 yds)
ze 116: 2.45 m (2³/4 yds)
ze 128: 2.55 m (2⁷/8 yds)
ze 140: 2.75 m (3¹/8 yds)
ze 152: 3.10 m (3¹/2 yds)
ias tape for hanger loop

CUTTING OUT
attern overviews
hese show you all pattern pieces with all lines and markings, as they appear on fold-out
attern sheet.
Front
Back
Neckband
Sleeve
Pocket
he number of times that a pattern piece should be cut out and any other specifications,
g. cut on the fold, are printed on each pattern piece.
 addition, you will need the following extra pieces (there are no pattern pieces for these -
ou draw them with tailor's chalk onto fabric in the dimensions listed below):
2 pocket bands for the adult version, each 4.5 cm (1³/4") wide and for
ze 34-40 resp. 44/46 ea. 20.5 cm (8¹/4") long
ze 42/44 resp. 48/50 ea. 21.5 cm (8¹/2") long
ze 46/48 resp. 52/54 ea. 22.5 cm (8³/4") long
pocket bands for the children's version, each 3 cm (1¹/4") wide and for
ze 104 ea. 13.5 cm (5¹/4") long
ze 116 ea. 14 cm (5¹/2") long
ze 128 ea. 15 cm (6") long
ze 140 ea. 16 cm (6¹/4") long
ze 152 ea. 18 cm (7") long
Tie-belt for adult version, 9 cm (3¹/2") wide, finished width 4.5 cm (1³/4"), and for
ze 34-40 resp. 44/46: 180 cm (71") long
ze 42/44 resp. 48/50: 190 cm (75") long
ze 46/48 resp. 52/54: 200 cm (79") long

Tie-belt for the children's version, 6 cm (2¹/2") wide, finished width 3 cm (1¹/4"), and for
Size 104: 115 cm (45¹/4") long
Size 116: 120 cm (47¹/4") long
Size 128: 125 cm (49¹/4") long
Size 140: 130 cm (51¹/4") long
Size 152: 140 cm (55¹/4") long
c) Strip on the grain for 2 belt carriers, 2 cm (⁷/8") wide (finished width 1 cm - ¹/2"), and for
adult version, all sizes, 36 cm (14¹/4") long
children's version, all sizes, 30 cm (12") long
3 cm (1¹/4") bias tape for hanger loop: 15 cm (6") long

Tip: bias tape can be also be used for belt carriers.

Each size has a different outline:
Adult version:
Size 34-40 resp. 44/46
Size 42/44 resp. 48/50
Size 46/48 resp. 52/54
Children's version:
Size 104
Size 116
Size 128
Size 140
Size 152

BEFORE CUTTING OUT
Important:
The broken outlines on front and back mean that these pattern pieces must be extended
to full length beginning at arrowheads. Add the following amounts to pattern pieces:
Adult version:
Front: 40 cm (15³/4") for **all sizes**
Back: 72 cm (28¹/2") for **all sizes**

Children's version:

Front:	Back:
Size 104: 15 cm (6")	**Size 104:** 40.5 cm (16")
Size 116: 23.5 cm (9")	**Size 116:** 50.5 cm (20")
Size 128: 23.5 cm (9")	**Size 128:** 52 cm (20¹/2")
Size 140: 29 cm (11¹/2")	**Size 140:** 58.5 cm (23")
Size 152: 34.5 cm (13³/4")	**Size 152:** 66.5 cm (26¹/4")

After lengthening front and back pattern pieces, connect the ends of side outlines to make
hemline. Width of hemline should be as follows (please make sure this is right!):

Hem edge on front:		on back:
Size 34-40 resp. 44/46:	40 cm (15³/4")	30 cm (12")
Size 42/44 resp. 48/50:	42 cm (16¹/2")	32 cm (12³/4")
Size 46/48 resp. 52/54:	44 cm (17¹/4")	34 cm (13¹/2")
Size 104:	30 cm (12")	22 cm (8³/4")
Size 116:	30.5 cm (12¹/4")	22.5 cm (8³/4")
Size 128:	31.5 cm (12¹/2")	23.5 cm (9")
Size 140:	32.5 cm (13")	24.5 cm (9³/4")
Size 152:	35 cm (13³/4")	26.5 cm (10¹/2")

CUT OUT AS FOLLOWS
As shown on our cutting layouts, some pieces are cut from a single fabric layer, some
from doubled layers. When cutting from doubled layers fold fabric **right** sides together.
The fold edge is call "fabric fold."
When cutting from a single fabric layer pin pieces onto the **right** fabric side. It is important
that those pattern pieces shown on layout with a solid outline be pinned PRINTED SIDE
UP onto fabric, those with broken outlines PRINTED SIDE DOWN onto fabric. This
guarantees that you cut out righthand and lefthand pieces. These pattern pieces represent
the right half of a human body only. Therefore, it will be necessary to turn pattern piece
for the back on the children's version at center back in order to cut out a full piece. **Don't
forget to add seam and hem allowances!**
See page 14 for detailed cutting instructions which explain everything step-by-step.

145

CONSTRUCTION

Please see our Illustrated Teaching Instructions on page 15.
Stitch shoulder seams. Overcast seam allowances (ills. 1 and 2) with an overlock machine or with wide-set zigzag stitch. Topstitch shoulder seams.
Attach sleeves before closing side seams - it's easier!
Stitch sleeves to armholes, **right** sides together (ill. 3).
Construct belt carriers (ill. 4). Overcast sleeve attachment seam allowances together and press into body of garment, topstitch into place. Baste belt carriers onto the **right** side of side seam edges. Pin side seams and underarm seams in sleeves (ill. 5).
When stitching side seams and underarm seams in sleeves, make sure that ends of sleeve attachment seams match!
Press side seam allowances into back, topstitch ³/₄ cm (³/₈") into place (ill. 6). Turn up hem and closing edge allowances, stitch into place (ill. 7).
Sleeves: fold extended facings to the **inside** along foldline, baste fold, baste and stitch open facing edge into place.
Pockets: stitch the **right** side of bands to the **wrong** side of upper pocket edges. Turn bands to the **right** side of pocket, baste seamed edge. Turn under open long edge of band, stitch into place (ill. 8). Press side and lower edge allowance on pockets to the **inside**. Baste pockets onto fronts where marked, topstitch ¹/₂ cm (¹/₄") into place.
Fold neckband in half lengthwise, **right** sides together. Stitch both ends. Turn band **right**

side out, baste and press edges (ill. 9). Stitch neckband onto the **right** side of neck edge (ill. 10). Trim neck edge allowance only. Press neckband allowances down into body of garment, topstitch into place (ill. 11).
Construct hanger loop: press both long edges of fabric strip ³/₄ cm (³/₈") to the **inside**. Then fold strip in half lengthwise, edges on the **inside**. Press. Edgestitch both long edges. Turn in ends. Stitch hanger loop onto neckband attachment seam at center back as shown in ill. 12.
Tie-belt: fold fabric strip for belt in half lengthwise, **right** sides together. Stitch both ends and open long edge closed, leaving 10 cm (4") open for turning. Trim seam allowances back to ¹/₂ cm (¹/₄") width, trim corners diagonally. Turn belt **right** side out, baste and press all edges. Slipstitch turning gap closed. Then topstitch ¹/₂ cm (¹/₄") along all belt edges.

Allowances:
Shoulder and side seams, underarm seams in sleeves 2 cm (⁷/₈"); front closing and hem edges 4 cm (1⁵/₈"); all other edges 1.5 cm (⁵/₈").

Cutting layout for all sizes

Adult version

Children's version

Style 2

3 shirts from one pattern, pages 13 and 20/21

Size 104 sheet A, red outline ⌁⌁⌁ pieces 39 to 42
Size 116 sheet B, red outline → → → pieces 39 to 42
Size 128 sheet C, red outline ·········· pieces 39 to 42
Size 140 sheet D, red outline ∿∿∿ pieces 39 to 42

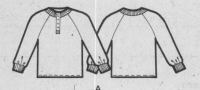

A   B + C

View C
Pieces for clown appliqué are printed in green on sheet A.

Pattern overview

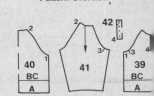

40 BC A   41   39 BC A

Pay careful attention to the lines and markings for the different views when tracing off pattern pieces. These are designated with the view letters.

Fabric requirements
View A
Shirt with polo closing
150 cm (59") wide cotton flannel:
Size 104: 0.60 m (³/₄ yd)
Size 116: 0.65 m (⁷/₈ yd)
Size 128: 0.75 m (⁷/₈ yd)
Size 140: 0.90 m (1 yd)
Tubular rib knit for neckband and wristbands, 160 cm (63") in circumference: **all sizes:** 0.15 m (¹/₄ yd)
View B
Red shirt with iron-on appliqué
160 cm (63") wide sweatshirting:
Size 104: 0.50 m (⁵/₈ yd)
Size 116: 0.55 m (³/₄ yd)
Size 128: 0.65 m (⁷/₈ yd)
Size 140: 0.80 m (⁷/₈ yd)
Tubular rib knit for hemband, neckband and wristbands, 160 cm (63") in circumference: **all sizes:** 0.15 m (¹/₄ yd)
View C
Black shirt with clown appliqué
160 cm (63") wide sweatshirting:
Size 104: 0.50 m (⁵/₈ yd)
Size 116: 0.55 m (³/₄ yd)
Size 128: 0.65 m (⁷/₈ yd)
Size 140: 0.80 m (⁷/₈ yd)
Tubular rib knit for hemband, neckband and wristbands, 110 cm (43¹/₂") in circumference: **all sizes:** 0.25 m (³/₈ yd)

Notions/Haberdashery
View A:
Fusible interfacing; 5 small, hammer-in snaps
View B:
1 iron-on appliqué motif
View C:
Fabric and trim remnants for clown appliqué; fusible interfacing; fusing agent.
Before cutting out:
Views A,B,C
All pieces for these garments except the extra pieces are to be cut from a SINGLE fabric layer as shown on the layouts. Always pin pattern pieces onto the **right** fabric side when cutting from a single layer. Those pattern pieces on layout with a solid outline are pinned PRINTED SIDE UP onto fabric, those with broken outlines are pinned PRINTED SIDE DOWN onto fabric.
The grain direction arrows printed for View A on pattern pieces correspond to the knit direction for Views B and C.

View A
For polo closing trim pattern piece 39 (front) along the vertical line (band attachment line) down to seam number 4, then cut across to center front fold. Cut out this piece with [?] cm (³/₈") on closing edges.

Cutting out:
39 Front (once on the fold) **A B C**
40 Back (once on the fold) **A B C**
41 Sleeve (twice) **A B C**
42 Closing band (cut twice on fold) **A**
Extra pieces:
There are no pattern pieces for these pieces. They are marked onto fabric with tailor's chalk and are designated on layout with the small letters **a, b, c.**
Views A,B,C
a) 2 wristbands, each 10 cm (4") wide, finished width 5 cm (2"):
Size 104 ea. 14.5 cm (5⁵/₈") long
Size 116 ea. 15 cm (6") long
Size 128 ea. 15.5 cm (6¹/₄") long
Size 140 ea. 16 cm (6¹/₂") long
View A
b) Neckband, 6 cm (2¹/₄") wide, finished width 3 cm (1¹/₄"):
Size 104 32 cm (12³/₄") long
Size 116 33 cm (13") long
Size 128 34 cm (13¹/₂") long
Size 140 35 cm (13³/₄") long
Views B & C
c) Neckband, 6 cm (2¹/₄") wide, finished width 3 cm (1¹/₄"):
Size 104 35 cm (13³/₄") long
Size 116 36 cm (14¹/₄") long
Size 128 37 cm (14¹/₂") long
Size 140 38 cm (15") long
d) Hemband, 10 cm wide, finished width 5 cm (2"):
Size 104 52 cm (20¹/₂") long
Size 116 56 cm (22¹/₄") long
Size 128 60 cm (23³/₄") long
Size 140 64 cm (25¹/₄") long
Please note:
View A
Iron fusible interfacing onto the **wrong** side of closing bands and lower end of front closing. See shaded areas on cutting layout.

Construction
See Illustrated Teaching Instructions on pages 20/21, ills. 1 - 12 and 1 - 4.
Views A,B,C
● Stitch side seams and underarm seams in sleeves (ill. 6). Overcast and press open seam allowances.
● Pin, baste and stitch sleeves to armholes, **right** sides together (ill. 7). Overcast seam allowances together and press into sleeves.

View A

● Fold neckband in half lengthwise, **wrong** sides together, and press, carefully shaping open edges into a curve to fit neck. Baste and stitch neckband to the **right** side of neck edge, stretching it slightly as you stitch. Overcast seam allowances together, press downward.

● Stitch closing bands to neckband ends and closing edges down to seam number 4, **right** sides together. Fold bands in half lengthwise, **right** sides together. Stitch upper end of each from fold over to attachment seam (ill. 1). Trim seam allowances back to 1/2 cm (1/4") width. Turn bands **right** side out.

● Clip seam allowance on front only in close to last stitch at each lower corner (ill. 2).

● Press band attachment seam allowances into bands. Fold bands along their foldline, turn under inner edge of each and baste into place over attachment seam. Press. From the **right** side of shirt edgestitch along both long edges and upper end of each band, securing inner layer (ill. 3).

● Pin right band onto left band, center-on-center. Stitch lower ends of bands to front from corner to corner, **right** sides together (ill. 4).

Views B & C

● Fold neckband in half lengthwise, **wrong** sides together, and press, shaping its open edges to a curve to fit neck. Open out neckband flat. Stitch its ends **right** sides together (ill. 8). Then fold again along foldline. Baste and stitch neckband to the **right** side of neck edge so that its seam lies at center back (ills. 9 and 10).

Views A,B,C

● Wristbands: stitch ends of each band **right** sides together, forming a ring. Fold bands in half lengthwise, **wrong** sides together. Stitch bands to the **right** side of lower sleeve edges, stretching as you stitch (ill. 11).

View A

● Press hem allowance to the **inside,** turn under raw edge (finished width 1 cm - 1/2"), topstitch 3/4 cm (3/8") into place.

● Hammer snaps into closing bands where marked, upper halves into right band, lower halves into left band (ill. 5). Fixing tools and directions are in the packet.

Views B & C

● Stitch ends of hemband **right** sides together, forming a ring. Fold hemband in half lengthwise, **wrong** sides together. Stitch hemband to the **right** side of lower shirt edge with overlock stitch, stretching band slightly as you stitch.

View B

● Pin iron-on appliqué motif onto front where desired, making sure that coated side lies on fabric. Press into place from the **right** side using a press cloth (ill. 12). Then press thoroughly from the **wrong** side to fuse motif permanently.

View C

Trace clown motif off the pattern sheet onto tissue paper. Iron interfacing onto the **wrong** side of front over the area where the appliqué will be attached, making sure you apply it with steam so that you can remove it later on. **This is important!** Make appliqué as explained on page 21, ills. 1 - 4. Attach rickrack, embroider eyes and sew on buttons last. Apply steam to the interfacing outside the appliqué, peel back and trim off along outer edge of appliqué.

Allowances:
Views A,B,C
All seams 1.5 cm (5/8"); remaining edges 1 cm (1/2").
View A
Hem 2 cm (7/8"); closing band attachment seam 3/4 cm (3/8").

Cutting layouts for all sizes

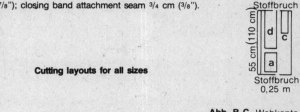

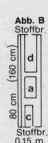

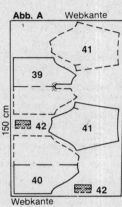

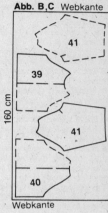

Style

3

2 children's pants from 1 pattern, pages 13 and 22/23

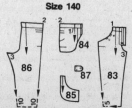

A

B

Side leg length from waist casing:
Views A & B
Size 104: 63 cm (24 3/4")
Size 116: 72 cm (28 1/2")
Size 128: 81 cm (32")
Size 140: 90 cm (35 1/2")

Pattern overviews

Sizes 104+116

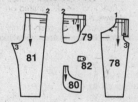

Size 128

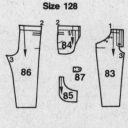

Size 140

Views A & B

When tracing off pattern pieces pay careful attention to the lines and markings for the differing views. These are designated by the view letters.

Size 140: extend front and back pant pattern pieces to the indicated length beginning at points of arrows. Take this into consideration when positioning tissue paper so that you'll have enough for each full piece without having to tape sections together. Connect the ends of extended lines on back piece to make hemline. Draw in front hemline over to extended edge. Compare lower leg width on your pieces with ours!
Lower leg width, back pants
Size 140: 18 cm (7")

Fabric requirements
View A
Plaid pants with zipper:
150 cm (59") wide, reversible doubleweave fabric:
Size 104: 0.80 m (7/8 yd)
Size 116: 0.90 m (1 yd)
Size 128: 1.00 m (1 1/8 yds)
Size 140: 1.10 m (1 1/4 yds)
View B
Unicolored girl's pants, without zipper:
150 cm (59") wide, reversible doubleweave fabric:
Size 104: 0.80 m (7/8 yd)
Size 116: 0.90 m (1 yd)
Size 128: 1.00 m (1 1/8 yds)
Size 140: 1.10 m (1 1/4 yds)

Notions/Haberdashery
Views A & B: 4 hammer-in studs; 12 mm (1/2") elastic, 90 cm (36") for **all sizes.**
View A: fusible interfacing; 1 hammer-in snap; 1 zipper:
Sizes 104+116: 14 cm (5 1/2") long
Sizes 128+140: 16 cm (6 1/2") long
Before cutting out:
Views A & B
Please note the differing center front lines on front pant piece and hip yoke for the differing views, for View A the right and left placket edges as well.

View A

Fold fabric in half lengthwise, **right** sides together, matching the plaid in both layers. Pin layers together at intervals so that plaid won't slip out of line. Pin pattern pieces onto fabric as shown on your layout, making sure that the marker line on side edge of front and back pant pieces as well as on hip yoke lie on the same bar in the plaid.-

Cutting out:

Figures in brackets refer to sizes 128 and 140.
78 (83) Pants, front (cut twice) **A B**
79 (84) Hip yoke (cut twice) **A B**
80 (85) Pocket pouch (cut twice) **A B**
81 (86) Pants, back (cut twice) **A B**
82 (87) Front tab (cut twice) **A**

Please note:
View A
Iron interfacing onto the **wrong** side of one tab piece. Shaded pattern pieces on layouts or sections of pattern pieces are to be interfaced.

Construction tips:
View A
Make sure that the plaid matches exactly at vertical seams. To prevent plaid from slipping out of line while stitching, insert pins perpendicular to seamline.

Construction:
See Illustrated Teaching Instructions on pp. 22/23, ills. 1 - 18.

Views A & B
● Stitch tucks on pocket opening, ill. 1.
● Pin pouch pieces to pocket opening edges, **right** sides together, ill. 2.
● Stitch pouch pieces into place. Trim seam allowances back to 1/2 cm (1/4") width, clip curves. Ill. 3.
● Fold pouch pieces over to the **inside.** Baste, press and topstitch seamed (pocket opening) edges. Baste pocket opening edges onto the **right** side of hip yokes, ill. 4.
● Stitch pouch pieces to hip yokes as marked on pattern, ill. 5.
● Baste pockets under side edges, matching marked seamlines. Stitch side seams. Ill. 6.
● Press side seam allowances into back pant pieces, topstitch into place. Ill. 7.

View A
● Stitch inside leg seams, press open the allowances. Insert one leg into the other, **right** sides together, matching side as well as inside leg seams. Double stitch crotch seam from upper back edge around to placket mark in front. Press open seam allowances in back down to curve.
● Baste hip yokes into place at front placket edges, left yoke along center front line, the right yoke over to foldline for underlap. Press allowance on upper edge of front pant pieces to the **inside.** Edgestitch fold edge onto hip yoke, continue and edgestitch pocket opening edge into place down to lowermost casing stitching line.
● Fold extended facing on upper edge of pants to the **inside** along foldline, press, turn under open edge, baste into place. Beginning and ending at pocket openings, topstitch along upper pant edge as marked, securing facing and thus making casings for elastic. Insert elastic into casings. Try on pants to check elastic fit. Baste elastic ends into place at pocket opening edges. Topstitch front pant pieces as marked, stitching remainder of waist casing into place. Topstitch along pocket opening edge to upper pant edge, securing elastic ends.
● Stitch tab pieces **right** sides together. Trim seam allowances. Turn tab **right** side out. Baste and topstitch edges. See ill. 16.
● Baste tab onto left placket edge (ill. 17), stitch into place along center front line.
● Press facing on placket edges to the **inside,** left facing along center front line, right facing along underlap foldline. Edgestitch right half of zipper under right placket edge using a zipper presser foot. Pin placket closed, center-on-center. Baste and stitch left half of zipper under left placket edge along marked line, catching in tab (ill. 18).

View B
● Stitch inside leg seams and crotch seam (ill. 8).
● Stitch hip yokes **right** sides together at center front seam (ill. 9).
● Stitch upper edge of front pants onto hip yoke along the foldline (ill. 10).
● Fold extended facing on upper pant edge to the **inside,** turn under raw edge, baste into place (ill. 11).
● Beginning and ending at pocket openings, topstitch facing into place along marked lines, making casings for elastic. Insert elastic into casings, baste ends into place at pocket openings. Try on pants, check elastic fit (ill. 12).
● Topstitch remainder of waist facing into place in front, stitching elastic ends into place at the same time (ill. 13).

Views A & B
● Stitch across casings to prevent elastic from twisting (ill. 14).
● Hammer studs into pocket opening edges where marked, taking care NOT to catch in hip yokes (ill. 15). For View A hammer snap into tab and right front pant piece. Fixing tools and instructions are in the packet.
● Turn up hem allowance twice 1 cm (1/2"), press, topstitch 3/4 cm (3/8") into place.

Allowances
Views A & B
Vertical seams and hems 2 cm (7/8"); crotch seam at curve and remaining edges 1 cm (1/2").

Cutting layouts for all sizes

Pattern piece numbers in brackets refer to sizes 128 and 140

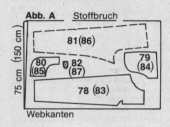

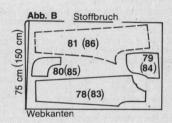

Place pattern pieces onto the fabric as shown on the pattern layout

As a general rule, pattern pieces are placed onto the fabric with their printed side up. Pattern pieces which have to be placed onto the fabric with their printed side down are drawn with a broken line on the pattern layout. This may become necessary in order to economize on fabric or in order to obtain two mirror-image pieces, eg one right sleeve and one left sleeve. Some pattern pieces have to be placed on the fabric fold. The fold line and the half of the pattern piece which has to be added to make a complete piece are also drawn with a broken line on the pattern layout.

Style
4

Child's skirt on pages 13 and 23

Skirt length from waist casing:
Size 104: 24.5 cm (9 1/2")
Size 116: 28 cm (11")
Size 128: 31.5 cm (12 1/2")
Size 140: 35 cm (13 3/4")

Pattern overview

| 46 | 45 | 44 | 43 |

Fabric requirements
140 cm (55") wide doubleweave:
Size 104: 0.40 m (1/2 yd)
Size 116: 0.45 m (5/8 yd)
Size 128: 0.50 m (5/8 yd)
Size 140: 0.55 m (3/4 yd)

Notions/Haberdashery:
90 cm (1 yd) of 12 mm (1/2") elastic; 4 hammer-in studs

Cutting out
43 Front skirt panel (cut twice)
44 Hip yoke (cut twice)
45 Pocket pouch (cut twice)
46 Back skirt panel (cut once on fold)

Construction
See Illustrated Teaching Instructions on page 23, ills. 1 - 3.
Please see illustrated instructions for style 3, View B on pages 22/23 for constructing hip yoke pockets and upper edge.
● Stitch and topstitch center front seam from upper edge down to slit mark (ill. 1).
● Fold and stitch tucks in pocket opening edges, x-onto-o, **right** sides together, press toward center front. Stitch pouch pieces to pocket opening edges so that upper edge of each lies on facing line on upper skirt edge (ill. 2).
● Trim seam allowances on pocket opening edges, clip curves.
● Fold pouch pieces over to the **inside.** Baste, press, edgestitch and topstitch 3/4 cm (3/8") along seamed (pocket opening) edges. Pin the **wrong** side of front skirt onto the **right** side of hip yokes so that pocket opening edges lie on placement lines. Baste opening edges into place.
● Stitch pouch pieces to hip yokes from side edge around to lowermost line for waist casing.
● Baste pockets into place at side seam edges, matching marked seamlines. Stitch side seams. Overcast seam allowances together, press into back skirt, edgestitch and topstitch 3/4 cm (3/8") into place.
● Stitch hip yokes **right** sides together at center front seam. Press open seam allowances.
● Press the allowance on upper edge of front skirt to the **inside** so that it touches foldline, edgestitch onto hip yoke. Continue and edgestitch pocket opening edges into place down to lowermost casing line.

● Press the extended facing on upper skirt edge to the **inside,** turn under its open edge, baste into place from pocket opening edge around the back to other pocket opening edge.
● From the **right** side of skirt stitch facing into place along both casing lines from one pocket opening edge around the back to the other pocket opening. Insert elastic into casings, baste into place at pocket openings. Try on skirt to determine final fit of elastic!
● Beginning and ending at upper edge of skirt, edgestitch again along pocket opening edges, securing elastic ends. Then topstitch front skirt along lowermost casing line, securing facing on inside.
● To prevent elastic from twisting, stitch across casings at side seams and center back and at center of each yoke if desired (ill. 14, page 23).
● Machine stitch hem and front slit allowances into place (ill. 3).
● Hammer studs into pocket opening edges where marked, taking care NOT to catch in hip yokes.

Cutting layout for all sizes

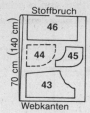

Stoffbruch
46
44 45
43
70 (140 cm)
Webkanten

Allowances
Seams and hem 1.5 cm (⅝"); all other edges 1 cm (½").

Style
5

Shirt & 2 dresses from pages 28/29 and 47

Sizes 36+38 sheet C, green outline —x—x—x— pieces 63 and 64
Sizes 40+42 sheet B, green outline •••••••••• pieces 63 and 64
Sizes 44+46 sheet A, green outline —o—o—o— pieces 63 and 64

Pattern overview

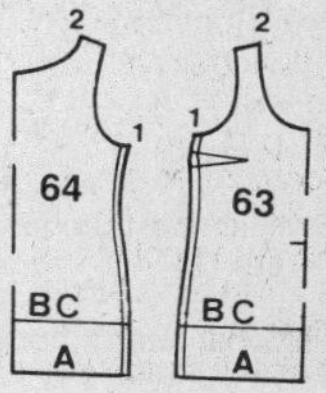

2 2
64 63
B C B C
A A

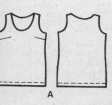

A

B+C

Length from waist to hem:
View A
sizes 36 to 46: 30 cm (12")
Views B & C
Sizes 36+38: 54 cm (21¼")
Sizes 40+42: 56 cm (22¼")
Sizes 44+46: 58 cm (23")

For this style 2 sizes, e.g. sizes 36 and 38, are together on one pattern. Therefore, pay careful attention to the different side seamlines when tracing off pattern pieces. Also pay careful attention to the hemlines and skirt attachment seamlines for the different views.

Fabric requirements
View A, beige shirt
170 cm (67") wide, viscose rayon/linen blend jersey:
All sizes: 0.80 m (⅞ yd)
View B, dress with striped skirt
140 cm (55") wide dotted cotton jersey for bodice:
Sizes 36+38: 0.80 m (⅞ yd)
Sizes 40+42: 0.85 m (1 yd)
Sizes 44+46: 0.90 m (1 yd)
140 cm (55") wide, vertically striped cotton jersey for skirt:
All sizes: 1.20 m (1⅜ yds)
View C, dress with dotted skirt
Tubular rib knit for bodice, 110 cm (43½") in circumference:
Sizes 36 to 42: 0.70 m (⅞ yd)
Sizes 44+46: 0.90 m (1 yd)
140 cm (55") wide dotted cotton jersey for skirt:
All sizes: 1.20 m (1⅜ yds)

Notions/Haberdashery
Views B & C
3 cm (1¼") bias tape or seam tape: 1.20 m (1⅜ yds) for **all sizes.**

See **General information** about **jersey fabrics** on pages 120/121.

Cutting out
Views A, B & C
63 Front (cut once on fold)
64 Back (cut once on fold)
Extra pieces
There are no pattern pieces for skirt panels and bias strips for finishing edges. These pieces are drawn with tailor's chalk directly onto fabric and are designated with the small letters **a, b** and **c** on layouts.
Views B & C
c) 3 skirt panels, for **all sizes** each 35 cm (13¾") long and 138 cm (54½") wide. Total width of skirt 414 cm (163½").
View B
a) 2 bias strips for finishing armholes, each 3 cm (1¼") wide and for
Size 36- 48 cm (19") long
Size 38- 50 cm (19¾") long
Size 40- 51 cm (20¼") long
Size 42- 53 cm (21") long
Size 44- 53 cm (21") long
Size 46- 54 cm (21¼") long
b) 3 cm (1¼") wide bias strip for finishing neck edge:
Sizes 36+38- totalling 80 cm (31½") in length
Sizes 40+42- totalling 82 cm (32½") in length
Sizes 44+46- totalling 83 cm (32¾") in length

Construction
See Illustrated Teaching Instructions on page 28, ills. 1-3.
Views A, B, C
● Stitch bust darts (ill. 1).
● Stitch shoulder seams, press open allowances.
View B
● Stitch bias strips for finishing neck edge **right** sides together on the grain (see page 92). Fold bias strips for neck and armhole edges in half lengthwise, **wrong** sides together. Press. Pin folded bias strips as facings onto the **right** side of neck and armhole edges so that their open edges lie on the allowance. Turn under ends of neck bias facing at one shoulder seam. Stitch bias facings into place with 1 cm (½") seam allowance.
● Trim seam allowances back to 3 mm (⅛") width. Fold bias facings to the **inside** and baste into place so that about 3 mm (⅛") of it is visible on the **right** side. From the **right** side of garment edgestitch along attachment seams, securing facings.
Views A & C
● Overcast neck and armhole edges, fold to the **inside.** Overcast fold edges with whipstitching. From the **right** side of garment topstitch edges with twin ballpoint needles, stitching very close to whipstitching (ill. 2). The bobbin thread will form a zigzag line.
Views A, B, C
● Stitch side seams. Press open the allowances, hand sew into place at armhole edges.
View A
● Fold hem allowance to the **inside.** Topstitch 3 cm (1¼") into place from the **right** side of garment using twin ballpoint needles.
Views B & C
● Stitch skirt panels **right** sides together at ends, forming a ring. Fold hem allowance to the **inside,** topstitch 3 cm (1¼") into place from the **right** side of skirt using twin ballpoint needles.
● Gather upper edge of skirt: run a row of machine basting 3 mm (⅛") on each side of marked seamline. Pull up the bobbin threads at both ends of this stitching until skirt matches bodice. Evenly distribute gathering. Stitch skirt to bodice, **right** sides together, catching in seam tape or stretched out bias tape (ill. 3). Press seam allowances up into bodice.

Cutting layouts

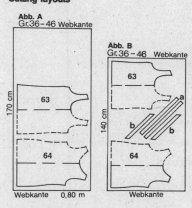

Abb. A
Gr. 36-46 Webkante
63
63
64
Webkante 0.80 m

Abb. B
Gr. 36-46 Webkante
63
a
b b
64
Webkante

Allowances
Seams 1.5 cm (⅝"); hems 3.5 cm (1½"); all other edges 1 cm (½").

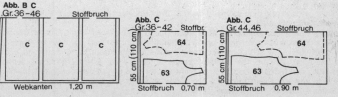

Abb. B C
Gr. 36-46 Stoffbruch
c c c
70 cm (140 cm)
Webkanten 1.20 m

Abb. C
Gr. 36-42 Stoffbr.
64
63
55 cm (110 cm)
Stoffbruch 0.70 m

Abb. C
Gr. 44,46 Stoffbruch
64
63
55 cm (110 cm)
Stoffbruch 0.90 m

Sizes 36+38 sheet C, green outline ················· pieces 69 to 76
Sizes 40+42 sheet B, green outline ⌇⌇⌇⌇⌇⌇⌇ pieces 69 to 76
Sizes 44+46 sheet A, green outline ——— — —— pieces 69 to 76

A   B   A, B

Pattern overview

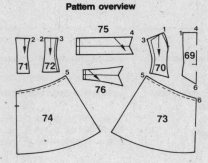

Skirt length from waist:
64 cm (25¼")

Petticoat length from waist casing: 66 cm (26")

For this style 2 sizes, e.g. sizes 36 and 38, are together on one pattern. Therefore, pay careful attention to the different size lines when tracing off pattern pieces 70, 72, 75 and 76.

Fabric requirements:
View A, dress with shoulder straps
Do not use stiff, unpliable fabric for this view. It would prevent the upper band from shaping properly.
150 cm (59") wide cotton broadcloth:
1.75 m (2 yds) for **all sizes.**
View B, dress with halter strap
150 cm (59") wide cotton broadcloth:
1.80 m (2 yds) for **all sizes.**
Views A & B, petticoat:
70 cm (28") wide petticoat fabric:
1.80 m (2 yds) for **all sizes.**

Notions/Haberdashery:
Views A & B
Dress: 40 cm (16") zipper; fusible interfacing; 2 staves or sections of boning, ea. 28 cm (11") long.
Petticoat: 1 cm (½") elastic to fit waist.

Cutting out:
69 Bodice, center front (cut once on fold) **A B**
70 Bodice, side front (cut twice) **A B**
71 Bodice, center back (cut twice) **A B**
72 Bodice, side back (cut twice) **A B**
73 Skirt, front (cut once on fold) **A B**
74 Skirt, back (cut twice) **A B**
75 Upper band (cut twice) **A**
76 Halter strap (cut twice) **B**
Extra pieces:
View A
a) 2 strips on the grain for straps, ea. 6 cm (2¼") wide, finished width 3 cm (1¼"):
Sizes 36+38 ea. 37 cm (14½") long
Sizes 40+42 ea. 40 cm (15¾") long
Sizes 44+46 ea. 43 cm (17") long
Views A & B
Petticoat: 1 panel 70 cm (27¾") long and 1.78 m (70¼") wide.
The length stated includes 2.5 cm (1") allowance for waist casing.
Please note:
The shaded pattern pieces or parts of pieces on layouts are to be interfaced.
Views A & B
Center front corner on upper edge of front skirt.
View B
Straps to foldline

Construction:
See Illustrated Teaching Instructions on pp. 34/35, ills. 1-15.
Views A & B
● Stitch section and side seams in bodice. Overcast seam allowances, press to one side, topstitch into place (ill. 1).
● Stitch side seams and center back seam in skirt up to placket mark. Clip allowance on upper skirt edge at center front point. Gather skirt: run a row of machine basting 3 mm (⅛") on each side of the marked seamline front center front point around to a back placket edge. Pull up the bobbin threads at both ends of these stitching sections, gathering skirt to match bodice. Knot gathering threads, evenly distribute gathering (ill. 2).
● Baste and stitch skirt to bodice (ills. 3 and 4). Press seam allowances up into bodice, topstitch ¾ cm (⅜") into place (ill. 5).

View A
● Stitch zipper under placket edges (ills. 6 and 7).
● Fold upper bands in half lengthwise, **right** sides together. Stitch ends. Turn bands right side out. Baste open (upper) long edges of each band together with diagonal (tailor's) basting (ill. 8), thus giving this edge the extra fullness necessary for curves.
● Slip staves (or boning) under side seam allowances (ill. 9).
● Baste and stitch bands to upper edge of bodice as in ills. 10 and 11. Press allowance down into bodice, topstitch into place. Sew band ends into place at center back (ill. 14).
● Construct straps as in ill. 12. Pin strap ends under upper edge of bodice touching section seams, in front to the side of section seams, in back to the center. Sew straps into place (ill. 13).
View B
● Slip staves (or boning) under side seam allowances (ill. 9).
● Press the allowance on upper bodice edge to the **inside,** turn under open edge 1 cm (½"), baste into place.
● Stitch straps **right** sides together at center seam. Fold strap along foldline, **right** sides together. Stitch open long edges together. Turn strap **right** side out. Press and topstitch ¾ cm (⅜") along both long edges. Pin strap under upper edge of side front bodice piece so that they just touch section seams. Baste into place.
● Edgestitch and topstitch ¾ cm (⅜") along upper bodice edge, securing strap ends.
● Press zipper placket allowances to the **inside.** Baste zipper under placket edges so that its teeth are covered (centered application), turning under upper ends of tapes. Using a zipper presser foot, topstitch ½ cm (¼") along placket edges, securing zipper.
Views A & B
● Machine finish hem as in ill. 15.
Petticoat:
● Stitch ends of petticoat panel **right** sides together, forming a ring. Leave 2.5 cm (1") open at upper end for inserting elastic.
● Press upper edge 2.5 cm (1") to the **inside,** turn under raw edge, baste. Topstitch 1.5 cm (⅝") along upper edge, securing allowance and thus making casing for elastic. Measure and cut elastic to fit, insert into casing. Sew elastic ends together.

Allowances:
View B: 2 cm (⅞") on upper edge of dress.
Views A & B: Hem and seams 1.5 cm (⅝"), all other edges 1 cm (½").

Cutting layouts for all sizes

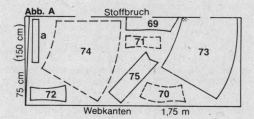

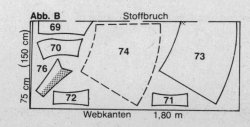

Style 7

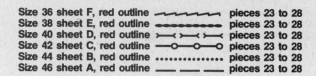

Size 36 sheet F, red outline ⌇⌇⌇⌇⌇ pieces 23 to 28
Size 38 sheet E, red outline ●━●━●━●━● pieces 23 to 28
Size 40 sheet D, red outline ⟩━━⟨⟩━━⟨ pieces 23 to 28
Size 42 sheet C, red outline ━○━━○━━○ pieces 23 to 28
Size 44 sheet B, red outline ·········· pieces 23 to 28
Size 46 sheet A, red outline ─ · ── · ── pieces 23 to 28

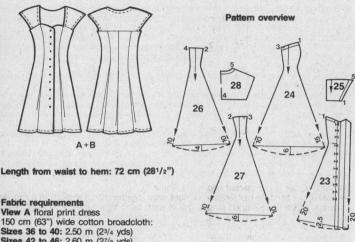

Pattern overview

A + B

Length from waist to hem: 72 cm (28½")

Fabric requirements
View A floral print dress
150 cm (63") wide cotton broadcloth:
Sizes 36 to 40: 2.50 m (2¾ yds)
Sizes 42 to 46: 2.60 m (2⅞ yds)
View B striped dress
150 cm (63") wide, vertically striped polished cotton:
Sizes 36 to 40: 2.50 m (2¾ yds)
Sizes 42 to 46: 2.60 m (2⅞ yds)

Notions/Haberdashery
Views A & B
11 buttons; fusible interfacing; shoulder pads

Before cutting out
Views A & B
Trace off extra pattern pieces for facings that are printed on upper edge of center and side front pieces as well as on neck edges of front and back yoke pieces. These pieces are designated with the same number as the main pattern piece on layout.
View B
Pay careful attention to the stripe direction when pinning pattern pieces onto fabric. Make sure that stripes match on lower edge of front shoulder yokes.

Extend pattern pieces for center front and back as well as for side front and back to full length by adding the amount printed on broken line at arrowhead on overview drawing. Connect the ends of these lines with a straight line in the following widths:

Center front (piece 23):
Size 36: 42 cm (16½")
Size 38: 42.5 cm (16¾")
Size 40: 43 cm (17")
Size 42: 43.5 cm (17¼")
Size 44: 44 cm (17¼")
Size 46: 44.5 cm (17½")
Side front (piece 24):
Size 36: 59 cm (23¼")
Size 38: 59.5 cm (23½")
Size 40: 60 cm (23¾")
Size 42: 60.5 cm (23¾")
Size 44: 61 cm (24")
Size 46: 61.5 cm (24¼")

Center back (piece 26):
Size 36: 48.5 cm (19¼")
Size 38: 49 cm (19¼")
Size 40: 49.5 cm (19½")
Size 42: 50 cm (19¾")
Size 44: 50.5 cm (20")
Size 46: 51 cm (20¼")
Side back (piece 27):
Size 36: 58 cm (23")
Size 38: 58.5 cm (23¼")
Size 40: 59 cm (23¼")
Size 42: 59.5 cm (23½")
Size 44: 60 cm (23¾")
Size 46: 60.5 cm (24")

Draw a line at the center of and perpendicular to this connecting line, 2.5 cm (1") long on center front piece, 6 cm (2¼") long on side front and side back pieces, 4 cm (1⅝") long on center back. Draw a curved line from ends of extension lines to this center point (see pattern overview drawings). This curved line is your hemline.

Cutting out
Views A & B
23 Center front (cut twice)
23 Center front facing (cut twice)
24 Side front (cut twice)
24 Side front facing (cut twice)
25 Front shoulder yoke (cut twice)
25 Front yoke facing (cut twice)
26 Center back (cut twice)
27 Side back (cut twice)
28 Back shoulder yoke (cut once on fold)
28 Back yoke facing (cut once on fold)
Please note:
Views A & B
Iron interfacing onto the **wrong** side of all facings EXCEPT extended facings on front closing edges. See shaded areas on layouts.

Construction
See Illustrated Teaching Instructions on page 35, ills. 1 - 7.
● Stitch front section seams. Press front extended facings to the **inside** (ill. 1).
● Stitch shoulder seams in yoke and neck facings. Press armhole allowances on yoke to the **inside**, turn under edge, topstitch 1 cm (½") into place. Stitch facing to neck edge, **right** sides together. Turn facing to the **inside** (ills. 2 and 3). Topstitch neck edge.
● Stitch back center and back section seams. Stitch back yoke to upper edge of back between marker lines, **right** sides together (ill. 4). Overcast seam allowances together, press downward.
● Turn front extended facings to the **outside**, pin into place. Baste front yokes to upper edge of side fronts between section seam and marker line, **right** sides together. Stitch center and side front facings **right** sides together at section seams. Pin and stitch these facings to upper front edges, **right** sides together, matching section seams and securing front yokes (ill. 5). Turn all facings to the **inside**. Stitch side seams, continue and stitch ends of side front facings to allowance on upper back edge (ill. 6).
● Turn up hem allowance twice 1 cm (½"), press, machine stitch into place.
● Topstitch along closing, neck and yoke attachment seam edges. Hand sew facing into place as in ill. 7.
● Work buttonholes into right closing edge where marked. Sew buttons onto left closing edge along center front line.
● Hand sew shoulder pads to shoulder seam allowances.

Allowances:
Views A & B
Vertical seams 1 cm (½"); shoulder seams, armholes, hem 2 cm (⅞"); all other edges 1 cm (½").

Cutting layouts for all sizes

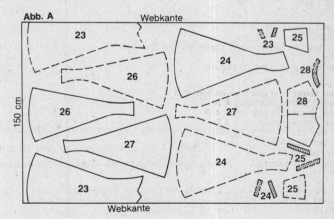

Abb. A Webkante

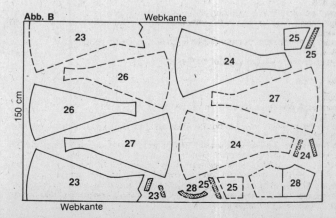

Abb. B Webkante

Style 8

Dress on page 37

Sizes 36+38 sheet F, green outline —o—o—o pieces 63 and 64
Sizes 40+42 sheet E, green outline —x—x—x pieces 63 and 64
Sizes 44+46 sheet D, green outline ∞∞∞ pieces 63 and 64

Pattern overviews

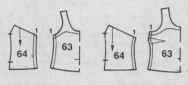

Sizes 36, 38   **Sizes 40 to 46 with bust darts**

Length from waist to hem 78 cm (30¾")

The pattern pieces for this style contain 2 sizes, e.g. 36 and 38. Therefore, pay careful attention to the different side seamlines when tracing off pattern pieces.

Fabric requirements
We recommend that this style be made up in jersey only.
140 cm (55") wide cotton jersey:
all sizes: 2.00 m (2¼ yds)

Notions/Haberdashery
4 cm (1⅝") bias tape: 1.10 m (1¼") for **all sizes.**
Important:
See pages 120/121 for tips on working with jersey.
Before cutting out:
Trace off facing marked on front bodice piece as an extra pattern piece. This piece will be designated with the same number as bodice front on layout. Cut out facing with a center front seam to economize on fabric.

Cutting out
63 Bodice, front (cut once on fold)
63 Front facing (cut twice)
64 Bodice, back (cut twice)
Extra pieces:
There are no pattern pieces for skirt panels and straps. These are drawn with tailor's chalk directly onto fabric and are designated with the small letters **a** and **b** on cutting layout.
a) 2 skirt panels, each 67 cm (26½") long and for
Sizes 36+38: 90 cm (35½") wide
Sizes 40+42: 100 cm (39½") wide
Sizes 44+46: 110 cm (43½") wide
b) 1 strap, 10 cm (4") wide (finished width 5 cm - 2") and for
Sizes 36+38: 50 cm (19¾") long
Sizes 40+42: 52 cm (20½") long
Sizes 44+46: 54 cm (21¼") long

Construction:
See Illustrated Teaching Instructions on page 36, ills. 1 - 11.
● Sizes 40 to 46: stitch bust darts. Knot threads at point.
● Stitch center back seam from lower edge up to lowermost slit mark. Press open seam allowances, press slit allowance to the **inside** and topstitch ¾ cm (⅜") into place (ill. 1).
● Construct strap (ill. 2). Topstitch ¾ cm (⅜") along both long edges of strap.
● Stitch facings **right** sides together at center front seam. Pin strap ends onto the **right** side of shoulder edges on front bodice, making sure that strap is not twisted. Pin, baste and stitch facing to front neck, shoulder and armhole edges, catching in straps (ill. 3). Turn facing to the **inside** (ill. 4).
● Slip center of strap into center back slit. Stitch upper end of center back seam from slit mark to upper edge (ill. 5).
● Stitch bodice side seams, continue and stitch front facing ends to extended facing on upper edge of back bodice (ill. 6). Tip: if the lower edge of facing is visible as an unsightly ridge on the right side, trim facing back to 1 cm (½") width along neck and armhole edges.
● Topstitch along neck, armhole and shoulder edges (ill. 7). Hand sew extended facing on upper back edge onto center back seam allowances.
● Stitch side seams in skirt. Gather upper skirt edge (ill. 8). Pin and stitch skirt to lower bodice edge, **right** sides together, catching in seam tape or stretched out bias tape on the **wrong** side of bodice (ill. 9). Press seam allowances up into bodice, topstitch ¾ cm (⅜") into place (ill. 10).
● Press hem allowance to the **inside**, topstitch 1.5 cm (⅝") into place from the **right** side of skirt using twin ballpoint needles. See your sewing machine manual for inserting and threading twin needles. The bobbin thread will form a zigzag line. You thus avoid stretching the fabric but the stitching retains elasticity.

Allowances
Hem and center back slit edges on bodice 2 cm (⅞"); 2 cm (⅞") extended facing on upper edge of back bodice; all seams 1.5 cm (⅝"); all other edges 1 cm (½").

Cutting layout for all sizes

Style 9

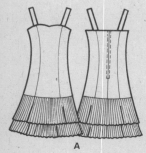

2 dresses from one pattern, pages 38 and 41

Sizes 36+38 sheet A, green outline — .... — .... pieces 47 to 51
Sizes 40+42 sheet B, green outline —o—o—o pieces 47 to 51
Sizes 44+46 sheet C, green outline ∿∿∿ pieces 47 to 51

A   B

Length from waist to hem:
Sizes 36+38: 56 cm (22¼")
Sizes 40+42: 58 cm (23")
Sizes 44+46: 60 cm (23¾")

Pattern overview

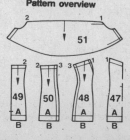

Diagram for pleated tiers

The numbers in parentheses ( ) pertain to sizes 40+42, those in brackets [ ] to sizes 44+46. The amounts stated are in centimeters.

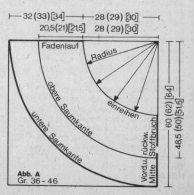

For this style 2 sizes, e.g. 36 and 38, are together on one pattern. Therefore, pay careful attention to the different size lines when tracing off pattern pieces. Pay careful attention to the lines and markings for the different views as well.

Here's how to make pattern pieces for tiers:

Beginning at the upper right corner of a square piece of tissue paper or plastic sheet, mark the radius for your size at upper and side edges and at 4 points between, 28 cm (15") to the left of the corner for sizes 36+38, for example. Connect these points with a curved line. This line is the upper edge of both tiers. Working from this line, mark the length for upper and lower tiers at upper and side edge and at several points between. Connect these points to make hemlines for tiers.

Fabric requirements:

View A dress with pleated tiers
112 cm (44¼") wide dobby weave polyester:
Sizes 36+38: 3.40 m (3¾ yds), **sizes 40 to 46:** 3.50 m (3⁷⁄₈ yds)
Tip: Before purchasing your fabric, please take into consideration that the permanence of commercial pleating depends upon the fabric type. Natural fiber fabrics such as cotton, silk and wool cannot be pleated permanently. 100% synthetic fabrics hold pleating best. In blends the higher the percentage of synthetic fibers the more permanent the pleats.
View B dotted dress with sleeves
150 cm (59") wide polished cotton:
Sizes 36+38: 2.20 m (2½ yds), **size 40 to 46:** 2.30 m (2⁵⁄₈ yds)
140 cm (55") wide tulle:
Sizes 36+38: 1.80 m (2 yds), **sizes 40+42:** 1.85 m (2¹⁄₈ yds), **sizes 44+46:** 1.90 m (2¹⁄₈ yds)
Remnant of lightcolored polished cotton with dark dots for bow.

Notions/Haberdashery:

Views A & B
40 cm (16") zipper; fusible interfacing
View B
1 cm (½") elastic:
Size 36: 1.30 m (1½ yds)
Size 38: 1.35 m (1⁵⁄₈ yds)
Size 40: 1.40 m (1⁵⁄₈ yds)
Size 42: 1.45 m (1¾ yds)
Sizes 44+46: 1.50 m (1¾ yds)
2.5 cm (1") bias tape for binding ruffle attachment seam:
Sizes 36+38: 1.05 m (1¼ yds)
Sizes 40+42: 1.15 m (1³⁄₈ yds)
Sizes 44+46: 1.25 m (1½ yds)

Before cutting out:

Views A & B
Trace off separate pattern pieces for the facings that are printed on upper edge of front and back pattern pieces. For View A trace off center and side facings, for View B center facings only. On the layouts these facings are marked with the same number as their main pattern piece.
View A
Tape pattern pieces for center and side front facings resp. center and side back facings together matching seam numbers. See layout as well.

Cutting out

47 Center front (cut once on fold) **A B**
47 Front facing (cut once on fold) **B**
48 Side front (cut twice) **A B**
47/48 Front facing (cut once on fold) **A**
49 Center back (cut twice) **A B**
49 Back facing (cut twice) **B**
50 Side back (cut twice) **A B**
49/50 Back facing (cut twice) **A**
51 Sleeve (cut twice) **B**
Upper hem tier (cut twice on fold) **A**
Lower hem tier (cut twice on fold) **A**

Extra pieces:

There are no pattern pieces for View A straps and View B skirt panels, tulle ruffle and bow "knot". These pieces are marked with tailor's chalk onto fabric and are designated on layout with the letters **a, b, c** and **d.**
View A
a) 2 straps, ea. 6 cm (2¼") wide, finished width 3 cm - 1¼"
Sizes 36+38 ea. 37 cm (14½") long
Sizes 40+42 ea. 40 cm (15¾") long
Sizes 44+46 ea. 43 cm (17") long
View B
b) 3 skirt panels, each 148 cm (58½") wide and for
Sizes 36+38 ea. 28 cm (11") long
Sizes 40+42 ea. 29 cm (11½") long
Sizes 44+46 ea. 30 cm (12") long
c) Strip on the grain for bow "knot", 7 cm (2¾") long and 5 cm (2") wide. Finished width 2.5 cm (1").
d) 3 panels for tulle ruffle, ea. 138 cm (54½") wide and for
Sizes 36+38 ea. 56 cm (22¼") long
Sizes 40+42 ea. 58 cm (23") long
Sizes 44+46 ea. 60 cm (23¾") long
From a lightcolored fabric remnant cut a strip on the grain for bow, 34 cm (13½") long and 14 cm (5½") wide. Finished width 7 cm (2¾").
Please note:
Views A & B
Iron interfacing onto the **wrong** side of front and back facings (see shaded pieces on cutting layout).
Commercial pleating
View A
Have hem tier panels commercially pleated in accordion or sunburst pleats. See our dealer/stockist list for the address of a pleating firm.

Construction:
View A
See Illustrated Teaching Instructions on page 38, ills. 1 - 12.
● Stitch center back seam up to placket mark, stitch front and back section seams and side seams.

● Fold straps in half lengthwise, **right** sides together. Stitch long edges of each together. Turn straps **right** side out, press (ill. 1). Pin straps onto **right** side of upper edge over front section seams so that an open end of each lies on upper edge allowance.
● Stitch front and back facings **right** sides together at side seams. Press open seam allowances. Pin and stitch facing to upper edge of dress, **right** sides together, catching in straps in front. Trim seam allowances, clip in close to seam at center front (ill. 3). Press seam allowances into facing. Edgestitch facing along its attachment seam, securing the allowances (ill. 4). Turn facing to the **inside,** press upper edge of dress.
● Press placket allowances to the **inside.** Baste zipper under placket edges, machine stitch into place (ill. 5). Hand sew zipper tapes and placket allowances onto facing (ill. 6).
● Stitch pleated sections for each hem tier **right** sides together at ends, forming a ring in each case. Seams should lie in the inner fold of a pleat (ill. 7). Trim seam allowances, overcast together.
● Trim hem allowance on both tiers back to ½ cm (¼") width, overcast, turn to the **inside,** machine stitch into place (ill. 8).
● Pin the **wrong** side of upper tier onto the **right** side of lower tier, baste upper edges together (ill. 9). Gather upper edge of tiers to match lower edge of bodice: run a row of machine basting 3 mm (¹⁄₈") on each side of marked seamline. Pull up the bobbin threads at both ends of this stitching until tiers match bodice. Evenly distribute gathering. Baste and stitch tiers to lower edge of bodice, **right** sides together (ill. 10). Overcast seam allowances together, press up into bodice (ill. 11).
● Pin straps under upper back edge at section seams, hand sew into place onto facing (ill. 12).

Cutting layouts for all sizes

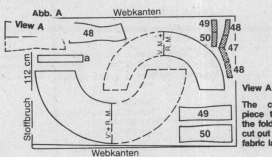

The center front bodice piece that extends beyond the fold on layout should be cut out LAST from a SINGLE fabric layer.

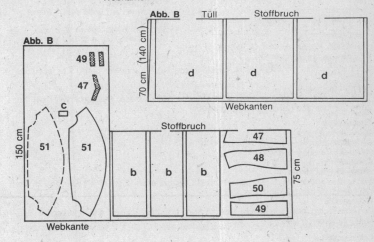

Allowances:
View B
Upper and lower sleeve edges 2 cm (⁷⁄₈"); skirt hem 1.5 cm (⁵⁄₈")
Views A & B
Center back, side and section seams 1.5 cm (⁵⁄₈"); all other seams and edges 1 cm (½").

Fadenlauf	straight grain
einreihen	gather
obere Saumkante	hem edge, upper tier
untere Saumkante	hem edge, lower tier
vord. u. rückw. Mitte	center front and back
Stoffbruch	fold
Radius	radius
Abb. A	View A
Gr. 36-46	sizes 36-46

153

View B

See Illustrated Teaching Instructions on page 41, ills. 1 - 6.

● Stitch center back seam up to placket mark.
● Stitch front and back facings to upper edge of center front and back bodice pieces, **right** sides together. Clip seam allowances in close to seam at center front.
● Stitch front and back section seams, continue and stitch center facings to allowance on upper edge of side pieces (ill. 1). Stitch side seams.
● Stitch underarm seams in sleeves, stitching between seamlines marked on upper and lower edges only. Press upper and lower allowances to the **inside,** turn under their raw edge, stitch into place along marked stitching line (ill. 2). Cut sections of elastic in the lengths stated below and insert into upper and lower sleeve edges:

For lower edges	For upper edges
Size 36 ea. 27 cm (10¾")	**Size 36** ea. 34 cm (13½")
Size 38 ea. 28 cm (11")	**Size 38** ea. 35 cm (13¾")
Size 40 ea. 29 cm (11½")	**Size 40** ea. 36 cm (14¼")
Size 42 ea. 30 cm (12")	**Size 42** ea. 37 cm (14½")
Size 44 ea. 31 cm (12¼")	**Size 44** ea. 38 cm (15")
Size 46 ea. 32 cm (12¾")	**Size 46** ea. 39 cm (15½")

● Stitch sleeves to armholes, matching seam numbers (ill. 3).
● Turn facings to the **inside,** baste and press upper bodice edges, continue and press

sleeve attachment seam allowances down into bodice. Edgestitch along upper edge of bodice and along sleeve attachment seams.
● Press placket allowances to the **inside.** Turn upper ends of zipper tapes to the **right** side of zipper. Then baste and stitch zipper under placket edges (ill. 4). Hand sew zipper tapes and placket allowance onto facing, making sure that stitches are not visible from the right side.
● Stitch panels for skirt and tulle ruffle **right** sides together at ends, forming a ring in each case. Hem lower edge of skirt: turn up hem allowance twice, press, topstitch ¾ cm (³/₈") into place. Fold tulle ruffle in half lengthwise, **wrong** sides together. Baste open (upper) edges together. Gather upper edge of skirt and tulle to match lower edge of bodice. Baste the **wrong** side of skirt onto the **right** side of tulle ruffle, basting upper edges together (ill. 5).
● After stitching skirt and ruffle to lower bodice edge, bind seam allowances with bias tape (ill. 6).
● **Bow:** fold fabric strips for bow and "knot" in half lengthwise, **right** sides together. Stitch open long edges together. Turn strips **right** side out and press so that the seam lies at one edge. Fold ends of bow strip toward the center of strip, overlap 1 cm (½") and hand sew together. Fold 3 tiny pleats into center of strip for "knot" and hand sew into place. Then wrap this strip around the center of bow, gathering as desired. Hand sew ends together on backside of bow. Hand sew bow onto skirt attachment seam at left front section seam.

Style
10

Jacket on page 38

Size 36/38 sheet A, green outline ● ● ● ● ● ● pieces 65 to 68
Size 40/42 sheet B, green outline 〰〰〰 pieces 65 to 68
Size 44/46 sheet C, green outline 〰〰〰 pieces 65 to 68

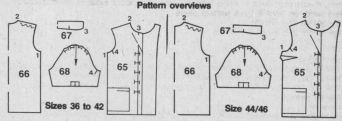

Pattern overviews

Sizes 36 to 42   **Size 44/46**

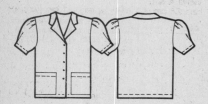

Total back length
Size 36/38: 78 cm (30¾")
Size 40/42: 80 cm (31½")
Size 44/46: 79 cm (31¼")

Fabric requirements:
Printed jacket:
112 cm (44¼") wide dobby weave polyester:
Sizes 36 to 42: 2.05 m (2³/₈ yds)
Size 44/46: 2.20 m (2½ yds)

Notions/Haberdashery:
5 buttons; fusible interfacing; stiff, fusible interfacing for shoulder puffs; 1 pr. shoulder pads.

Before cutting out:
Trace off pocket printed on front as a separate pattern piece. This piece will have the same number as the front on cutting layout.

Cutting out:
65 Front (cut twice)
65 Pocket (cut twice)
66 Back (cut once on fold)
67 Collar (cut twice on fold)
68 Sleeve (cut twice)
Stiff fusible interfacing: for shoulder puffs cut 2 strips, each 12 cm (4¾") wide and 25 cm (10") long. Finished width 6 cm (2³/₈").
Please note:
Iron interfacing onto the **wrong** side of front extended facings and undercollar. See shaded pieces on layout.

Construction:
See Illustrated Teaching Instructions on page 40, ills. 1 - 11.
● Iron interfacing onto the **wrong** side of front extended facings (ill. 1).
● Stitch collar layers **right** sides together along outer edges. Trim seam allowances at corners diagonally. Turn collar **right** side out, baste and press seamed edges. Holding rounded over fingers, take diagonal (tailor) basting along collar "roll" (ill. 2). Edgestitch along seamed edges.
● For size 44/46 stitch **bust darts.** Press their allowances downward.
● Stitch shoulder and side seams. Turn up hem allowance once 1 cm (½") and then 2 cm (⅞"), press, machine stitch into place.
● Pockets: press open long edge on pocket self-facing ¾ cm (³/₈") to the **inside.** Turn facing to the **right** side of pocket, stitch ends to side edges of pocket. Trim seam allowance at upper corners diagonally. Turn self-facing to the **inside,** press. Continue and press side and lower edge allowances to the **inside.** Stitch facing into place along — line. Pin pockets onto fronts where marked, edgestitch into place.
● Baste collar onto the **right** side of neck edge between marker lines 3. Marker lines on collar should match shoulder seams. Turn extended facings to the **outside,** baste into place at neck edge over collar (ill. 3). Stitch along neck edge, securing collar and facings. Turn facings to the **inside,** baste and press seamed (neck) and fold (closing) edges. Press side edge of each facing to the **inside,** stitch into place (ill. 4). Edgestitch along closing and neck edges. Hand sew facing ends onto shoulder seams and hem allowance.
● Sleeves: stitch underarm seams. Stitch x-lines of each pleat **right** sides together from lower edge up to pleat mark (ill. 6). Press pleats so that x-lines lie on o-line. Stitch sleeve hems (ill. 7). Fold pleats into sleeve caps, x-onto-o, and baste. Set in sleeves, basting and stitching from the sleeve side (ill. 8).
● Shoulder puffs: fold strips of stiff interfacing in half lengthwise, **coated** sides together, press. Fold pleats into strip. Sew puffs into place (ills. 9 and 10).
● Work buttonholes into right closing edge where marked. Sew buttons onto left closing edge along center front line.
● Sew shoulder pads into place (ill. 11).

Allowances:
Seams 1.5 cm (⅝"); hem and sleeve hems 3 cm (1¼"); self-facing on upper pocket edge 4 cm (1⅝"); all other edges 1 cm (½").

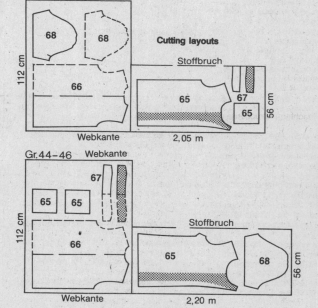

Cutting layouts

Never cut out without adding the necessary seam allowances

Not even when the pattern is one size too large. On a simple dress with two side seams and a centre back seam, there are six edges which require at least 1.5 to 2 cm / ½ to 1 inch seam allowance each. This means the dress will be 9 to 12 cm / 3½ to 4½ ins tighter if you cut out without adding the allowances. Any two sizes differ, however, only 4 cm / 1½ ins in bust width. Consult our dressmaking manual "Sewing made easy", order number K 620, for details on altering patterns.

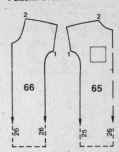

Size 36/38 sheet D, green outline ⟶○⟶○⟶○ pieces 65 and 66
Size 40/42 sheet E, green outline ○○○○○○ pieces 65 and 66
Size 44/46 sheet F, green outline ∿∿∿∿∿∿ pieces 65 and 66

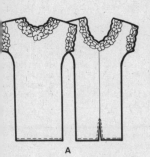
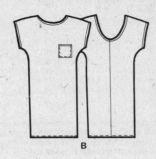

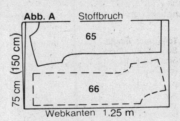

A

B

Views A & B
Length from waist to hem: 68 cm (26³/₄")

View A:
Motif outlines for cutwork embroidery are printed in green on sheet D.

Extend pattern pieces for front and back to full length by adding the amount printed at arrowheads. When tracing off pattern pieces make sure that you have enough tissue paper for the entire pieces, otherwise you'll have to tape pieces together. Connect the ends of extension lines to make hemline. Hemline should measure as follows:

Hem width on front & back pattern piece
Size 36/38: 24.5 cm (9³/₄")
Size 40/42: 26.5 cm (10¹/₂")
Size 44/46: 28.5 cm (11¹/₄")

Fabric requirements
View A: dress with cutwork embroidery
150 cm (59") wide cotton/linen blend:
All sizes: 1.25 m (1¹/₂ yds)
View B: pink dress
140 cm (55") wide cotton jersey:
Size 36/38: 1.40 m (1⁵/₈ yds)
Sizes 40 to 46: 1.50 m (1³/₄ yds)

Notions/Haberdashery
View A Fusible interfacing for reinforcing embroidery; raglan shoulder pads
View B 12 mm (¹/₂") braid:
Sizes 36 to 42: 2.10 m (2³/₈ yds)
Size 44/46: 2.20 m (2¹/₂ yds)
Before cutting out:
View B trace off pocket printed on pattern piece 65 as a separate pattern piece. This piece is also designated with the number 65 on layout.

Cutting out
65 Front (cut once on fold) A B
65 Pocket (cut once) B
66 Back (cut twice) A B

Construction
See Illustrated Teaching Instructions on page 44, ills. 1 - 10.
View A
● Stitch center back seam, leaving a 14 cm (5¹/₂") long slit open in lower end. Stitch shoulder seams. Overcast and press open all seam and slit allowances.
● Embroidery: it is very important that you reinforce the embroidered areas with fusible interfacing. Trace embroidery motifs onto the **uncoated** side of interfacing. Then arrange motifs onto the **wrong** side of neck edge, matching center front and center back. Shoulder marks in motif should match shoulder seams in dress. Make sure that the **coated** side of interfacing lies on **wrong** side of dress. For sizes 40/42 and 44/46 it will be necessary to extend the scallops on sleeve edges over to side seamlines. Iron interfacing into place with steam (ill. 1) so that you can later remove it.
● Mark embroidery motifs onto the **right** fabric side by machine stitching from the **wrong** side exactly in all motif lines (ill. 2) with a normal, straight stitch setting. From the **right** side machine embroider over these lines with the satin stitch setting (ill. 3). **It is important** that you test stitch first to get the right setting. Embroider the short lines in the motif first, then the leaves and blossoms, making sure that the end of one line is always covered by the next line that you embroider. Try to embroider as much at one time as possible, avoiding interruptions in the stitching, connecting as many lines as possible. At the end of some outlines, the blossoms, for example, leave needle in fabric, raise presser foot, turn fabric, lower presser foot and continue embroidering. Embroider scalloped edge last.
● Cutwork: remove fusible interfacing as in ill. 4. Trim allowances on neck and sleeve edges back to scalloping (ill. 5). The shaded areas in the motif (see pattern sheet) indicate where fabric is to be cut out. VERY CAREFULLY cut out fabric with sharply pointed scissors, getting into all corners but taking care NOT to damage embroidery (ill. 6).
● Stitch side seams, making sure that ends of sleeve embroidery match exactly. Trim seam allowances back to 1 cm (¹/₂") width, overcast, press open. Press hem and slit allowances to the **inside**. Turn under raw ends of slit allowances, baste into place. From the **right** side of dress topstitch 2 cm (⁷/₈") along hem edge, ³/₄ cm (³/₈") along slit edges with twin needles in both cases, securing the allowances (ill. 7).
● Try on dress. Pin raglan shoulder pads into place, adjusting their position to best suit your figure and the dress. Then hand sew pads to shoulder seam allowances.
View B
● Stitch center back seam. Pre-shape braid with a warm iron to fit neck edge. Stitch braid

onto the **wrong** side of neck allowance so that its shorter edge lies on neck seamline. Trim neck edge allowance back to ¹/₂ cm (¹/₄") width. Fold braid and allowance to the **right** side of dress, baste and stitch into place (braid covers allowance). See ills. 8 and 9.
● Stitch shoulder seams. Press open seam allowances, hand sew into place at neck edge.
● Stitch remainder of braid to upper edge of pocket and to sleeve edges in the same manner as for neck edges. Press side and lower edge allowances on pocket to the **inside**. Stitch pocket onto left half of front where marked (ill. 10).
● Stitch side seams. Press open seam. allowances, hand sew into place at lower sleeve edges. Press hem allowance to the **inside**, topstitch 2 cm (⁷/₈") into place from the **right** side of dress using twin needles.
● Try on dress. Pin raglan shoulder pads into place, adjusting their position to best suit your figure and the dress. Then hand sew pads to shoulder seam allowances.

Cutting layouts for all sizes

Abb. A Stoffbruch

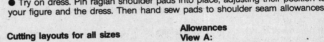

65

66

150 cm

75 cm

Webkanten 1,25 m

Abb. B Stoffbruch

65

66

65

70 cm (140 cm)

Webkanten

Allowances
View A:
1.5 cm (⁵/₈") on seams.
View B:
1 cm (¹/₂") on seams.
Views A & B:
hem 2.5 cm (1"), all other edges 1 cm (¹/₂").

Which interfacing for which fabric?

FABRIC WEIGHT	SUGGESTED FABRICS	RECOMMENDED VILENE INTERFACING	DESCRIPTION
Very light weight fabrics	Silks, viscose blends, polyesters, extra fine cottons, challis, georgette, sheer fabris	Optima silkysoft 327 – Fusible – White	Has no grainline Non stretch Luxury Soft Handle Washable & Dry Cleanable
Delicate Fabrics	Voile, chiffon, crepe de chine, georgette, lawn, silk, cotton, polycotton, polyester	Ultrasoft 308 – Fusible – White	Has no grainline, soft to touch, gentle yet stable control, washable, dry cleanable.
Soft, Delicate or Light weight	Voile, Chiffon, Crepe de chine, georgette, silk, lawn, knits, jersey, polyester	Light Sew-in 310 – White / 311 – Charcoal	Has grainline – Lengthwise stability, Crosswise stretch. No grainline 300 White, 310 Charcoal 310 White, 311 Charcoal Washable, dry cleanable
Light to medium	Challis, jersey, double knits, poplin, wool, wool blends, linen, corduroy, velvet	Ultrasoft – Medium 315 – Fusible – White or Medium Sew-in 312 – White	Has grainline – Lengthwise stability and crosswise. No grainline Washable and Dry. cleanable
Medium to Heavy	Gaberdine, tweeds, double knits, suit and coat weight, wools and woollen mixtures	Ultrasoft – Medium 315 – Fusible – White Ultrasoft – Heavy 316 – Fusible – White or Heavy Sew-in.	Has grainline – Lengthwise stability and crosswise. No grainline – Washable and Dry cleanable.
Light to Medium	Cotton and cotton blend fabrics	Medium Iron-on 304 – White	No grainline – light, crisp, handle, washable only
Medium to Heavy	Cotton and cotton blend fabrics	Firm Iron-on 305 – White	No grainline – Firm, crisp, handle, Washable only

Style
12

Dress & jacket from one pattern on pages 46/47

Size 36 sheet A, red outline ━━━━━━━ pieces 17 to 22
Size 38 sheet B, red outline ∿∿∿∿∿ pieces 17 to 22
Size 40 sheet C, red outline ─ ···· ─ ···· pieces 17 to 22
Size 42 sheet D, red outline ∧∧∧∧∧∧ pieces 17 to 22
Size 44 sheet E, red outline ── ·· ── ·· pieces 17 to 22
Size 46 sheet F, red outline ⟩━⟨━⟩━⟨ pieces 17 to 22

Pattern overview

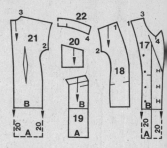

A
B

Length from waist to hem:
Sizes 36+38: 56 cm (22¼")
Sizes 40+42: 58 cm (23")
Sizes 44+46: 59 cm (23¼")

Back jacket length:
Size 36: 76.5 cm (30⅛")
Size 38: 77 cm (30⅜")
Size 40: 78.5 cm (31")
Size 42: 79 cm (31¼")
Size 44: 80.5 cm (31¾")
Size 46: 81 cm (32")

View A: extend pattern pieces 17 and 21 to full length by adding the amounts printed at arrowheads. When tracing off pattern pieces make sure you have enough tissue paper for the entire pattern piece. Otherwise you'll have to tape pattern sections together. Connect ends of extension lines with a straight line to make hemline. Hem width of pattern pieces should be as follows:
Center front (piece 17)
Sizes 36 to 46: 16 cm (6½")
Back (piece 21):
Size 36: 24.5 cm (9⅝")
Size 38: 25.5 cm (10")
Size 40: 26.5 cm (10½")
Size 42: 27.5 cm (10⅞")
Size 44: 28.5 cm (11¼")
Size 46: 29.5 cm (11⅝")
Views A & B
Pay careful attention to the lines and markings for the different views when tracing off pattern pieces. On pattern sheet these are always designated with the view letter.

Fabric requirements
View A, red dress
150 cm (59") wide crinkled viscose rayon/linen blend:
Sizes 36 to 40: 2.10 m (2⅜ yds)
Sizes 42 to 46: 2.30 m (2⅝ yds)
View B, jacket
150 cm (59") wide crinkled viscose rayon/linen blend:
Sizes 36 to 40: 1.80 m (2 yds)
Sizes 42 to 46: 1.90 m (2⅛ yds)

Notions/Haberdashery
View A: 8 buttons
View B: 6 buttons
Views A & B: lining remnant for pocket pouches; fusible interfacing; 1 flat button for inside; shoulder pads
Before cutting out
Center front (piece 17) will be cut out four (4) times, as left and right center front and corresponding facings (see layout).

Cutting out
Views A & B
17 Center front (cut 4 times)
18 Upper side front (cut twice)
19 Lower side front (cut twice)
20 Pocket pouch (cut twice from lining)
21 Back (cut twice)
22 Collar (cut twice on fold)
Please note:
Views A & B
Iron interfacing onto the **wrong** side of front facings (cut from piece 17), onto extended facing on lower side front, onto one collar layer (undercollar). See shaded pieces and areas on layout.

Construction
See Illustrated Teaching Instructions on page 48, ills. 1 - 11.
Views A & B
● Stitch lining pouch pieces to extended facing on pocket opening edge of lower side front pieces, **right** sides together. Press seam allowances into lining. Fold facings to the **inside**, baste and press fold edge (ill. 1). From the **right** side edgestitch and topstitch along pocket opening edges as marked. Stitch lower edge of lining pouch pieces to lower edge of upper side fronts, **right** sides together. Baste lower side fronts onto upper side fronts at side edges, matching marked seamlines (ill. 2).
● Stitch side fronts to center fronts at section seams, catching in pocket pouches (ill. 3).

● Stitch center back seam, darts and shoulder seams. Press sleeve hem allowances to the **inside**, turn under edge, machine stitch into place. Stitch side seams (ill. 4).
● Press hem allowance to the **inside**, blindstitch into place.
● Stitch collar layers **right** sides together. Turn collar **right** side out (ill. 5). Holding undercollar rounded over fingers, secure upper collar with diagonal (tailor's) basting taken along collar "roll." Then edgestitch along seamed edges of collar.
● Stitch interfaced center front facings to lapel and closing edges, **right** sides together, stitching to marker line on lapels. Clip allowances in close to last stitch at each marker line. Turn facings to the **inside**, baste and press seamed edges (ill. 6). Tip: press open seam allowances on facing attachment seams from lower edge up to lapel points, or as close to them as you can get. Then see how much easier it is to baste closing and lapel edges!
● Press allowance on lower ends of facings to the **inside** (ill. 7).
● Baste collar (both layers) onto the **right** side of neck edge (ill. 8). Turn facings to the **outside** and baste to neck edge over collar. Stitch along neck edge from corner to corner, securing collar and facings. Turn facings to the **inside**. Holding each front rounded over fingers, secure facings with diagonal (tailor's) basting taken along lapel foldlines (ill. 9).
● Edgestitch along closing, lapel and neck edges, securing collar attachment seam allowances across back neck. Baste facings onto shoulder and section seam allowances. From the **right** side edgestitch center fronts along section seams, securing facings. Stitch in shoulder seam grooves over to collar attachment seam, securing facing ends (ill. 10). Hand sew lower facing ends onto hem allowance.
● Hand sew lapel points to collar as in ill. 11.
● Work buttonholes into right closing edge as marked. Work a buttonhole into left closing edge at uppermost marking. Sew buttons onto both fronts where marked. Sew flat button onto the **inside** of right front underneath third button from the bottom to secure underlap.
● Try on dress resp. jacket. Pin shoulder pads into place, adjusting their position to best suit your figure and the garment. Then hand sew to shoulder seam allowances and facings.

Allowances
Views A & B
Seams 1.5 cm (⅝"); hem 4 cm (1⅝"); sleeve edges 2.5 cm (1"); all other edges 1 cm (½").

Cutting layouts

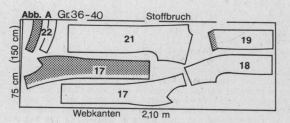

Abb. A Gr. 36-40 — Stoffbruch — Webkanten — 2,10 m

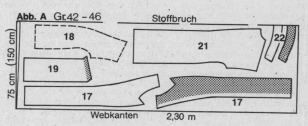

Abb. A Gr. 42-46 — Stoffbruch — Webkanten — 2,30 m

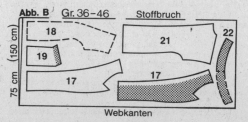

Abb. B Gr. 36-46 — Stoffbruch — Webkanten

Style 13

4 skirts on pages 47, 66 and 67

Sizes 36+38 sheet F, green outline ○○○○○○○ pieces 67 and 68
Sizes 40+42 sheet E, green outline ─ .... ─ .... pieces 67 and 68
Sizes 44+46 sheet D, green outline ∧∧∧∧∧∧∧ pieces 67 and 68

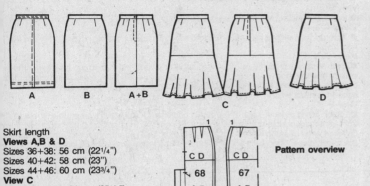

Skirt length
Views A, B & D
Sizes 36+38: 56 cm (22¼")
Sizes 40+42: 58 cm (23")
Sizes 44+46: 60 cm (23¾")
View C
Sizes 36 to 46: 64 cm (25¼")

Pattern overview

The pattern pieces for front and back skirt panels contain 2 sizes. Therefore, pay careful attention to the differing side seamlines when tracing off pattern pieces. Also note the lines and markings for the different views. These are designated on pattern sheet with view letters.

Scale drawing for full-circle tier(s), View D

The scale drawing for the full-circle tier, View C, can be found on page 69.

Make pattern piece for full circle tier as follows

Note the radius for your size. Beginning at the upper righthand corner of a square piece of tissue paper or plastic sheet mark the radius at upper and side edges and at 4 points between. Connect these points with a curved line. This line will be the upper edge of tier. From this line mark the length of tier for your size at upper and side edges and at 4 points between. Connect these lines to make the hemline of tier.

├ Size 46: 32 cm (12¾")─┼─18 cm──┤ 18 cm (7")
├ Size 44: 32 cm (12¾")─┼─17,4 cm──┤ 17.4 cm (6⅞")
├ Size 42: 30 cm (12")─┼─16,8 cm──┤ 16.8 cm (6⅝")
├ Size 40: 30 cm (12")─┼─16,1 cm──┤ 16.1 cm (6⅜")
├ Size 38: 28 cm (11")─┼─15,5 cm──┤ 15.5 cm (6")
├ Size 36: 28 cm (11")─┼─14,9 cm──┤ 14.9 cm (5¾")

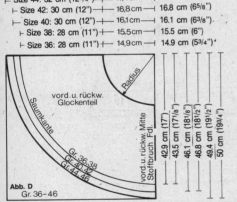

Allowances
View A: 3 cm (1¼") hem allowance.
View B: 4 cm (1⅝") hem allowance.
Views C & D: 1.5 cm (⅝") hem allowance.
All views: seams 1.5 cm (⅝"); all other edges 1 cm (½").

Cutting layouts

Fabric requirements
View A Jeans skirt
150 cm (59") wide denim:
All sizes: 0.75 m (⅞ yd)
View B Brown straight skirt
150 cm (59") wide, crinkled viscose rayon:
All sizes: 0.75 m (⅞ yd)
140 cm (55") wide lining fabric:
All sizes: 0.65 m (⅞ yd)
View C Beige skirt with full circle tier
145 cm (57") wide viscose rayon/linen blend:
Sizes 36+38: 1.40 m (1⅝ yds)
Sizes 40+42: 1.45 m (1¾ yds)
Sizes 44+46: 1.55 m (1¾ yds)

View D Black skirt with full circle tier
150 cm (59") wide challis:
Sizes 36+38: 1.10 m (1¼ yds)
Sizes 40+42: 1.20 m (1⅜ yds)
Sizes 44+46: 1.30 m (1½ yds)

Notions/Haberdashery
All views
Fusible waistband interfacing; 20 cm (8") zipper; 1 button.
Before cutting out
Views A & B Note facing and underlap+facing on right and left vent edges on back skirt panels.

Cutting out
67 Front skirt panel (cut twice) **A**
67 Front skirt panel (cut once on fold) **B C D**
68 Back skirt panel (cut twice) **A B C D**
Full circle panel (cut twice on fold) **C D**
View B
Lining: cut front and back panels once on the fold.
Extra piece
There is no pattern piece for waistband. This piece is drawn with tailor's chalk directly onto the fabric in the dimensions stated below and is designated with the small letter **a** on the cutting layout.
All views
a) Waistband, 6 cm (2¼") wide, finished width 3 cm (1¼"), and for
Size 36: 71 cm (28") long   **Size 42:** 83 cm (32¾") long
Size 38: 75 cm (29¾") long   **Size 44:** 87 cm (34¼") long
Size 40: 79 cm (31¼") long   **Size 46:** 91 cm (36") long
These lengths include 3 cm (1¼") for underlap.
Please note:
All views
Iron interfacing onto the **wrong** side of waistband (see the shaded piece on cutting layout).

vord. u. rückw. Glockenteil: front & back tier

Radius: radius

vord. u. rückw. Mitte: center front & back

Stoffbruch: fold

Fdl.: straight grain

Abb.: View D

Gr. 36-46: Sizes 36 to 46

Saumkante: hem edge

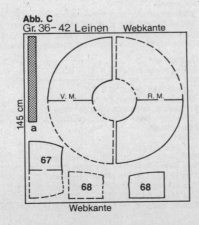

Abb. C
Gr. 36-42 Leinen

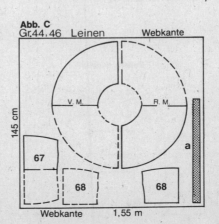

Abb. C
Gr. 44,46 Leinen

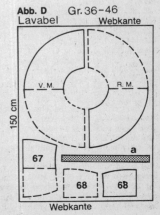

Abb. D Gr. 36-46
Lavabel

Construction
See Illustrated Teaching Instructions on page 69, ills. 1 - 8.
View A
● Stitch center front seam. Press allowances into right panel, edgestitch and topstitch ¾ cm (³/₈") into place.
Views A & B
● Stitch darts, press their allowances toward center front resp. center back (ill. 1). Stitch center back seam between placket and vent marks, backstitching seam ends. Press seam allowances into left panel. For View A edgestitch left panel along center seam from zipper placket down to vent. Stitch side seams for both views.
Views C & D
● Stitch darts, side seams and center back seam in skirt, side seams in tier as well. Press dart allowances toward center front resp. center back, press open side seam allowances. Press center back seam allowances into left panel. Stitch tier to lower skirt edge, **right** sides together, matching side seams (ill. 8). Press seam allowances up into skirt, edgestitch into place.
All views
● Insert zipper: press allowance on right placket edge to the **inside**. Baste and edgestitch right half of zipper under right placket edge so that edge lies very close to zipper teeth (ill. 2). Pin placket closed, center-on-center. Baste and stitch zipper under left placket edge, stitching 1.5 cm (⁵/₈") from edge (ill. 3).
View B
● Lining: stitch darts and seams. Pin lining into skirt, **wrong** sides together, matching darts and side seams. Slash along center back of lining exactly over zipper teeth or coil, clip diagonally ½ cm (¼") to the right and the left of center at lower end of placket. Turn under lining, hand sew onto zipper tapes.

All views
● Baste and stitch interfaced waistband to upper edge of skirt, **right** sides together. Fold waistband in half lengthwise, **right** sides together. Stitch both ends and lower edge of underlap. Trim seam allowances, trim corners diagonally (ill. 4). Turn waistband **right** out, fold along foldline, turn under open edge of inner layer and baste into place over attachment seam (ill. 5). For View A topstitch ¾ cm (³/₈") as well.
● Work buttonhole into left end of waistband 1 cm (½") from end. Sew button onto underlap.
View A
● Press hem allowance to the **inside**, topstitch 2 cm (⁷/₈") and 2.7 cm (1¹/₈") into place.
View B
● Press hem allowance to the **inside**, blindstitch into place.
Views C & D
● Turn up hem allowance twice (finished width 1 cm - ½"), press, topstitch ¾ cm (³/₈") into place.
Views A & B
● Back vent: press facing on right vent edge and vent underlap to the **inside**, hand sew onto hem allowance (ill. 6). From the **right** side topstitch left back panel along slanted line at upper end of vent, securing underlap and facing (ill. 7). For View A edgestitch along left edge of vent as well.
View B
● Attach lining at vent: slash lining along center back from lower edge up to 2 cm (⁷/₈") from vent mark. At this point cut diagonally 2.5 cm (1") to upper right and upper left. Turn up lower edge of lining twice so that lining is 2 cm (⁷/₈") shorter than skirt, press, machine stitch into place. Then turn under lining and hand sew onto vent facings.

Style 14

3 dresses from one pattern on pages 50 and 51

Size 36/38 sheet D, green outline ●—●—●—● pieces 69 to 72
Size 40/42 sheet E, green outline ·············· pieces 69 to 72
Size 44/46 sheet F, green outline — — — — pieces 69 to 72

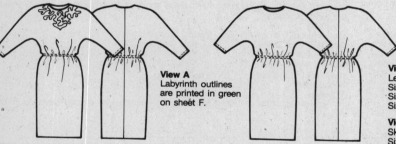

View A
Labyrinth outlines are printed in green on sheet F.

Views A & B
Length from waist casing to hem:
Size 36/38: 60 cm (23¾")
Size 40/42: 62 cm (24½")
Size 44/46: 64 cm (25¼")
View C
Skirt length:
Size 36/38: 60 cm (23¾")
Size 40/42: 62 cm (24½")
Size 44/46: 64 cm (25¼")

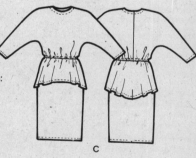

All views
Pay careful attention to the lines and markings for the different views when tracing off pattern pieces. View B sleeve length is shorter due to the fabric width.
Views A & B
Extend pattern pieces for front and back to full length by adding the amount printed at arrowheads. Make sure that you have enough tissue paper so that you can trace off pattern pieces in full size, thus avoiding taping together sections later on. Connect ends of extension lines to make hemline. Hem widths are as follows (please make sure these are right!):
Hem width for front and back pattern piece:
Size 36/38: each 24 cm (9½")
Size 40/42: each 26 cm (10¼")
Size 44/46: each 28 cm (11)

Fabric requirements
All three views should be made up in a stretchable knit fabric only.
View A Red dress
140 cm (55") wide jersey:
Size 36/38: 1.65 m (1⁷/₈ yds)
Size 40/42: 1.70 m (1⁷/₈ yds)
Size 44/46: 1.75 m (2 yds)
View B Black dress
130 cm (51") wide angora jersey:
Size 36/38: 1.70 m (1⁷/₈ yds)
Size 40/42: 1.75 m (2 yds)
Size 44/46: 1.80 m (2 yds)
View C Skirt & peplumed top
140 cm (55") wide dotted jersey for top:
Size 36/38: 1.60 m (1¾ yds)
Size 40/42: 1.65 m (1⁷/₈ yds)
Size 44/46: 1.70 m (1⁷/₈ yds)
140 cm (55") wide unicolored jersey for skirt:
Size 36/38: 0.70 m (⁷/₈ yd)
Sizes 40 to 46: 0.75 m (⁷/₈ yd)
140 cm (55") wide jersey lining for skirt:
Size 36/38: 0.65 m (⁷/₈ yd)
Sizes 40 to 46: 0.70 m (⁷/₈ yd)

Pattern overview

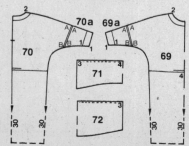

Notions/Haberdashery
All views: Fusible interfacing; 20 cm (8") zipper; 1 cm (½") elastic to fit waist; raglan shoulder pads.
View A: ¾ cm (³/₈") wide, supple tubular braid- 4.50 m (5 yds); approx. 90 small black beads for motif.
Views A & B: 3 cm (1¼") bias tape for waist casing:
Size 36/38: 1.15 m (1³/₈ yds)
Size 40/42: 1.20 m (1³/₈ yds)
Size 44/46: 1.25 m (1½ yds)
View B: 1 purchased lace collar.
View C: 3 cm (1¼") elastic for skirt to fit waist.
Before cutting out
Trace off neck facings marked on front and back pattern pieces as separate pattern pieces. These pieces are designated with the same number as the main pattern piece on the layout.
Tape sections for front pattern piece (pieces 69 and 69a) as well as for back pattern piece (pieces 70 and 70a) together at the attachment lines, matching letters A as well as B. Pay careful attention to the "Maschenlauf" (knit direction) arrows or lines on pattern pieces when pinning them onto jersey. These should run parallel to the selvage.

Cutting out
69 Front (cut once on fold) **A B C**
69 Front neck facing (cut once on fold) **A B C**
70 Back (cut twice) **A B C**
70 Back neck facing (cut twice) **A B C**
71 Peplum, front (cut once on fold) **C**
72 Peplum, back (cut once on fold) **C**
Extra pieces
View C
a) 2 skirt panels, for
Size 36 each 46 cm (18¼") wide and 67 cm (26½") long
Size 38 each 48 cm (19") wide and 67 cm (26½") long
Size 40 each 50 cm (19¾") wide and 69 cm (27¼") long
Size 42 each 52 cm (20¼") wide and 69 cm (27¼") long
Size 44 each 54 cm (21¼") wide and 71 cm (28") long
Size 46 each 56 cm (22¼") wide and 71 cm (28") long

…ese lengths include 4 cm (1¼") for extended waist facing, later elastic casing. There are …side seams, enabling you to taper the skirt at the hem if desired.
…ning: cut out lining panels 7 cm (2¾") shorter than fabric skirt panels but in the same …idth.

…ease note
…n interfacing onto the **wrong** side of front and back neck facings before stitching …cings together. See shaded pieces on cutting layouts.

…onstruction
…e Illustrated Teaching Instructions on page 49, ills. 1 - 10.

…l views
…Stitch center back seam from lower edge up to placket mark, leaving placket opening. …ress open seam allowances, press placket allowances to the **inside**. Baste zipper under …acket edges so that its teeth are covered (centered application). Work from the **right** side …nd use a zipper presser foot. Beginning at upper end of left placket edge, topstitch zipper …e cm (¼") into place.
…Stitch shoulder/upper sleeve seams. Stitch neck facings together at shoulder seams. …ress open seam allowances. Stitch facing to neck edge, **right** sides together (ill. 1). Trim …nd clip seam allowances, press into facing, edgestitch into place from the right side (ill. …. This step is sometimes called "understitching." Fold facing to the **inside,** hand sew …nto shoulder seam allowances, hand sew ends onto zipper tapes (ill. 3).

…ew A
…For easier handling, sew on braid BEFORE closing side seams. Trace labyrinth lines …ot bead position) onto tissue paper with burda's iron-on transfer pencil. Mark the center …ont line with pencil onto tracing paper as well. Pin tissue paper, labyrinth lines down, …nto the **right** side of front, matching center front lines. Press the wrong side of the …aper, transferring the lines onto front (ill. 4). Hand sew braid into place (ills. 5 and 6).

…ews A & B
…Stitch side seams and underarm seams in sleeves. Stitch bias tape onto the **wrong** side … dress over lines marked at waist level to make casing for elastic (ill. 7). Insert elastic into …asing, sew ends together.
…Fold sleeve hem allowances to the **inside,** baste into place. From the **right** side of dress …pstitch 2 cm (⅞") along lower sleeve edges with twin ballpoint needles, securing …lowances. Press hem allowance to the **inside,** blindstitch into place.

● Try on dress. Pin raglan shoulder pads into place, adjusting their position to best suit your figure and the dress. Then hand sew pads to shoulder/upper sleeve seam allowances.

View B
● Hand sew purchased lace collar to neck edge of black dress to lend it a new look.

View C
● Top: stitch shoulder/upper sleeve seams, side seams and underarm seams in sleeves. Stitch center back seam, leaving zipper placket open. Press open seam allowances, press placket allowances to the **inside**. Baste zipper under placket edges so that its teeth are covered (centered application). Work from the **right** side and use a zipper presser foot. Beginning at upper end of left placket edge, topstitch zipper ½ cm (¼") into place.
● Stitch neck facings together at shoulder seams. Stitch facing to neck edge (ill. 1). Trim seam allowances, press into facing, edgestitch into place (ill. 2). This step is sometimes called "understitching." Fold facing to the **inside,** hand sew onto shoulder seam allowances, sew ends onto zipper tapes (ill. 3). From the **right** side of garment topstitch 2 cm (⅞") along neck edge with twin ballpoint needles, securing facing. **Tip:** you can assure exact topstitching if you thread trace the topstitching line beforehand or use the guidelines on the throat plate of your machine.
● Stitch peplum side seams. Gather upper edge of peplum: run a row of machine basting 3 mm (⅛") on each side of the marked seamline. Pull up the bobbin threads at both ends of this stitching until peplum matches lower edge of top. Knot gathering threads, evenly distribute gathering. Stitch peplum to top, **right** sides together, matching side seams, center front and center back (ill. 8).
● Press seam allowances into top, topstitch into place to make casing for elastic. Insert elastic into casing (ill. 9). Sew elastic ends together.
● Stitch hem in peplum (ill. 10). Fold sleeve hem allowances to the **inside,** baste into place. From the **right** side of garment topstitch 2 cm (⅞") along lower sleeve edges with twin ballpoint needles, securing allowances.
● Try on top. Pin raglan shoulder pads into place, adjusting their position to best suit your figure and the garment. Then hand sew pads to shoulder/upper sleeve seam allowances.
● Skirt: stitch side seams, leaving 4 cm (1⅝") open at upper end of one seam for inserting waist elastic.
● Stitch side seams in skirt lining. Stitch lining to extended waist facing on skirt with 1 cm (½") seam allowance, **right** sides together, matching side seams. Fold waist casing and lining to the **inside.** Baste and topstitch facing 3.2 cm (1½") into place, making casing for elastic. Insert elastic into casing through open side seam, sew ends together.
● Press hem allowance to the **inside.** From the **right** side of skirt topstitch 2.5 cm (1") along hem edge with twin ballpoint needles, securing allowance. Turn up lower lining edge twice so that lining is 2 cm (⅞") shorter than skirt, press, machine stitch into place.

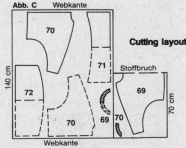

Abb. A,B Webkante

70

70

70

69

69

69

70

Webkante

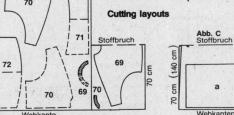

Abb. C Webkante

70

71

72

140 cm

69

70

69 70

Webkante

Cutting layouts Stoffbruch

70 cm

Abb. C Stoffbruch

a

70 cm (140 cm)

Webkanten

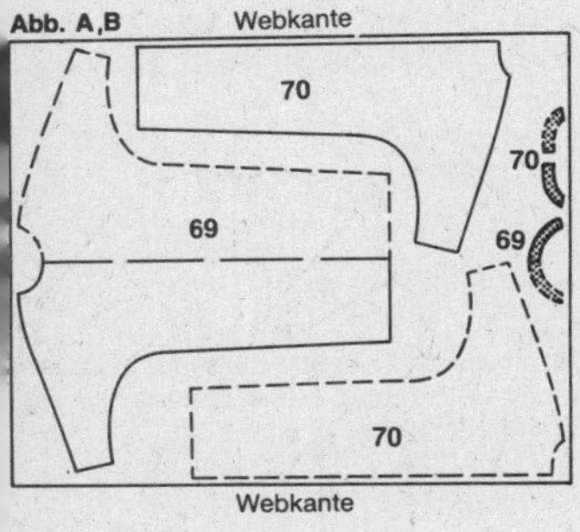

Allowances
Views A & B: hem 4 cm (1⅝").
View C: upper edge of peplum, lower edge of top 2 cm (⅞"); lower peplum edge 2.5 cm (1"); upper edge of skirt without allowance; skirt hem 3 cm (1¼").
All views: seams 1.5 cm 8⅝"); sleeve hems 2.5 cm (1"); all other edges 1 cm (½").

Making bias strips

…ias strips are available by the yard in a …ide range of colours. But you can also …ake them at home from fabric remnants. …he raw edges of your fabric remnant …hould be exactly on the crosswise grain. …his will make cutting out and joining the …trips easier. Fold fabric edge over in such … way that warp and weft threads meet. …he fabric fold is then guaranteed to be on …he bias. Draw lines marking the width of …our bias strips onto the fabric parallel to …he fabric fold. Pin fabric layers …etween the lines. Cut fabric fold open. …ut out bias strip along the lines. If your …abric is extremely lightweight, or the …abric layers tend to shift, cut out bias …trips from a single layer of fabric.

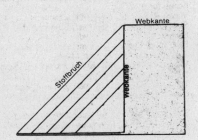

Webkante

Stoffbruch Webkante

Joining bias strips
Match ends with right sides together and stitch together.

Secure the ends of the stitching with a few backstitches.

---

1 2 3 4 5 6 7
Inches

1 2 3 4 5 6 7 8 9 10 11 12 13 14 15 16 17 18
centimeters

Style 15

A dress, 2 shirts and 2 skirts from one pattern on pages 52 and 53

Size 36/38 sheet D, green outline ∿∿∿ pieces 47 to 51
Size 40/42 sheet E, green outline ∧∧∧ pieces 47 to 51
Size 44/46 sheet F, green outline —....—.... pieces 47 to 51

Pattern overviews

Size 36/38

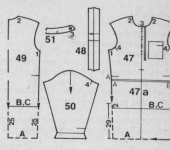

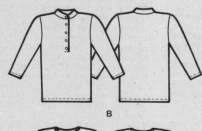

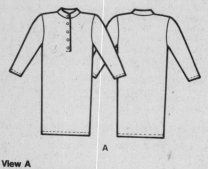

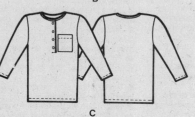

Size 40 to 46

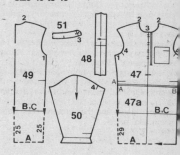

View A
Length from waist to hem:
Size 36/38: 60 cm (23¾")
Size 40/42: 62 cm (24½")
Size 44/46: 64 cm (25¼")
Views B & C
Back length of shirt:
Size 36/38: 75.5 cm (29¾")
Size 40/42: 77.5 cm (30½")
Size 44/46: 79.5 cm (31¼")
Skirt length from waist casing: approx. 78 cm (30¾")

Pay careful attention to the lines and markings for the different views when tracing off pattern pieces. These are designated with the view letter.
Extend pattern pieces for front and back by the amount printed at arrowhead. Make sure you have enough tissue paper for the entire pattern piece. Otherwise you'll have to tape sections together. Connect ends of extension lines on back to make hemline. Connect end of extension line on front to existing hemline. Hemline width should measure as follows (make sure this is right!):
Back hemline:
Size 36/38: 24.5 cm (9¾")
Size 40/42: 26.5 cm (10½")
Size 44/46: 28.5 cm (11¼")

Fabric requirements
View A Violet dress
150 cm (59") wide violet wool jersey:
All sizes: 1.80 m (2 yds)
150 cm (59") wide green wool jersey:
All sizes: 0.15 m (¼ yd)
View B Printed skirt and shirt 160 cm (63") wide viscose rayon jersey:
Size 36/38: 2.90 m (3¼ yds)
Sizes 40 to 46: 3.00 m (3⅜ yds)
View C Striped skirt and shirt
140 cm (55") wide, color coordinated jerseys:
Horizontally striped jersey:
All sizes: 1.50 m (1¾ yds)
Unicolored jersey
Size 36: 2.00 m (2¼ yds)
Sizes 38 to 46: 2.10 m (2⅜ yds)

Notions/Haberdashery
All views: fusible interfacing; seam tape or bias tape for shoulder seams; raglan shoulder pads.
Views A & B: 5 buttons
Views B & C: 2 cm (⅞") elastic to fit waist
View C: 4 buttons

Before cutting out
All views
Tape pattern pieces 47 and 47a together at the attachment edges, matching letters A as well as B.
Our layouts show that some pieces are cut from a single fabric layer. In this case pin the pattern pieces onto the **right** fabric side. Those pieces on layout with a solid outline are pinned PRINTED SIDE UP, those with a broken outline PRINTED SIDE DOWN onto fabric. It is important that lines for polo closing lie on left half of front. Pattern piece 49 (back) is only one half of the back. Therefore it will be necessary to turn it over when cutting out to get the back in one piece.
Pay careful attention to knit direction lines and arrows when pinning pattern pieces onto jersey.
View C
Trace off pocket printed on piece 47 as an extra pattern piece. This piece will have the same number as the front on layout.
When pinning pattern pieces onto fabric, make sure that the stripe marks on front and back pattern pieces lie on the same stripe in fabric. To cut out sleeves and pocket, fold remaining fabric in half lengthwise, **right** sides together, matching stripes exactly. Then pin pocket and sleeve pattern pieces into place and cut out. Make sure that stripes on pocket match those at pocket attachment lines on front.

Cutting out
47 Front (cut once) A B C
47 Pocket (cut once) C
Front facing (cut once) A B C
49 Back (cut once on fold) A B C
50 Sleeve (cut twice) A B C
51 Standing collar (cut twice on fold) A B
Extra pieces
There are no pattern pieces for skirt panels, hip yokes and binding strips for neck edge. These are to be drawn with tailor's chalk directly onto fabric in the dimensions stated below and are designated on layouts with the small letters **a, b, c** and **d.**
Views B & C
a) 2 hip yokes, each 19 cm (7½") long and for
Size 36: ea. 48 cm (19") wide
Size 38: ea. 50 cm (19¾") wide
Size 40: ea. 52 cm (20½") wide
Size 42: ea. 54 cm (21¼") wide
Size 44: ea. 56 cm (22¼") wide
Size 46: ea. 58 cm (23") wide
These amounts include 3 cm (1¼") for waist casing
View B
b) 2 skirt panels, each 64 cm (25¼") long and for
Size 36: ea. 132 cm (52") wide
Size 38: one 132 cm (52") wide and one 143 cm (56½") wide
Size 40: ea. 143 cm (56½") wide
Size 42: one 143 cm (56½") wide and one 154 cm (61") wide
Size 44: ea. 154 cm (61") wide
Size 46: one 147 cm (58") wide and one 158 cm (62½") wide
View C
c) 2 skirt panels, each 64 cm (25¼") long and for
Size 36: ea. 132 cm (52") wide
3 skirt panels, each 64 cm (25¼") long and for
Size 38: two 132 cm (52") wide and one 11 cm (4½") wide
Size 40: two 132 cm (52") wide and one 22 cm (9") wide
Size 42: two 132 cm (52") wide and one 33 cm (13") wide
Size 44: two 132 cm (52") wide and one 44 cm (17¼") wide
Size 46: two 132 cm (52") wide and one 55 cm (21¾") wide
d) 4 cm (1⅝") wide fabric strips for binding neck edge:
Size 36/38: 53 cm (21") long
Size 40/42: 55 cm (21¾") long
Size 44/46: 56 cm (22¼") long
Please note:
Iron interfacing onto the **wrong** side of fabric (see shaded pieces and areas on layouts)
All views
Onto one half of front facing, onto lower end of front closing lines.
Views A & B
Onto one collar layer (this will become the outer layer).

Tips for handling jersey are located on pages 120/121.

Construction
See Illustrated Teaching Instructions on page 54, ills. 1 - 10.
All views
● **Dress/Shirt:** iron interfacing onto the **wrong** side of front over lower end of closing lines. Slash front along slit line. Stitch facing to slit edges (ill. 1).
● Fold facing along its foldlines to the **inside,** turn under its inner edge, pin into place (ill. 2). Edgestitch facing along its attachment seam. Fold facing on right closing edge to the

inside. Topstitch lower end of closing as explained in ill. 3, for View C making sure you stitch exactly in stripe direction.

View C
● Pocket: fold self-facing on upper pocket edge to the **outside**, stitch ends to pocket. Turn facing back to **inside**, baste and press, continue and press side and lower edge allowances to the **inside**. From the **right** side topstitch along upper pocket edge with twin ballpoint needles as marked, securing facing. Baste pocket onto front where marked, matching stripes. Edgestitch pocket into place. Tip: to prevent pocket (and stripes) from slipping out of line while stitching, insert pins perpendicular to pocket edges and stitch across them.

All views
● Stitch shoulder and side seams, catching in seam tape or stretched out bias tape on front at shoulder seams.

Views A & B
● Construct collar. Baste facing on right closing edge into place at neck edge. Attach collar (ills. 4 and 5). Turn under open edge of inner collar layer, baste into place over attachment seam (ill. 6), hand sew into place along attachment seam for View A. Then edgestitch collar ends and upper edge. For View B edgestitch along all collar edges, securing its inner layer.

View C
● Fold facing on right closing edge to the **inside**, baste into place at neck edge. Bind neck edge: baste foldover braid onto the **right** side of neck edge so that one edge lies on neck seamline. Stitch braid into place with ³/₄ cm (³/₈") seam allowance. Trim neck allowance back to marked seamline, i.e. braid edge. Press braid upward. Turn in ends of braid, then fold braid over neck edge to the **inside**. Turn under edge of braid and baste into place so that it extends 2 mm (1/16") beyond attachment seam. From the **right** side of shirt stitch in braid attachment seam groove, securing inner layer.

All views
● Stitch underarm seams in sleeves. Press garment and sleeve hem allowances to the **inside.** From the **right** side topstitch 2.5 cm (1") along hem and sleeve hem edges with twin ballpoint needles, securing hem allowances. Set in sleeves, making sure that seam numbers match and stitching from the sleeve side.
● Work buttonholes into right closing edge and right collar end (Views A and B) as marked. Sew buttons onto facing of left closing edge so that they lie at upper end of buttonhole. For Views A and B sew a button onto the center front line of left collar end.
● Try on dress resp. shirt. Pin shoulder pads into place, adjusting their position to best suit your figure and the garment. Then hand sew pads to sleeve attachment and shoulder seam allowances.

Views B & C
● Skirt: stitch side seams in hip yoke (ill. 7).
● Stitch skirt panels **right** sides together at section seams, forming a ring. Fold pleats into upper edge of skirt (ill. 8). Outer pleat folds should be 4 cm (1⁵/₈") wide, inner folds 7 cm

(2³/₄") wide EXCEPT for **View B, size 46.** In this case inner pleat folds should be 6.5 cm (2¹/₂").
Number of pleats:

Size 36: 24 pleats;	Size 38: 25 pleats
Size 40: 26 pleats;	Size 42: 27 pleats
Size 44: 28 pleats;	Size 46: 29 pleats

● Pin and baste pleats into place. Baste and stitch hip yoke to upper skirt edge, **right** sides together, so that side seams in hip yoke each match a pleat fold. Press seam allowances up into yoke, baste into place (ill. 9). From the **right** side of skirt topstitch yoke 2.5 cm (1") along its attachment seam with twin ballpoint needles, securing the allowances.
● Press allowance on upper hip yoke edge to the **inside**, turn under its raw edge and stitch in place, ill. 10. Insert elastic, overlap ends and hand-sew together.
● Turn in hem, press and baste in place. From the **right** side of the skirt, topstitch hem 2.5 cm (1") along edge with twin ballpoint needles, thus securing it.

Allowances
All views: seams of dress resp. shirt 1.5 cm (1⁵/₈"); hem and sleeve hems 3 cm (1¹/₄"); all other edges 1 cm (¹/₂").
Views B & C: upper edge of skirt panels, lower edge of hip yoke and hem 3 cm (1¹/₄").
View C: 4 cm (1⁵/₈") on upper pocket edge as self-facing, 1 cm (¹/₂") on all other pocket edges.

Cutting layouts

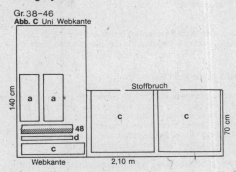

Gr. 38-46
Abb. C Uni Webkante

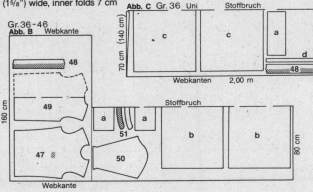

Abb. C Gr. 36 Uni

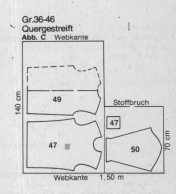

Gr.36-46
Quergestreift
Abb. C Webkante

Gr. 36-46
Abb. A Lila Webkante

Grün
Gr. 36-46
Abb. A Webkante

Gr. 36-46
Abb. B Webkante

Style
16

2 blouses from one pattern, page 56

Size 36/38 sheet C, green outline ——— — pieces 52 to 59
Size 40/42 sheet B, green outline ············· pieces 52 to 59
Size 44/46 sheet A, green outline ～～～ pieces 52 to 59

Pattern overview

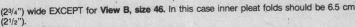

Fabric requirements
View A Unicolored blouse
150 cm (59") wide covert fabric:
All sizes: 1.45 m (1⁵/₈ yds)
View B Plaid blouse
150 cm (59") wide shirting flannel:
All sizes: 1.10 m (1¹/₄ yds)
150 cm (59") wide denim for yoke and collar:
All sizes: 0.50 m (⁵/₈ yd)

Back blouse length:
Size 36/38: 64.5 cm (25¹/₂")
Size 40/42: 65.5 cm (26")
Size 44/46: 66.5 cm (26¹/₄")

Notions/Haberdashery
Views A & B
Fusible interfacing; 9 small hammer-in snaps; raglan shoulder pads.
View A
21 studs.
View B
2 metal zippers, ea. 12 cm (5") long; 2 metal collar corners.

Before cutting out
View B
Trace off pocket pouch printed on front yoke as an extra pattern piece. On cutting layout this piece will have the same number as front yoke.
Fold plaid flannel in half lengthwise, **right** sides together. Pin layers together so that the plaid matches exactly. Then pin pattern pieces into place as shown on layout, making sure that the plaid marks on pattern pieces lie on the same bars in the plaid.

Cutting out
52 Front (cut twice) A B
53 Sleeve, front (cut twice) A B
54 Back (cut once on fold) A B
55 Sleeve, back (cut twice) A B
56 Yoke, front (cut twice) A B
56 Pocket pouch (cut 4 times) B
57 Yoke, back (cut once on fold) A B
58 Collar stand (cut twice on fold) A B
59 Collar (cut twice on fold) A B

Extra pieces
Views A & B
a) 2 cuffs, each 8 cm (3") wide, finished width 4 cm (1⅝"), and for
Size 36/38 ea. 22 cm (8¾") long
Size 40/42 ea. 23 cm (9") long
Size 44/46 ea. 24 cm (9½") long
These lengths include 2 cm (⅞") for underlap.

Please note
Views A & B
Iron interfacing onto the **wrong** side of extended facings on fronts and front yoke pieces, onto one collar and one stand layer, onto one half of each cuff. See shaded areas and pieces on layout.

Construction
See Illustrated Teaching Instructions on page 55, ills. 1 - 5.
View B
● Work zipper pockets into front yoke pieces: baste a pouch piece onto each front yoke over zipper lines, **right** sides together. From the **wrong** side of yoke stitch exactly in zipper lines, securing pouch piece. Slash between these stitching lines, stopping 1 cm (½") short of ends. Clip diagonally to each corner, forming small triangles at opening ends. Pull pouch pieces through openings to the **inside**. Baste and press seamed edges. Baste zippers under opening edges so that their teeth are visible and that pulls lie at upper end of openings. Edgestitch and topstitch ¾ cm (⅜") along opening edges, securing zippers. Pin other pouch pieces onto attached pieces, **right** sides together. Working with

yoke piece on top and folded back, stitch pieces for each pouch together along all edges. Overcast pouch allowances together.

Views A & B
● Baste and stitch front sleeve pieces to front armhole edges from side seam edge up to seam number 2, **right** sides together. Baste and stitch back sleeve pieces to back armhole edges in the same manner, stitching up to seam number 3. Overcast seam allowances together, press into front resp. back. Iron a strip of fusible interfacing onto the **wrong** side of upper edge on front, back and sleeve pieces (ill. 1).
● Press the allowance on lower edge of front and back yoke pieces to the **inside**. Stitch the **wrong** side of yokes onto the **right** side of fronts, sleeves pieces and back (ill. 2).
● Stitch shoulder and upper sleeve seams down to slit mark. Press open seam allowances, press slit allowances to the **inside**, topstitch ½ cm (¼") into place. Stitch side seams and underarm seams in sleeves.
● Turn up hem allowance twice ¾ cm (⅜"), press, machine stitch into place.
● Fold front closing edges to the **inside** along foldline, baste and press. Then fold again to the **inside** along facing line, baste and press. Edgestitch along closing edges, then topstitch as marked, securing facings.
● Fold cuffs in half lengthwise, **right** sides together. Stitch both ends of each and open long edges together for 2 cm (⅞") at one end for underlap. Make sure you have a righthand and a lefthand cuff! Trim seam allowances, trim corners diagonally. Clip in close to last stitch at underlap. Turn cuffs **right** side out, baste and press seamed and fold edges. Fold tucks into lower sleeve edges, x-onto-o, and baste. Baste and stitch interfaced cuff halves to lower sleeve edges so that underlap extends at back slit edge. Press seam allowances into cuffs. Turn under open edge of inner cuff layers, baste into place over attachment seam. Edgestitch and topstitch ¾ cm (⅜") along all cuff edges, securing inner layer of each.
● Stitch collar layers **right** sides together along outer edges, matching marked seamlines. Turn collar. Baste, press, edgestitch and topstitch ¾ cm (⅜") along its seamed edges (ill. 3). Baste open edges together. Baste and stitch stand layers **right** sides together, catching in collar (ill. 4). Turn stand **right** side out. Stitch interfaced stand layer to neck edge, **right** sides together. Turn under open edge of inner stand layer, baste into place over attachment seam. Edgestitch along all stand edges, securing its inner layer (ill. 5).
● Hammer snaps into closing edges at center front lines where marked, upper halves into right closing edge, lower halves into left edge. Hammer snaps into cuff ends as well. Fixing tools and instructions are in the packet.
● Try on blouse. Pin raglan shoulder pads into place, adjusting their position to best suit your figure and the blouse. Then hand sew pads to shoulder seam allowances.
View A
● Hammer 3 studs into each collar corner, 5 studs into lower edge of each front yoke at center point, 5 studs into lower edge of back yoke at center point. Hammer studs into place between topstitching rows.

Allowances
Shoulder and side seams, upper and lower sleeve seams 1.5 cm (⅝"); hem 1.5 cm (⅝"); all other edges 1 cm (½").

Cutting layouts for all sizes

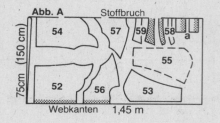

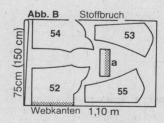

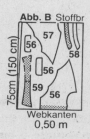

Style 17

6-gored skirt and petticoat, pages 56 and 57

Size 36 sheet F, red outline ➝ ➝ ➝ pieces 37 and 38
Size 38 sheet E, red outline ∿∿∿∿ piece 37
Size 40 sheet D, red outline —·····—···· piece 37
Size 42 sheet C, red outline ⊂⊃⊂⊃⊂⊃ piece 37
Size 44 sheet B, red outline —×—×—× piece 37
Size 46 sheet A, red outline —○—○—○ piece 37

Pattern overview

Skirt length from lower topstitching line: 82 cm (32½")
Petticoat length from elastic casing: 86 cm (34")

The petticoat pattern piece (38) is the same for all sizes and is printed on sheet F, together with pattern piece for size 36 skirt.

Extend skirt pattern piece to full length by adding the amount printed at arrowheads. Make sure you have enough tissue paper to trace off entire pattern piece to avoid taping sections together later on. Connect the ends of extension lines with a straight line, making hemline. This line should measure as follows:

Lower edge width of pattern piece 37
Size 36: 42.5 cm (16¾")
Size 38: 43 cm (17")
Size 40: 43.5 cm (17⅛")
Size 42: 44.5 cm (17½")
Size 44: 45 cm (17¾")
Size 46: 45.5 cm (18")

At the center of this hemline draw a 2.5 cm (1") long line, perpendicular to and below line. Connect ends of extension lines with this line, making curved hemline.

Fabric requirements
Skirt
150 cm (59") wide denim:
All sizes: 2.00 m (2¼ yds)
Petticoat
140 cm (55") lining fabric:
All sizes: 1.65 m (1⅞ yds)
150 cm (59") wide plaid cotton flannel for hem ruffle:
All sizes: 0.55 m (¾ yd)

162

Notions/Haberdashery
2 zippers, each 25 cm (10") long; ¾ cm (⅜") elastic to fit waist for petticoat.

Cutting out
37 Skirt panel (cut 6 times)
38 Petticoat panel (cut twice on the fold)

Extra pieces
There are no pattern pieces for hem ruffle on petticoat and belt carriers on skirt. These pieces are draw directly onto fabric with tailor's chalk in the dimensions stated below and are designated on layout with the small letters **a** and **b.**

Skirt:
a) Fabric strip on the grain for 5 belt carriers, 35 cm (14") long and 6 cm (2¼") wide.

Petticoat:
b) For hem ruffle 3 pieces, each 148 cm (58½") wide and 14 cm (5½") long.

Please note
When cutting out hem ruffle make sure that the plaid matches at ends of sections.

Construction
See Illustrated Teaching Instructions on page 55, lower ill. 1.

Skirt:
● Stitch skirt panels **right** sides together at section and side seams, leaving zipper placket open in each front section seam from foldline down 25 cm (10"). Overcast and press open seam and placket allowances. Baste zipper under placket edges so that their teeth are visible. Edgestitch and topstitch ¾ cm (⅜") along placket edges, securing zippers (ill. 1).
● Press extended facing on upper skirt edge to the **inside** along foldline, topstitch into place along marked line. Then edgestitch and topstitch ¾ cm (⅜") along upper skirt edge.
● Fold strip for belt carriers in half lengthwise, **right** sides together. Stitch 2 cm (⅞") from fold. Turn strip **right** side out. Press strip, edgestitch and topstitch ¾ cm (⅜") along

both its long edges. Cut strip into 5 equal pieces. Overcast both ends of each carrier and turn under 1 cm (½"). Pin carriers onto the **right** side of skirt, 2 cm (⅞") below upper edge and placed at the center of side front and all back panels. Stitch carrier ends into place so that carriers stand away from skirt a bit.
● Turn up hem allowance twice ¾ cm (⅜"), press, machine stitch into place.

Petticoat:
● Stitch side seams, leaving upper end of one seam open in facing width. Press open seam allowances. Press facing on upper edge to the **inside,** turn under open edge, stitch into place as marked. Measure and cut elastic to fit waist, insert into casing through open side seam. Sew elastic ends together.
● Stitch hem ruffle sections **right** sides together at ends, forming a ring. Tip: to prevent the plaid from slipping out of line while stitching, insert pins across seamline and stitch across them. Turn up ruffle hem allowance twice ¾ cm (⅜"), press, machine stitch into place.
● Gather upper edge of ruffle: run 2 rows of machine basting along upper edge, spaced ½ cm (¼") apart. Pull up the bobbin threads at both ends of this stitching until ruffle matches lower edge of petticoat. Knot gathering threads, evenly distribute gathering. Baste and stitch ruffle to lower edge of petticoat, stitching between rows of gathering stitching. Overcast seam allowances together, press up into skirt, edgestitch into place.

Allowances
Skirt: seams 1.5 cm (⅝"); hem 1 cm (½"); all other edges 1 cm (½").
Petticoat: side seams 1.5 cm (⅝"); upper edge 2 cm (⅞"); lower edge of hem ruffle 1.5 cm (⅝"); all other edges 1 cm (½").

Cutting layouts for all sizes

Those pieces extending beyond the fold on layout should be cut out LAST from a SINGLE fabric layer.

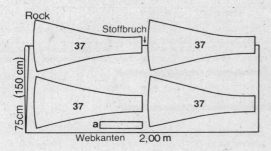

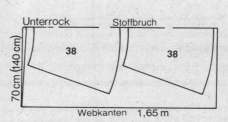

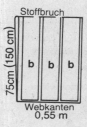

Style 18

Blouse on page 59

Size 36/38 sheet F, green outline •••••••••••••• pieces 52 to 59
Size 40/42 sheet E, green outline 〜〜〜〜〜 pieces 52 to 59
Size 44/46 sheet D, green outline — — — — pieces 52 to 59

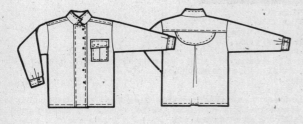

Fabric requirements
140 cm (55") wide, unicolored crinkled cotton:
All sizes: 1.85 m (2⅛ yds)

Notions/Haberdashery
Fusible interfacing; 13 buttons; raglan shoulder pads.

Extend pattern pieces for front and back to full length by adding the amount printed at arrowheads. Make sure you have enough tissue paper to trace off entire pieces to avoid taping sections together later on. Connect ends of extension lines with a straight line to make hemline. Hem width should be as follows:
Size 36/38: 23.5 cm (9¼") & 30.5 cm (12")
Size 40/42: 25.5 cm (10") & 32.5 cm (12⅞")
Size 44/46: 27.5 cm (10¾") & 34.5 cm (13⅝")

Before cutting out
Trace off pocket flap marked on front as a separate pattern piece. On layout this piece is designated with the same number as front.

Pattern overview

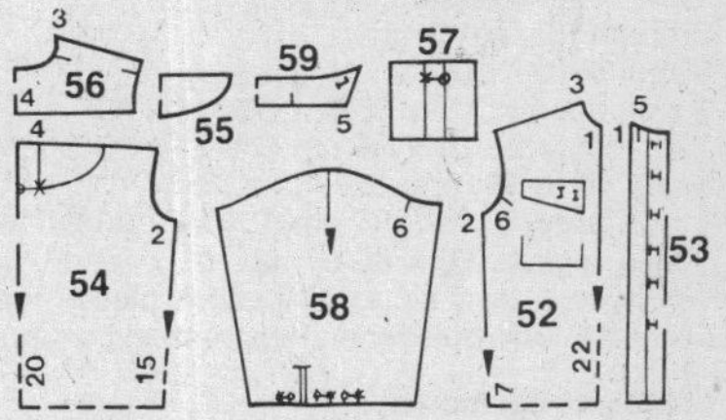

Cutting out
52 Front (cut twice)
52 Pocket flap (cut twice)
53 Front closing band (cut twice on fold)
54 Back (cut once on fold)
55 Back patch (cut once on fold)
56 Back yoke (cut twice on fold)
57 Pocket (cut once)
58 Sleeve (cut twice)
59 Collar (cut twice on fold)

Extra pieces
There are no pattern pieces for cuffs and sleeve slit binding. These pieces are drawn directly onto fabric with tailor's chalk in the dimensions stated below and are designated on layout with the small letters **a** and **b.**
a) 2 cuffs, each 11 cm (4½") wide, finished width 5.5 cm (2¼"), and for
Size 36/38 ea. 23 cm (9") long
Size 40/42 ea. 24 cm (9½") long
Size 44/46 ea. 25 cm (10") long
b) 2 strips on the grain for sleeve slit binding, each 20 cm (8") long and 3 cm (1¼") wide.

Please note
Iron interfacing onto the **wrong** side of one half of each cuff and closing band as well as onto one flap and one collar piece. See shaded pieces and areas on layout.

Construction
See Illustrated Teaching Instructions on page 58, ills. 1 - 11.
● Fold back lengthwise, **right** sides together, matching x-lines of pleat. Stitch these together from upper edge down to x-mark. Press pleat so that seam lies on o-line.
● Baste the allowance on curved edge of back patch to the **inside.** Baste the **wrong** side of patch onto the **right** side of back where marked, edgestitch and topstitch curved edge ¾ cm (⅜") into place (ill. 1).

● Baste one yoke layer to upper back edge, **right** sides together. Baste the **right** side of other layer to the **wrong** side of upper back edge. Stitch along this edge, stitching all 3 pieces together (ill. 2). Press yoke layers up over their attachment seam. Baste and stitch outer layer to upper edge of fronts, **right** sides together. Turn under front edges of inner layer, baste into place over front attachment seams (ill. 3). From the **right** side edgestitch and topstitch yoke ¾ cm (³⁄₈") along its attachment seams, securing inner layer. Baste yoke layers together along neck and armhole edges.

● Sleeve slits: fold binding strips in half lengthwise, **wrong** sides together, press. Slash lower edge of each sleeve along marked line. Spread slit edges apart, edgestitch onto open edges of binding strip, **right** sides together. Fold binding strip over slit edge to the **inside**, baste into place over its attachment seam. From the **right** side of sleeve edgestitch slit binding along its attachment seam, securing its inner layer.

● Stitch sleeves to armholes (ill. 4). Press seam allowances into blouse, edgestitch into place. Stitch side seams and underarm seams in sleeves (ill. 5).

● Front closing bands: stitch interfaced band halves to front closing edges, **right** sides together. Press seam allowances into bands. Fold bands in half lengthwise, **right** sides together. Stitch upper end of each from fold over to marker line (seam number 5). Trim seam allowances, trim corners diagonally, clip in close to last stitch at each marker line (ill. 6).

● Turn up hem allowance twice ¾ cm (³⁄₈"), press, machine stitch into place. Turn front bands **right** side out, fold along foldline. Turn under open edge of inner band layers, baste into place over attacment seam. From the **right** side of blouse edgestitch and topstitch ¾ cm (³⁄₈") along all band edges, securing inner layer.

● Construct collar (ill. 8). Attach collar (ill. 9). Edgestitch and topstitch collar ¾ cm (³⁄₈") along ends and upper edge, edgestitch along attachment seam.

● Pocket with flap: fold pleat into pocket, x-onto-o, press. Edgestitch outer pleat fold. Turn in allowance on upper pocket edge twice ¾ cm (³⁄₈"), press, machine stitch into place. Overcast other allowances. Stitch flap pieces **right** sides together along ends and slanted lower edges (ill. 10). Trim seam allowances at corners diagonally. Turn flap **right** side out. Baste, press, edgestitch and topstitch ¾ cm (³⁄₈") along its seamed edges. Overcast open edges together. Press allowances on side and lower pocket edges to the **inside**. Baste pocket onto left front where marked, edgestitch and topstitch ¾ cm (³⁄₈") into

place. Stitch flap, interfaced layer down, onto front along attachment line (ill. 11). Press flap down over pocket. Topstitch flap ¾ cm (³⁄₈") along its attachment seam.

● Fold cuffs in half lengthwise, **right** sides together. Stitch both ends. Trim seam allowances, trim corners diagonally. Turn cuffs **right** side out. Fold tucks into lower sleeve edges, x-onto-o, and baste. Fold binding on slit edge furthest from underarm seam to the **inside**, baste into place. Baste and stitch interfaced cuff layer to lower sleeve edge, **right** sides together. Press seam allowances into cuffs. Turn under open edge of inner cuff layers, baste into place over attachment seams. From the **right** side of sleeve edgestitch and topstitch ¾ cm (³⁄₈") along all cuff edges, securing inner layer of each.

● Work buttonholes into right closing band, right end of collar, into cuffs and pocket flap where marked. Work 2 into each cuff, 1.5 cm (⁵⁄₈") from end. Sew on buttons.

● Try on blouse. Pin shoulder pads into place, adjusting their position to best suit your figure and the blouse. Then hand sew pads to yoke attachment seam allowances.

Allowances

Seams, hem and upper pocket edge 1.5 cm (⁵⁄₈"), all other edges 1 cm (½").

Cutting layout for all sizes

Those pieces extending beyond the fold on layout should be cut out LAST from a SINGLE fabric layer.

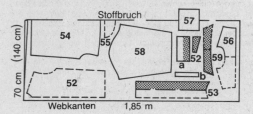

Stoffbruch
(140 cm) 70 cm
54 55 57 58 52 56 59 a 52 b 53
Webkanten 1,85 m

Style 19

2 skirts from one pattern, pages 59, 61 and 65

Sizes 36+38 sheet F, green outline ～～～～ pieces 73 to 75
Sizes 40+42 sheet E, green outline ‒‒‒‒‒‒ pieces 73 to 75
Sizes 44+46 sheet D, green outline ～～～～ pieces 73 to 75

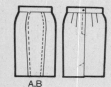

A,B

Skirt length: 58 cm (23")

Pattern overview

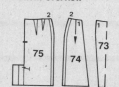

For this style there are two sizes, e.g. sizes 36 and 38, on one pattern. Therefore, pay careful attention to the differing side seamlines when tracing off pattern pieces.

Leather requirements
View A Leather skirt
Smooth (nappa) leather:
Sizes 36+38: approx. 14 sq. ft. =
1 skin approx. 65 x 85 cm (25¾" x 33½") = 6.5 sq. ft.
1 skin approx. 75 x 85 cm (29¾" x 33½") = 7.5 sq. ft.
Sizes 40 to 46: approx. 15 sq. ft. =
1 skin approx. 70 x 85 cm (27¾" x 33½") = 7 sq. ft.
1 skin approx. 80 x 85 cm (31½" x 33½") = 8 sq. ft.
Tip: always take along all pattern pieces for the planned garment when shopping for leather! Study our general instructions on how to handle leather located on page 124.

Fabric requirements
View B Black flannel skirt
140 cm (55") wide wool flannel:
Sizes 36+38: 0.75 m (⁷⁄₈ yd)
Sizes 40 to 46: 0.90 m (1 yd)
140 cm (55") wide lining:
All sizes: 0.65 m (⁷⁄₈ yd)

Notions/Haberdashery
Views A & B
Fusible waistband interfacing; 20 cm (8") zipper.
View A
Leather or textile glue.
Before cutting out
Views A & B
Pay careful attention to the vent underlap and facing on back skirt panels, i.e. left and right edges of vent are different.
View A
Before cutting out your leather skirt, sew it up in muslin or cheap fabric first and try on, making any necessary adjustments. Transfer these alterations to your pattern pieces, then cut out leather. Always cut from a single layer of leather. Tape pattern pieces onto the

wrong side of skins as shown on layout. Make sure you always have lefthand and righthand pieces! Attain this by cutting out once with pattern piece PRINTED SIDE UP on leather and once PRINTED SIDE DOWN. Mark all lines and allowances with ballpoint pen.

Cutting out
Views A & B
73 Center front panel (cut once on fold) *
74 Side front panel (cut twice) *
75 Back panel (cut twice) *
Cut out all pieces with * from lining as well, cutting out back panel once on the fold.
Extra pieces There is no pattern piece for waistband. Draw this piece with tailor's chalk directly onto fabric in the dimensions stated below. On layout this piece is designated with the small letter **a**.
Views A & B
a) Waistband, 8 cm (3") wide, finished width 4 cm (1⁵⁄₈"), and for
Size 36: 71 cm (28") long
Size 38: 75 cm (29¾") long
Size 40: 79 cm (31¼") long
Size 42: 83 cm (32¾") long
Size 44: 87 cm (34¼") long
Size 46: 91 cm (36") long
These lengths include 3 cm (1¼") for underlap.
View A: it will be necessary to cut out waistband in sections and piece together later on. This seam should match a side seam in skirt.
Please note
Views A & B
Iron interfacing onto the **wrong** side of waistband (see shaded piece on layout), for View B stitching waistband sections **right** sides together at ends and pressing open seam allowances BEFORE applying interfacing.

Construction
See Illustrated Teaching Instructions on page 59, ills. 1 - 3.
Views A and B
● Stitch side front panels to center front panel **right** sides together at section seams. Press seam allowances into center panel, topstitch 2 cm (⁷⁄₈") into place (ill. 1). For View A trim seam allowances back to this topstitching (ill. 2).
● Stitch center back seam between placket and vent marks, backstitching seam ends. Press allowances and vent facings into left panel. Stitch back darts, press their allowances toward center back.
● Insert zipper: fold allowance on right placket edge to the **inside** so that fold extends 4 mm (⅛") beyond placket seamline. Baste and edgestitch right half of zipper under right placket edge so that edge lies very close to teeth. Use a zipper presser foot. Close zipper. Pin resp. tape placket closed so that left placket edge lies on seamline marked on right edge. Baste and stitch left half of zipper under left placket edge, stitching 1.5 cm (⁵⁄₈") from edge.
● Lining: stitch front section seams, back darts and side seams. Press open seam allowances, press dart allowances toward center back. Pin lining into skirt, **wrong** sides together, matching darts and seams. Slash back lining along center of zipper. At lower end of zipper clip diagonally ½ cm (¼") to the right and left. Turn under lining, hand sew onto zipper tapes. Baste to upper skirt edge.

Baste and stitch waistband to upper skirt edge, **right** sides together, so that underlap extends at right edge of zipper placket. Press seam allowances into waistband. Fold waistband in half lengthwise, **right** sides together. Stitch both ends and lower edge of underlap. Trim seam allowances, trim corners diagonally. Turn waistband **right** side out, baste and press seamed and fold edges.

View A
 Clip allowance on open edge of inner waistband layer in close to last stitch at underlap. Baste inner layer into place, open edged, over attachment seam. From the **right** side of skirt edgestitch waistband along its attachment seam, securing inner layer. Trim allowance on inner layer back close to this stitching.

View B
 Turn under open edge of inner waistband layer, baste into place over attachment seam. From the **right** side of skirt edgestitch along all waistband edges, securing its inner layer.
Both views
 Press hem allowance to the **inside,** for View A glue into place (ill. 3). For View B blindstitch hem allowance into place.

● Back vent: press vent facings to the **inside,** hand sew onto hem allowance. From the **right** side of skirt topstitch left back panel at upper end of vent as marked, securing facing and underlap.
● Turn up lower lining edge twice so that lining is 2 cm (⁷/₈″) shorter than skirt, press, machine stitch into place. Slash back lining along center of vent from lower edge up to 2 cm (⁷/₈″) short of vent mark. Clip diagonally 2.5 cm (1″) to the right and to the left at upper end. Turn under lining and hand sew onto vent facings.
● Work buttonhole into left waistband end, 1 cm (¹/₂″) from end. Sew button onto underlap.

Allowances
Views A & B
Front section seams 2.5 cm (1″); side and center back seams 1.5 cm (⁵/₈″); hem 4 cm (1⁵/₈″); all other edges 1 cm (¹/₂″).

The measurements given in brackets for view A refer to the sizes 40 to 46.

Cutting layouts

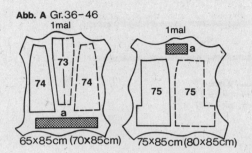

Abb. A Gr. 36–46
1mal / 1mal
65×85cm (70×85cm)   75×85cm (80×85cm)

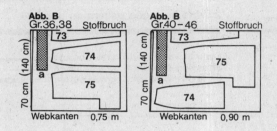

Abb. B Gr. 36, 38   Stoffbruch
70 cm (140 cm)   Webkanten   0,75 m
Abb. B Gr. 40–46   Stoffbruch
70 cm (140 cm)   Webkanten   0,90 m

Style 20

Jacket on pages 60 and 61

Size 36 sheet A, red outline ∿∿∿∿∿∿ pieces 29 to 32
Size 38 sheet B, red outline ●–●–●–● pieces 29 to 32
Size 40 sheet C, red outline ≻–≺–≻–≺ pieces 29 to 32
Size 42 sheet D, red outline —o—o—o pieces 29 to 32
Size 44 sheet E, red outline ⊂⊃⊂⊃⊂⊃ pieces 29 to 32
Size 46 sheet F, red outline ___ ___ pieces 29 to 32

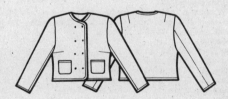

Back jacket length
Size 36: 50 cm (19³/₄″)
Size 38: 51 cm (20¹/₄″)
Size 40: 52 cm (20¹/₂″)
Size 42: 53 cm (21″)
Size 44: 54 cm (21¹/₄″)
Size 46: 55 cm (21³/₄″)

Fabric requirements
150 cm (59″) wide houndstooth check wool:
Sizes 36+38: 1.50 m (1³/₄ yds)
Sizes 40+42: 1.55 m (1³/₄ yds)
Sizes 44+46: 1.60 m (1³/₄ yds)
140 cm (55″) wide lining:
All sizes: 1.20 m (1³/₈ yds)

Notions/Haberdashery
Fusible interfacing; fusible polyester fleece; 8 buttons; shoulder pads.
Before cutting out
Trace off pocket on front and front and back facings as separate pattern pieces. On the layout these pieces are designated with the same numbers as the main pattern pieces. Fold fabric in half lengthwise, **right** sides together. Pin layers together so that the checks match.

Cutting out
29 Front (cut twice) *
29 Front facing (cut twice)
29 Front pocket (cut 4 times)
30 Back (cut once on the fold) *
30 Back facing (cut once on fold)
31 Upper sleeve (cut twice) *
32 Under sleeve (cut twice) *
Cut pieces with * out from lining as well (minus facing width).
Extra pieces
There are not pattern pieces for bias strips for binding upper pocket, lower sleeve and outer jacket edges. These are drawn with tailor's chalk directly onto fabric in the dimensions stated below and are designated on layout with the small letters **a, b** and **c.**
a) Bias strips for binding hem, closing and neck edges, 4 cm (1⁵/₈″) wide and for
Sizes 36+38 totalling 2.50 m (2³/₄ yds) in length
Sizes 40+42 totalling 2.70 m (3 yds) in length
Sizes 44+46 totalling 2.90 m (3¹/₄ yds) in length

Pattern overview

30   32   31   4 29

b) 2 bias strips for binding lower sleeve edges, each 4 cm (1⁵/₈″) wide and for
Sizes 36+38 ea. 27 cm (10³/₄″) long
Sizes 40+42 ea. 28 cm (11″) long
Sizes 44+46 ea. 29 cm (11¹/₂″) long
c) 2 bias strips for binding upper pocket edges, each 4 cm (1⁵/₈″) wide and for
Sizes 36+38 ea. 13 cm (5″) long
Sizes 40 to 46 ea. 14 cm (5¹/₂″) long
Please note
Iron interfacing onto the **wrong** side of fronts and onto back neck facing (see shaded pieces on layout). In addition, iron interfacing strips onto hem allowances of sleeves and back.
Important: allow interfaced pieces to cool for approx. 30 minutes after applying interfacing and before handling. Then pin pattern pieces back onto interfaced pieces and trace seamlines and markings onto interfacing.

Construction
See Illustrated Teaching Instructions on page 62, ills. 1 - 11.
● Stitch front and back darts to points. Knot threads at points. Trim front dart allowances (ill. 1). Press back dart allowances toward center back.
● Stitch shoulder seams, easing in back shoulder edges. Stitch side seams. Press open all seam allowances.
● Stitch front and back facings **right** sides together at shoulder seams (ill. 2).
● Press allowance to the **inside,** blindstitch into place. Baste facing onto closing and neck edges, **wrong** sides together, matching shoulder seams (ills. 3 and 4).
● Topstitch along outer edges of jacket, securing facing. Stitch bias strips for binding outer edges **right** sides together on the grain. Press open seam allowances. Baste and stitch bias strip onto the **right** side of outer jacket edges (ill. 5). Fold bias strip over to the **inside,** turn under its raw edge, hand sew into place along its attachment seam (ill. 6).
● Construct pockets (ill. 7). Bind upper edge of each (illus 8). Baste pockets onto fronts where marked, edgestitch into place.
● Sleeves: stretch front edge of upper sleeve pieces with a warm iron until they match corresponding edge on under sleeve (ill. 9). Stitch upper sleeve pieces to under sleeve pieces **right** sides together at upper seam (seam number 3), easing in upper sleeve at elbow level. Stitch underarm seams in sleeves. Tip: seam allowances in sleeves should be no wider than 1 cm (¹/₂″), otherwise sleeves will not fall as nicely. Press sleeve hem allowances to the **inside,** blindstitch into place. Topstitch 1 cm (¹/₂″) along lower sleeve edges, then bind them with bias strip (ills. 5 and 6).
● Set in sleeves, easing in caps between easing dots and catching in a bias strip of lining or bias tape along upper half of armhole (ill. 10). Press bias strip into jacket.
● Try on jacket. Pin shoulder pads into place, adjusting their position to best suit your figure and the jacket. Then hand sew to sleeve attachment and shoulder seam allowances.

● **Lining:** stitch darts and seams. Set in sleeves. Pin lining into jacket, **wrong** sides together, matching darts and seams. Hand sew sleeve attachment seam allowances of jacket and lining together at caps and side seams. Turn under lining and hand sew onto neck and closing facing down to 5 cm (2") from hem. Turn up lower lining edge 1 cm (1/2"), press. Slip lower lining edge upward, slipstitch onto upper edge of jacket hem allowance. Then finish sewing lining onto front facings (see lining instructions for style 22 on page 64, ills. 9 - 12).
● Work buttonholes into right front where marked. Sew buttons onto both fronts as marked.

Allowances
Side and shoulder seams 1.5 cm (5/8"); NO allowance on closing, neck and upper pocket edges; 3 cm (1 1/4") hem allowance beginning and ending 3 cm (1 1/4") from center front lines (see ill. 3); sleeve hems 3 cm (1 1/4"), all other edges 1 cm (1/2").

Cutting layout for all sizes

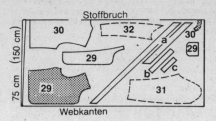

Style 21

2 skirts from one pattern on page 60

Sizes 36+38 sheet A, green outline ———————— piece 77
Sizes 40+42 sheet B, green outline —x—x—x—x— piece 77
Sizes 44+46 sheet C, green outline ⚬⚬⚬⚬⚬⚬ piece 77

Pattern overview

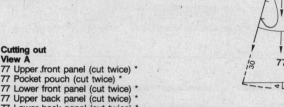

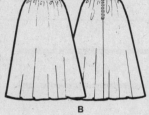

A   B

Views A & B
Skirt length: 80 cm (31 1/2")

Pay careful attention to the lines and markings for the differing views when tracing off pattern pieces for front and back panels. Extend pattern piece to full length by adding the amount printed at arrowheads. Make sure you have enough tissue paper to trace off the entire pattern piece, thus avoiding taping sections together later on. Connect the ends of extended lines with a straight line which should measure as follows (make sure this is right!):
Width for lower edge of pattern piece 77:
Sizes 36+38: 64.5 cm (25 1/2")
Sizes 40+42: 66.5 cm (26 1/4")
Sizes 44+46: 68.5 cm (27")
At the center of this line draw a line extending 4 cm (1 5/8") below the line. Connect ends of extension lines with this line, forming a curved line which is now the hemline of pattern piece.

Leather requirements
View A Leather skirt
Suede:**All sizes:** approx. 37.5 sq.ft. or 5 skins, ea. approx. 70x80 cm (27 3/4" x 31 1/2") = 6.5 sq. ft. 1 skin approx. 50x80 cm (19 3/4" x 31 1/2") = 5 sq. ft.
Tip: Take along all pattern pieces for the garment planned when shopping for leather. Study our general instructions for leather located on pages 124/125.

Fabric requirements
View B Printed skirt 140 cm (55") wide, viscose rayon crêpe:
All sizes: 1.95 m (2 1/4 yds)
Views A & B
140 cm (55") wide lining:
Sizes 36+38: 1.50 m (1 3/4 yds)
Sizes 40+42: 1.55 m (1 3/4 yds)
Sizes 44+46: 1.65 m (1 7/8 yds)

Notions/Haberdashery
Views A & B
Fusible waistband interfacing; 20 cm (8") zipper; 2 buttons.
View A
1 belt buckle with prong, 2.5 cm (1") high; leather or textile glue.
Before cutting out
Views A & B
Pattern piece 77 is used to cut out front and back skirt panels. Trace off the pocket pouch printed on pattern piece 77 as a separate pattern piece. On the layout this piece will also be designated with the number 77.
View A
Cut skirt pattern piece apart along the horizontal seamline. You will now have upper and lower front panels, upper and lower back panels. All panels will be designated with the number 77 on layouts.
Tip: Before cutting out your leather skirt, make it up in muslin or other cheap fabric first and try on for fitting. Pin any necessary alterations on test skirt, then transfer them onto pattern pieces. Then tape pattern pieces onto the **wrong** side of a single layer of leather as shown on layout. Make sure that you have righthand and lefthand panels by placing pattern pieces once PRINTED SIDE UP onto leather and once PRINTED SIDE DOWN. Mark all seamlines and allowances onto leather with ballpoint pen.

Cutting out
View A
77 Upper front panel (cut twice) *
77 Pocket pouch (cut twice) *
77 Lower front panel (cut twice) *
77 Upper back panel (cut twice) *
77 Lower back panel (cut twice) *
* = Cut out these pieces from lining as well, taping the sections for front resp. back pane back together first. There are no horizontal section seams in lining.
Front lining panel (cut once on fold)
Back lining panel (cut twice)

Cutting out
View B:
77 Front panel (cut once on fold) *
77 Pocket pouch (cut 4 times)
77 Back panel (cut twice) *
* = Cut out these pieces from lining as well.
Extra pieces
There are no pattern pieces for waistband and belt. These pieces are drawn with tailor's chalk directly onto fabric in the dimensions stated below and are designated on layout with the small letters **a**, **b** and **c**.
View A
a) Waistband, 12 cm (4 1/2") wide, finished width 6 cm (2 1/4").

Length of front section:	Length of left back section:	Length of right back section:
Size 36: 35 cm (13 3/4")	**Size 36:** 17 cm (6 1/2")	**Size 36:** 20 cm (8")
Size 38: 37 cm (14 1/2")	**Size 38:** 18 cm (7")	**Size 38:** 21 cm (8 1/2")
Size 40: 39 cm (15 1/2")	**Size 40:** 19 cm (7 1/2")	**Size 40:** 22 cm (9")
Size 42: 41 cm (16 1/4")	**Size 42:** 20 cm (8")	**Size 42:** 23 cm (9 3/8")
Size 44: 43 cm (17")	**Size 44:** 21 cm (8 1/2")	**Size 44:** 24 cm (9 3/4")
Size 46: 45 cm (17 3/4")	**Size 46:** 22 cm (9")	**Size 46:** 25 cm (10")

Lengths for right back section include 3 cm (1 1/4") for underlap.
b) Belt, 5.5 cm (2 1/4") wide.

Length of right section:	Length of left section:
Sizes 36+38: 38 cm (15")	**Sizes 36+38:** 12 cm (4 1/2")
Sizes 40+42: 41 cm (16 1/4")	**Sizes 40+42:** 13 cm (5")
Sizes 44+46: 44 cm (17 1/4")	**Sizes 44+46:** 14 cm (5 1/2")

View B
c) Waistband, 12 cm (4 1/2") wide, finished width 6 cm (2 1/4").
Length of entire waistband:
Size 36: 72 cm (28 1/2")
Size 38: 76 cm (30")
Size 40: 80 cm (31 1/2")
Size 42: 84 cm (33")
Size 44: 88 cm (34 3/4")
Size 46: 92 cm (36 1/4")
These lengths include 3 cm (1 1/4") for underlap.
Please note:
View A Iron interfacing onto waistband AFTER sections have been stitched together at side seams, catching in belt sections. Iron interfacing onto waistband half with belt only (see shaded areas on layouts).
Important: before applying leather or textile glue to your leather, TEST GLUE FIRST on a scrap of your leather.
Being as the skirt panels are cut out without hem allowance, do not cut off threads at lower end of vertical seams too short so that you can tie them off and secure on the underside.
View B
Iron interfacing onto the **wrong** side of one half of waistband. See shaded area on layout.

Construction
See Illustrated Teaching Instructions on page 63, ills. 1 - 11.
View A
● Stitch upper skirt panels to the corresponding lower panels, **right** sides together. Topstitch above and below section seams (ill. 1).

• Stitch center front seam, center back seam from placket mark down to lower edge. orizontal section seams should match exactly in both cases. Press open seam llowances (under a press cloth!), press placket allowances to the **inside** and glue into lace. Topstitch front skirt 1/2 cm (1/4") on each side of center seam.
• Stitch side seams, leaving pockets open (ill. 2).
• Seam pockets: pin and stitch lining pouch pieces to front side seam allowances etween marker lines, **right** sides together, stitching exactly in marked seamline along pening edge, on allowance above and below opening. Press lining pouch pieces into ont skirt. Topstitch front skirt 1/2 cm (1/4") along side seams, securing allowances (ill. 3). in leather pouch pieces onto back allowance of side seams, **right** sides together. From e **right** side edgestitch back skirt along pocket opening edges, securing leather pouch ieces. Stitch pieces for each pouch together (ill. 4). Pin pouches into place at upper skirt dge.
• Tape zipper under back placket edges. From the **right** side topstitch 1/2 cm (1/4") along oth sides of center back seam and placket, securing zipper and allowances (ill. 5). Use a pper presser foot. At hem edge tie off thread ends of vertical seams and topstitching and ure on inside.
• Trim front end of RIGHT belt section diagonally. Fold the allowance on upper and wer edges of both belt sections and end of right section to the **inside** and glue into lace. Sew buckle onto end of left section (ill. 6). Stitch waistband sections **right** sides ogether at side seams, catching in belt sections (ill. 7). Press open seam allowances nder a press cloth!). Then iron waistband interfacing onto the **wrong** side of waistband alf with belt.
• **Lining:** stitch center back seam up to placket mark, stitch side seams. Press open seam llowances, press placket allowances to the **inside.** Insert lining into skirt, **wrong** sides ogether, matching seams. Pin to upper skirt edge. Gather upper skirt edge by running a w of machine basting 3 mm (1/8") on each side of the marked seamline. Pull up the obbin threads at both ends of this stitching until skirt matches waistband minus underlap l. 8).
• Baste and stitch interfaced waistband layer to upper skirt edge, **right** sides together, so at side seams match and underlap extends at right edge of placket. Fold waistband in alf lengthwise, **right** sides together. Stitch both ends (ill. 9). Turn waistband **right** side out, press. From the **right** side of skirt edgestitch along all waistband edges, securing its inner layer. Trim allowance on inner waistband layer back to this stitching (ill. 10).
● Hand sew lining onto zipper tapes (ill. 11). Turn up lower lining edge twice (lining should be 2 cm - 7/8" shorter than skirt), press, machine stitch into place.
● Work 2 buttonholes into waistband, 1 cm (1/2") from left end. Sew buttons onto underlap.

View B

● Stitch center back seam from lower edge up to placket mark. Leave placket open. Press open seam allowances, press placket allowances to the **inside.** Stitch side seams, leaving pockets open between marker lines. Press open seam allowances.
● Seam pockets: stitch pouch pieces to front and back side seam allowances, in marked seamline between marker lines, close to seam from upper marker line to upper edge. Press pouch pieces into front skirt, stitch together.
● Baste zipper under placket edges so that its teeth are covered (centered application). Machine stitch zipper into place using a zipper presser foot.
● **Lining:** construct and insert in the same manner as for View A. Gather upper skirt edge likewise as in View A.
● Baste and stitch interfaced waistband half to upper skirt edge, **right** sides together, so that its underlap extends at right edge of placket. Fold waistband in half lengthwise, **right** sides together. Stitch both ends and lower edge of underlap. Trim seam allowances, trim corners diagonally. Turn waistband **right** side out, baste and press fold edges. Turn under open edge of its inner layer, baste into place over attachment seam. From the **right** side of skirt edgestitch along all waistband edges, securing inner layer.
● Hand sew lining onto zipper tapes. Hem lining as explained in View A.
● Work 2 buttonholes into left end of waistband, sew buttons onto underlap (see View A).

Allowances
View A
NO hem allowance; all seams and edges 1 cm (1/2").
View B
Vertical seams and hem 1.5 cm (5/8"), all other edges 1 cm (1/2").

Cutting layouts for all sizes

Abb. A
2mal
a
77
70 x 80 cm
ca. 6,5 qfs
1mal
a
77
70 x 80 cm
ca. 6,5 qfs
1mal
b
77
70 x 80 cm
ca. 6,5 qfs
1mal
77
70 x 80 cm
ca. 6,5 qfs
1mal
77
50 x 80 cm
ca. 5 qfs
Abb. B
Stoffbruch
(140 cm)
70 cm
c
Webkanten
1,95 m

Style 22

Collarless jacket on page 65

Size 36 sheet F, red outline **pieces 33 to 36**
Size 38 sheet E, red outline **pieces 33 to 36**
Size 40 sheet D, red outline **pieces 33 to 36**
Size 42 sheet C, red outline **pieces 33 to 36**
Size 44 sheet B, red outline **pieces 33 to 36**
Size 46 sheet A, red outline **pieces 33 to 36**

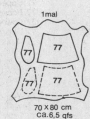

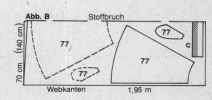

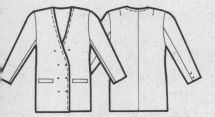

Back jacket length
Size 36: 79 cm (31 1/4")
Size 38: 80 cm (31 1/2")
Size 40: 81 cm (32")
Size 42: 81 cm (32")
Size 44: 82 cm (32 1/2")
Size 46: 82 cm (32 1/2")

xtend back pattern piece to the full length by adding the amount printed at arrowheads. onnect the ends of these lines with a straight line to make hemline which should easure as follows (make sure this is right!):
em width of back pattern piece:
ze 36: 26.5 cm (10 1/2")
ze 38: 27.5 cm (10 7/8")
ze 40: 28.5 cm (11 1/4")
ze 42: 29.5 cm (11 5/8")
ze 44: 30 cm (12")
ze 46: 31 cm (12 1/4")

Pattern overviews

Sizes 36, 38 and 40 | **Sizes 42, 44 and 46**

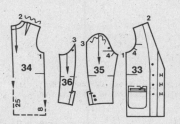

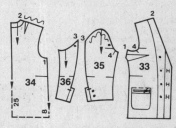

34
35
36
33
25
8
34
35
36
33
25
8

Fabric requirements
150 cm (59") wide glen checked wool:
Sizes 36+38: 1.70 m (1 7/8 yds)
Sizes 40+42+44: 1.80 m (2 yds)
Size 46: 1.90 m (2 1/8 yds)
140 cm (55") wide lining:
All sizes: 1.50 m (1 3/4 yds)

Notions/Haberdashery
Fusible interfacing; 8 large and 4 small buttons; 1 small, flat button for inside; 1 pair shoulder pads; polyester fleece.

Before cutting out
Trace off facing, pocket pouch and pocket welt printed on front pattern piece as well as neck facing on back as separate pattern pieces. On the layout these pieces are designated with the same number as front resp. back.
Fold fabric in half lengthwise, **right** sides together, matching the plaid in both layers exactly. Pin layers together at intervals to insure that plaid won't slip out of line. Then pin pattern pieces into place as shown on layout making sure that the plaid matching lines on main pieces lie on the same bar of plaid.

Cutting out
33 Front (cut twice) *
33 Front facing (cut twice)
33 Pocket welt (cut twice on fold)
33 Pocket pouch (cut twice) *
34 Back (cut twice) *
34 Back neck facing (cut once on fold)
35 Upper sleeve (cut twice) *
36 Under sleeve (cut twice) *
* = Cut out these pieces from lining as well, cutting out front and back minus facing but with 1 cm (1/2") allowance on these edges. Cut out lining sleeves without vent facing.

Please note
Iron interfacing onto the **wrong** side of fronts, back neck facing, one half of each pocket welt, vent facing on upper sleeve pieces and vent underlap on under sleeve pieces. See shaded areas and pieces on layout. In addition, cut strips of interfacing to match hem allowance on back and sleeve pieces. Iron onto hem allowances. **Important!** Allow all interfaced pieces to cool for at least 30 minutes after applying interfacing. Then pin pattern pieces onto these pieces and trace all seamlines and markings onto interfacing.

Construction
See Illustrated Teaching Instructions on page 64, ills. 1 - 12.
● **Welt pockets:** complete as explained for Style 27.

● **Sizes 42 to 46:** stitch bust darts. Trim dart allowances back to 1 cm (1/2") width a press open. See Style 20, page 62, ill. 1.
● **All sizes:** stitch back shoulder darts, press their allowances toward center back.
● Stitch center back, side and shoulder seams, easing in back shoulder edges. Stitch front and back facings together at shoulder seams (ill. 1).
● Baste hem allowance to the **inside,** press, blindstitch into place. Stitch facing to closing and neck edges, **right** sides together. Turn facing to the **inside,** baste and press seam edges (ill. 2). Turn up lower ends of facing, pin onto hem allowance. Topstitch alo closing and neck edges, hand sew facing onto hem allowance (ill. 3).
● Stitch sleeve seams, leaving vent open in back seam where marked. **Tip:** Sleeve sea allowances should be no wider than 1 cm (1/2"). Otherwise sleeves will not fall proper!
● Sleeve vents: clip seam allowance on under sleeve pieces in close to seam at corn above vent. Turn sleeve hem allowance to the **outside** and stitch its ends to vent underla and facing (ill. 4). Turn hem allowance back to the **inside,** press, blindstitch into plac Press vent facing to the **inside.** Hand sew onto hem allowance and underlap (ill. 5). Se smaller buttons onto vent edge on upper sleeves, catching in underlap (ill. 6).
● Set in sleeves, easing in sleeve caps where marked. Catch in a 13 cm (5") long bi strip at upper edge of each armhole. Always baste and stitch from the sleeve side (ill. Overcast seam allowances together by hand. Press bias strip into jacket.
● Try on jacket. Pin shoulder pads into place, adjusting their position to best suit yo figure and the jacket. Hand sew pads to sleeve attachment and shoulder sea allowances. Hand sew fleece strip into place on sleeve side of attachment seam (see ill. on p. 62). Hand sew facings onto shoulder pads (ill. 9).
● **Lining:** stitch darts and seams. Set in sleeves. Pin lining into jacket, **wrong** sid together, matching darts and seams. Hand sew lining to sleeve attachment sea allowances at caps and side seams. Turn under lining and hand sew onto facing (ill. 1 Attach lining to hem and sleeve hem allowances as in ills. 11 and 12.
● Work buttonholes into right closing edge where marked. Work a buttonhole into le front at uppermost marking.
● Sew buttons onto both fronts where marked. Sew a small, flat button onto the **inside** RIGHT front underneath second button from the top to secure underlap.

Allowances
Center back, side and shoulder seams 1.5 cm (5/8"); hem and sleeve hems 4 cm (1 5/8"); other seams and edges 1 cm (1/2").

Cutting layouts

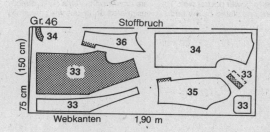

Gr. 36 - 44   Stoffbruch
(150 cm) 75 cm
34   35   34   33   33   36   33   33
Webkanten

Gr. 46   Stoffbruch
(150 cm) 75 cm
34   36   34   33   33   35   33   33
Webkanten   1,90 m

Style 23

3 blazers from one pattern on pages 66 and 67

Size 36 sheet A, red outline ~~~~~~~~ pieces 1 to 11
Size 38 sheet B, red outline ∿∿∿∿∿ pieces 1 to 11
Size 40 sheet C, red outline ———— pieces 1 to 11
Size 42 sheet D, red outline ●●●●●● pieces 1 to 11
Size 44 sheet E, red outline —·····— pieces 1 to 11
Size 46 sheet F, red outline ·········· pieces 1 to 11

A + B

C

Back jacket length
All views
Size 36: 76 cm (30")
Size 38: 77 cm (30 1/2")
Size 40: 77.5 cm (30 5/8")
Size 42: 78 cm (30 3/4")
Size 44: 78.5 cm (31")
Size 46: 79 cm (31 1/4")

Pattern overview

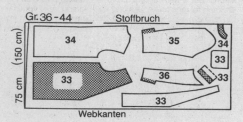

Fabric requirements
View A Houndstooth blazer:
145 cm (57") wide houndstooth printed
All sizes: 2.10 m (2 3/8 yds)
140 cm (55") wide lining:
All sizes: 1.45 m (1 5/8 yds)
View B Floral print blazer:
150 cm (59") wide viscose rayon/linen bl
All sizes: 2.00 m (2 1/4 yds)
140 cm (55") wide lining:
All sizes: 1.45 m (1 5/8 yds)
View C Plaid blazer:
150 cm (59") plaid crêpe:
Sizes 36+38+40: 1.75 m (2 yds)
Sizes 42+44+46: 1.90 m (2 1/8 yds)

Notions/Haberdashery
All views
Fusible interfacing; 8 large buttons; 1 flat button for inside; shoulder pads; polyester fleece for shaping sleeve caps; bias tape for reinforcing armholes.
Views A & B
6 smaller buttons for sleeves.
View C
Lining remnant for pockets; 2 smaller buttons for sleeves.

Before cutting out
All views
Pay careful attention to the different grain direction arrows on collar pattern piece. Upper collar should be cut out on the straight grain, undercollar on the bias.

Fold fabric in half lengthwise, **right** sides together, matching plaid exactly. Pin fabric layers together at intervals to insure that plaid doesn't slip out of line. Then pin pattern pieces onto place as shown on layout, making sure that plaid matching lines on major pieces lie on the same bar in the plaid. Plaid on pocket welts should match the plaid at pocket opening lines on front. To match plaid on upper welt proceed as follows: fold pattern piece 4 along its foldline so that printed side is on the outside. Place this piece onto cut out left front along attachment line. Trace the plaid at this point onto pattern piece. Then cut out welt, matching these plaid markings.

Cutting out
- 1 Front (cut twice) **A B C** *
- 2 Side panel (cut twice) **A B C** *
- 3 Back (cut twice) **A B C** *
- 4 Upper pocket welt (cut once) **A B C**
- 5 Upper pocket pouch (cut once) **A B C** *
- 6 Lower pocket pouch (cut twice) **A B C** *
- 7 Front facing (cut twice) **A B C**
- 8 Upper collar (cut once on the fold) **A B C**
- 9 Under collar (cut twice) **A B C**
- 10 Upper sleeve (cut twice) **A B** *
- 11 Under sleeve (cut twice) **A B** *
- 11 Sleeve (cut twice) **C**

* = Cut out these pieces from lining as well, cutting out front pieces minus facing. To do so fold darts into front pattern piece and pin. Then place facing pattern piece onto front pattern piece, printed sides together, and trace inner long edge of facing onto front. Cut out lining fronts over to this line plus 1 cm (1/2") allowance. Cut out back lining once on the fold. For movement pleat in center back place pattern piece 2 cm (7/8") from lining fold, making sure that grain direction arrow is parallel to lining fold. Cut out lining sleeves without vent facing and underlap.

Extra pieces
There is no pattern piece for lower pocket welt. These are drawn with tailor's chalk directly onto fabric in the dimensions stated below and are designated on layout with the small letter **a.**
All views
2 pocket welts, 6 cm (2 1/4") wide, finished width 3 cm (1 1/8"), and for
- Size 36 ea. 14 cm (5 1/2") long
- Size 38 ea. 14.5 cm (5 3/4") long
- Size 40 ea. 15 cm (6") long
- Size 42 ea. 15.5 cm (6 1/8") long
- Size 44 ea. 16 cm (6 3/8") long
- Size 46 ea. 16.5 cm (6 1/2") long

Please note
All views
Apply interfacing BEFORE tracing seamlines and markings onto garment pieces. Iron interfacing onto the **wrong** side of fronts, side panels, one half of each pocket welt, undercollar (stitch undercollar pieces together at center seam and press open allowances beforehand). See shaded pieces and areas on layout. Allow pieces to cool for at least 30 minutes before tracing seamlines and markings onto interfacing. Cut out strips of interfacing to match hem allowance on sleeves and back. Iron these strips into place.

Views A & B
Iron interfacing onto sleeve hem allowances and vent facings. Allow interfaced pieces to cool for at least 30 minutes before handling.

Important
Before stitching sleeve seams, place upper sleeve pieces **right** sides together and stretch their front edge with steam to match corresponding edge on under sleeve pieces. Ease in upper sleeve pieces at back seams.

Tip
Before cutting out check the position of lower welt pocket. Tape pattern pieces for front, side panel and back together, edge to edge. Fold and pin darts. Pin a welt onto front pattern piece along attachment line. Try on pattern in front of a mirror. If you are shorter than 1.68 m (5'6") and the lower pockets are too low, proceed as follows: draw a line onto front pattern piece from center front line over to section seam that cuts through the center of waist dart and is perpendicular to center front line. Measure the distance from pocket opening line to the desired position. Draw a second line at this distance below and parallel to first line. Fold front pattern piece so that these lines match. Fold pattern piece for side panel and back by the same amount at the same level. Re-mark buttonhole and button position onto front pattern piece.

Construction
See Illustrated Teaching Instructions on page 68, ills. 1 - 11.
All views
- Stitch upper front darts (ill. 1). Stitch waist darts, press their allowances toward center front.
- Stitch side panels to fronts **right** sides together at section seams.
- Lower welt pockets: fold welts in half lengthwise, **right** sides together. Stitch both ends of each (ill. 2). Turn welts **right** side out, baste and press seamed and fold edges, for Views A and B topstitch 1/2 cm (1/4") along these edges. Stitch welts, interfaced layer down, onto the **right** side of fronts along attachment line. Stitch lining pouch pieces into place over welts, stitching in welt attachment seam. Stitch fabric pouch pieces onto fronts, **right** sides together, so that their straight edge touches welt and seam is 1 cm (1/2") above welt attachment seam. Upper stitching lines should be 1/2 cm (1/4") shorter at both ends than lower ones. Backstitch seam ends. Slash fronts between these stitching lines. Clip diagonally to each last stitch, forming small triangles at opening ends (ill. 3). Do NOT cut or clip pocket pieces. Pull pouch pieces through openings to the **inside**. Fold opening end triangles to the **inside**. Baste pieces for each pouch together, trim evenly. Working with front on top and folded back, stitch pouch pieces together. Begin and end directly above opening end triangles and stitch across the base of each. Press welts up over openings, sew ends into place (ill. 4). Complete breast pocket in left front in the same manner. When constructing welt, trim seam allowances at upper corners diagonally before turning.
- Stitch center back seam. Stitch side panels to back **right** sides together at section seams. Baste hem allowance to the **inside**, press, blindstitch into place.
- Stitch facings to fronts along closing and lapel edges (ill. 5). Turn facings to the **inside**, baste and press seamed edges. **Tip:** Press open facing attachment seam allowances from lower edge up to lapel point before basting closing and lapel edges. Turn up lower facing edges, hand sew onto hem allowance.
- Stitch shoulder seams.
- Stitch collar layers **right** sides together along outer edges. Trim seam allowances, trim corners diagonally. Turn collar **right** side out. Baste, press and topstitch 1/2 cm (1/4") along its seamed edges. Holding undercollar rounded over fingers, secure upper collar with diagonal (tailor's) basting taken along collar "roll." Baste collar onto the **right** side of neck edge. Turn facings to the **outside** and baste to neck edge over collar (ill. 6). Stitch along neck edge, securing facing and collar. Turn facings back to the **inside**. Holding each front rounded over fingers, secure facing with diagonal (tailor's) basting taken along lapel foldline. For Views A and B topstitch 1/2 cm (1/4") along closing and lapel edges.
Views A & B
- Sleeves: stitch sleeve seams, leaving vent open in back seam as marked. Ease in upper sleeve pieces at back seams. Clip seam allowance on under sleeve in close to seam at corner above vent and complete vent as in ills. 7 and 8. Blindstitch sleeve hem allowances into place.
View C
- Fold each sleeve so that x-lines of pleat lie **right** sides together. Stitch lines together from lower edge up to pleat mark, backstitching seam ends. Open out sleeves flat and press in pleats so that seam lies on o-line. Stitch underarm seams in sleeves. Press hem allowances to the **inside**, blindstitch into place. Sew a button onto each sleeve pleat, 2 cm (7/8") above hem edge.

Allowances
All views
Seams 2 cm (7/8"); hem and sleeve hems 4 cm (1 5/8"); all other seams and edges 1 cm (1/2").

Cutting layouts

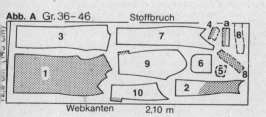

Abb. A Gr. 36–46   Stoffbruch
Webkanten   2,10 m

Abb. B Gr. 36–46   Stoffbruch
75 cm (150 cm)
Webkanten   2,00 m

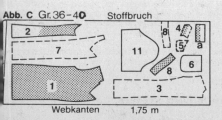

Abb. C Gr. 36–40   Stoffbruch
Webkanten   1,75 m

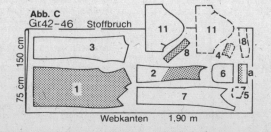

Abb. C Gr. 42–46   Stoffbruch
75 cm   150 cm
Webkanten   1,90 m

Those pattern pieces extending beyond the fold on layout (in this case the sleeves) should be cut out LAST from a SINGLE fabric layer, pinned onto the right fabric side.

All views

● Set in sleeves: baste sleeves into armholes, **right** sides together, easing in sleeve caps where marked. Catch in a 12 cm (5") long section of bias tape or a bias fabric strip on the jacket side of attachment seam at sleeve cap. Working from the sleeve side, stitch sleeves into place. Press bias tape resp. strip into jacket. Cut 2 strips of polyester fleece, ea. 6 cm (2¼") wide and 15 cm (6") long. Pin and hand sew these onto the sleeve side of attachment seams, centering over seam and sewing onto allowance. Try on jacket. Pin shoulder pads into place, adjusting their position to best suit your figure and the jacket. Straight edge of pads should extend approx. 1 cm (½") beyond sleeve attachment seam into sleeve cap. Hand sew facings onto pads (ill. 9).

● Lining: fold back lining piece in half lengthwise, **right** sides together. To make movement pleat stitch 5 cm (2") at upper and lower edges, 2 cm (⅞") in from fold. Open out back flat and press pleat to one side. Stitch all seams in lining, remembering that front shoulder edges will be narrower than back ones because lining is cut out without facing. Set in sleeves.

● Hanger loop: cut a bias strip from lining, 10 cm (4") long and 2 cm (⅞") wide. Fold the strip in half lengthwise, **right** sides together. Stitch ¾ cm (⅜") from its fold. Turn strip **right** side out, press, stretching as much as possible. Pin hanger loop onto collar attachment seam at center back so that its ends lie on collar allowance. Hand sew into place. Pin lining into jacket, **wrong** sides together. Hand sew sleeve attachment seam allowances of jacket and lining together at underarms, hand sew lining onto shoulder pads. Then hand sew lining onto facings, collar attachment seam and hem allowance (ill. 10 and 11). Slip lower edge of sleeve lining upward, slipstitch onto upper edge of sleeve hem allowance.

● Work buttonholes into right closing edge where marked. Work one into left closing edge at uppermost marking as well. Sew buttons onto both fronts where marked. Sew small, flat button onto the **inside** of right front underneath second button from the top to secure underlap.

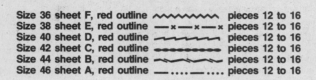

Style
24

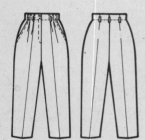

Side leg length
Size 36: 102 cm (40¼")
Sizes 38+40: 103 cm (40¾")
Sizes 42+44: 104 cm (41")
Size 46: 105 cm (41½")

Pattern overviews

Sizes 36 to 44

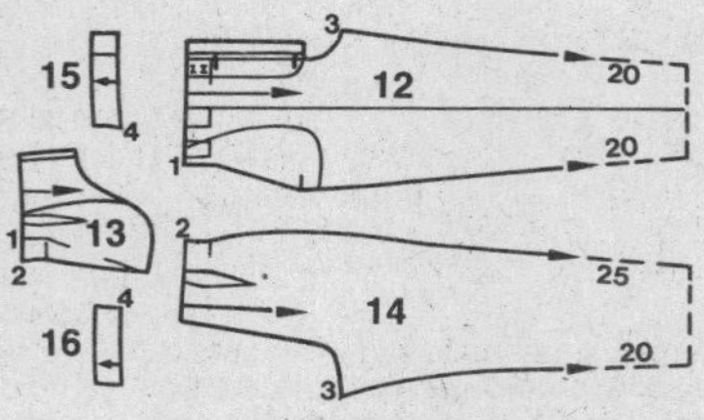

Size 46

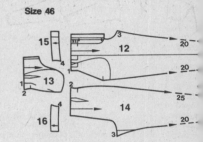

Extend front and back pant pattern pieces to the full length by adding the amount printed at arrowheads. Make sure you have enough tissue paper to trace off entire pattern pieces, avoiding taping sections together later on. Connect ends of extension lines with a straight line to make hemline that should measure as follows (make sure this is right!):
Hem width on front and back pant pieces:
Size 36: 20.5 cm (8⅛")
Size 38: 21 cm (8¼")
Size 40: 21.5 cm (8½")
Size 42: 22 cm (8⅝")
Size 44: 22.5 cm (8⅞")
Size 46: 23 cm (9")

Fabric requirements
150 cm (59") wide viscose rayon gabardine:
Sizes 36+38: 1.45 m (1⅝ yds)
Size 40: 1.50 m (1¾ yds)
Size 42: 1.55 m (1¾ yds)
Sizes 44+46: 1.60 m (1¾ yds)

Notions/Haberdashery
2 buttons; fusible interfacing; 1 zipper, 20 cm (8") long for **sizes 36 to 40**, 22 cm (9") long for **sizes 42 to 46**.

Before cutting out
Trace off pouch piece printed on front pant piece as a separate pattern piece. For **size 46** cut off back pant pattern piece and cut out separately (you save fabric this way). On the layout these pieces are designated with the same number as front and back pant pieces.
Make sure that grain direction arrows on pattern pieces EXACTLY match selvages when pinning pieces onto fabric.

Cutting out
12 Pants, front (cut twice)
12 Pocket pouch (cut twice)
13 Hip yoke (cut twice)
14 Pants, back (cut twice)
14 Back gusset for size 46 (cut twice)
15 Front waist facing (cut twice)
16 Back waist facing (cut twice)

Extra pieces
There are no pattern pieces for placket underlap and belt carriers. These are drawn directly onto fabric with tailor's chalk in the dimensions stated below and are designated on layout with the small letters **a** and **b**.
a) 2 placket underlap pieces, each 2.5 cm (1") wide and for
Sizes 36 to 40 ea. 25 cm (10") long
Sizes 42 to 46 ea. 27 cm (10¾") long
b) 5 belt carriers, each 7 cm (2¾") long and 3 cm (1¼") wide. Finished width 1.5 cm (⅝").

Please note
the differing lines for right and left placket edges on pattern pieces for front pants, hip yoke and front waist facing.
Iron interfacing onto the **wrong** side of front and back waist facings, onto pocket pouch pieces along opening edge. See shaded pieces and areas on layout.

Construction
See Illustrated Teaching Instructions on page 70, ills. 1 - 8.
● Fold front pant pieces **wrong** sides together along line for crease. Press in crease making sure that it is perfectly straight. **Important:** after pressing in crease allow each front pant piece to cool completely while still folded.
● Fold and stitch pleats into upper edge of front pant pieces, x-onto-o, **right** sides together, stitching down to pleat mark only. Backstitch seam ends (ill. 1). Press pleats toward center front. From the **right** side topstitch ½ cm (¼") along pleat seams.
● Stitch pouch pieces to front pant pieces along pocket opening edge, **right** sides together (ill. 2). Fold pouch pieces over to the **inside**. Baste, press and topstitch along seamed (pocket opening) edges.
● Stitch darts in back pant pieces and hip yokes. Knot thread ends at dart points. Press hip yoke darts toward side edge, back darts toward center back. Baste front pant piece onto the **right** side of the corresponding hip yoke so that pocket opening edge of each lies on placement line marked on hip yoke. Stitch pouch pieces to hip yokes. Baste pockets into place at upper and front edges (ill. 3), matching marked seamlines.
● **Size 46:** stitch gussets to back pant pieces, **right** sides together. Press open seam allowances.
● Baste and stitch front pant pieces to back pieces **right** sides together at side and inside leg seams. Insert one leg into the other, **right** sides together, matching side and inside leg seams. Stitch front crotch seam from placket mark down to inside leg seams.
● Turn right placket facing to the **outside** along foldline, pin into place. Stitch front waist facings to back facings **right** sides together at side seams. Stitch waist facings to upper edge of pant sections, **right** sides together, matching side seams (ill. 4). Press seam allowances into facings, edgestitch into place.
● Stitch placket underlap pieces **right** sides together at ends and one long edge, stitching one end as a curve. Turn underlap **right** side out. Baste, press and edgestitch along seamed edges. Turn right placket facing and allowance on left placket edge to the **inside**, press. Baste left half of zipper under left placket edge between placket marks so that edge lies very close to zipper teeth. Place placket underlap under left placket edge so that its open edge is even with zipper tape and straight end matches waist facing attachment seam. Edgestitch along left edge of placket, securing zipper and underlap. Use zipper presser foot. Close zipper. Pin placket closed, center-on-center. Baste and stitch right half of zipper to right placket facing, taking care NOT to catch in pant front (ill. 5). Open out front flat. Topstitch right placket edge as marked, securing facing.
● Insert one leg into the other, **right** sides together. Stitch remainder of crotch seam and center seam in waist facing (ill. 6).
● Fold waist facing to the **inside**, hand sew onto seam allowances, onto right placket facing, onto placket underlap (ill. 7).

Fold belt carriers in half lengthwise, **right** sides together. Stitch open long edge of each. rim seam allowances. Turn carriers **right** side out. press, edgestitch both long edges of ach. Overcast carrier ends. From the **right** side of pants topstitch along upper edge as narked, securing waist facing. Sew carriers into place in front over centermost pleats, in ack over darts and center back seam (ill. 8).

● Work buttonholes into right placket edge where marked. Sew buttons onto underlap.
● Press hem allowances to the **inside**, blindstitch into place.

Allowances
Seams 2 cm (⁷/₈"); hem 4 cm (1⁵/₈"); all other edges 1 cm (¹/₂").

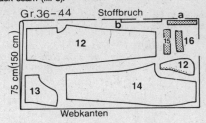

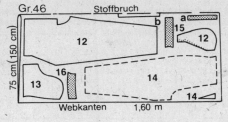

Cutting layouts

---

2 wrap blouses on page 71

Style
25

Sizes 36/38 sheet A, green outline 〜〜〜〜〜 pieces 60 to 62
Sizes 40/42 sheet B, green outline ⟶ ⟶ ⟶ pieces 60 to 62
Sizes 44/46 sheet C, green outline ─···─ ···─ pieces 60 to 62

Pattern overview

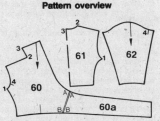

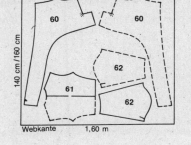

Allowances:
1.5 cm (⁵/₈") on all seams and edges.

Cutting layout for all sizes

ape pattern pieces 60 and 60a together at the attachment lines, matching the letters A as well as B.

abric requirements:
Make up these garments in jersey only!
ed wrap blouse:
60 cm (63") wide viscose rayon jersey:
ll sizes: 1.60 m (1³/₄ yds)
ilver wrap blouse:
40 cm (55") wide lamé jersey:
ll sizes: 1.60 m (1³/₄ yds)
mportant: Press lamé jersey on the **wrong side only** under a press cloth!
Construction tips for knits are located on pages 120 and 121.

Notions/Haberdashery:
eam tape or stretched bias tape for shoulder seams; raglan shoulder pads; fusible nterfacing remnants for reinforcing collar corners.

Before cutting out:
Pay careful attention to the "knit direction" lines and arrows when pinning pattern pieces onto fabric. These must run exactly parallel to the selvages.

Cutting out:
0 Front/tie band (cut twice)
1 Back (cut once on the fold)
2 Sleeve (cut twice)
Please note:
ron small squares of fusible interfacing onto the **wrong** side of fronts over corners at the ase of extended collar (see shaded areas on pattern pieces on layout).

Construction:
See Illustrated Teaching Instructions on page 70, ills. 1 - 4.
● Stitch shoulder seams from armhole in to corner at base of collar. Clip front shoulder allowance in close to last stitch at corner (ill. 1).
● Stitch front pieces **right** sides together at center seam in extended collar. Press seam llowances to one side. Trim underlying allowance back to ¹/₂ cm (¹/₄") width. Turn under vider (upper) allowance layer, baste into place over trimmed layer. From the **right** side dgestitch and topstitch ³/₄ cm (³/₈") along center seam in collar, securing the allowances. Stitch extended collar to back neck edge from corner to corner, **right** sides together, beginning and ending exactly in last stitch of each shoulder seam. Press seam allowances nto collar. Trim, baste and topstitch allowances ³/₄ cm (³/₈") into place in the same manner as for center seam in collar (ill. 2).
● Stitch side seams. Overcast the allowance on collar, closing, tie-band and hem edges f blouse, baste to the **inside** (mitering at corners), topstitch 1 cm (¹/₂") into place (ill. 3).
● Stitch underarm seams in sleeves. Press sleeve hem allowances to the **inside**, topstitch cm (⁷/₈") into place with twin ballpoint needles, stitching from the **right** sleeve side. Pin, aste and stitch sleeves to armholes, **right** sides together, matching seam numbers as well s marked seamlines. Underarm and side seams should match as well. Press seam llowances into blouse, edgestitch into place (ill. 4).
● Try on blouse. Pin raglan shoulder pads into place, adjusting their position to best suit our figure and the blouse. Then hand sew pads to shoulder seam allowances.

Which interfacing for which fabric?

FABRIC WEIGHT	SUGGESTED FABRICS	RECOMMENDED VILENE INTERFACING	DESCRIPTION
Very light weight fabrics	Silks, viscose blends, polyesters, extra fine cottons, challis, georgette, sheer fabris	Optima silkysoft 327 – Fusible – White	Has no grainline Non stretch Luxury Soft Handle Washable & Dry Cleanable
Delicate Fabrics	Voile, chiffon, crepe de chine, georgette, lawn, silk, cotton, polycotton, polyester	Ultrasoft 308 – Fusible – White	Has no grainline, soft to touch, gentle yet stable control, washable, dry cleanable.
Soft, Delicate or Light weight	Voile, Chiffon, Crepe de chine, georgette, silk, lawn, knits, jersey, polyester	Light Sew-in 310 – White	Has grainline – Lengthwise stability, Crosswise stretch
		311 – Charcoal	No grainline 300 White, 310 Charcoal 310 White, 311 Charcoal Washable, dry cleanable
Light to medium	Challis, jersey, double knits, poplin, wool, wool blends, linen, corduroy, velvet	Ultrasoft – Medium 315 – Fusible – White or Medium Sew-in 312 – White	Has grainline – Lengthwise stability and crosswise. No grainline Washable and Dry cleanable
Medium to Heavy	Gaberdine, tweeds, double knits, suit and coat weight, wools and woollen mixtures	Ultrasoft – Medium 315 – Fusible – White Ultrasoft – Heavy 316 – Fusible – White or Heavy Sew-in.	Has grainline – Lengthwise stability and crosswise. No grainline – Washable and Dry cleanable.
Light to Medium	Cotton and cotton blend fabrics	Medium Iron-on 304 – White	No grainline – light, crisp, handle, washable only
Medium to Heavy	Cotton and cotton blend fabrics	Firm Iron-on 305 – White	No grainline – Firm, crisp, handle, Washable only

168 C

Style 26

6 shirts from one pattern on pages 72 and 73

Size 36/38 sheet D, green outline —····—···· pieces 60 to 62
Size 40/42 sheet E, green outline —o—o—o pieces 60 to 62
Size 44/46 sheet F, green outline —x—x—x pieces 60 to 62

Cutting layout for all sizes

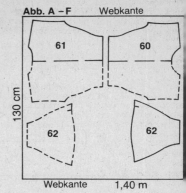

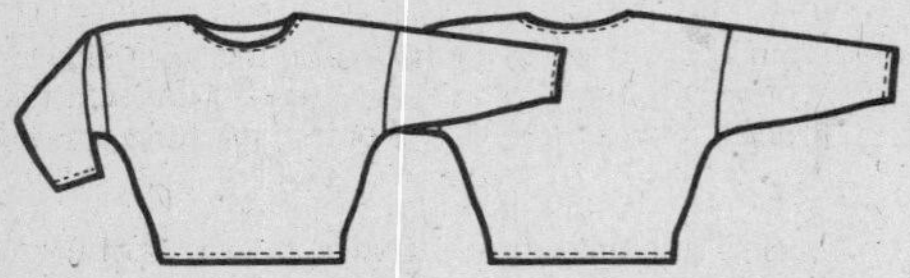

Abb. A – F   Webkante

130 cm

61   60
62   62

Webkante   1,40 m

Pattern overview

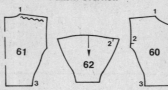

61   62   60

View B
The snake motif is printed in red on pattern sheet E.
View C
The palm motif is printed in green on pattern sheet E.

Fabric requirements:
All views:
130 cm (51") wide cotton jersey:
All sizes: 1.40 m (1⅝ yds)

Notions/Haberdashery:
View A: 1 appliqué motif (cloud).
View B: permanent textile paints, one bottle each of metallic pearl white, metallic green, metallic copper and gold; 2 sew on rhinestones for the snake's eyes; fusible interfacing; burda's blue transfer pencil; wax paper.
View C: textile felt pens in brown, light green and dark green; 15 wooden beads; fusible interfacing; burda's blue transfer pencil; wax paper.
View D: sheet of iron-on metallic dots, 10x20 cm (4" x 8").
View E: 1 sequinned appliqué motif.
View F: 12 sew-on rhinestones.

Cutting out:
All views
60 Front (cut once on the fold)
61 Back (cut once on the fold)
62 Sleeve (cut twice)
Please note:
View B
You can mix textile paints as desired. To paint the snake as illustrated we mixed metallic green with gold and metallic copper with metallic pearl white. Mix a quarter bottle of each color together with a ratio of 1 to 1.
Views B & C
Paint motifs onto front before closing side seams. Stitch left shoulder seam of View B beforehand, being as the snake motif extends over this shoulder onto the back.
To facilitate application of textile paints, iron fusible interfacing onto the **wrong** side of fabric (with steam!) first. Remove after the paints have thoroughly dried. Then press the motif from the **wrong** side, making it permanent.
Important:
Please follow the instructions for textile paints carefully.

Construction:
See Illustrated Teaching Instructions on page 73, ills. 1 - 7.
All views
● Turn in allowance on front and back neck edges twice, baste into place. From the **right** side of shirt topstitch ¾ cm (⅜") along neck edges with twin ballpoint needles, securing allowances.
View B
● Stitch left shoulder seam, press open the allowances. Trace snake motif onto wax paper with burda's transfer pencil. Iron interfacing onto the **wrong** side of t-shirt (with steam!) over the area where motif will be painted (ill. 3). Pin wax paper, motif side down, onto the **right** side of shirt. Press paper, transferring motif onto shirt (ill. 4). Paint motif (ill. 5). Allow to dry thoroughly. Re-heat and peel off interfacing. Press motif from the **wrong** side. Hand sew rhinestone eyes into place (ill. 6).
View C
● Transfer palm motif onto front as explained for View B and color with textile felt pens (ill. 7).
All views
● Stitch shoulder seams, press open the allowances, hand sew into place at neck edge.
● Stitch sleeves to armholes, **right** sides together, matching seam numbers exactly. Press seam allowances into shirt, edgestitch into place.
● Stitch side seams and underarm seams in sleeves, matching ends of sleeve attachment seams as well as marked seamlines. Fold hem and sleeve hem allowances 1 cm (½") and then 2 cm (⅞") to the **inside**, baste into place, press. From the **right** side of shirt topstitch 18 mm (¾") along hem and lower sleeve edges with twin ballpoint needles, securing allowances.
Views A & E
● Pin appliqué motif onto shirt and hand sew into place with tiny back stitches taken along outer edge of motif.
View D
● Cut sheet with metallic dots into strips and arrange as shown in the illustration on page 72. Iron into place (ill. 1 on page 73). Peel away paper (ill. 2).
View F
● Hand sew rhinestones onto front as shown in the illustration on page 72.

Allowances:
Neck edge and all seams 1.5 cm (⅝"); hem and sleeve hems 3 cm (1¼").

Style 27

Jacket and coat from one pattern on pages 74 and 75

Size 36/38 sheet F, red outline —····—···· pieces 43 to 46
Size 40/42 sheet E, red outline ·············· pieces 43 to 46
Size 44   sheet F, red outline ∿∿∿∿ pieces 39 to 42
Size 46   sheet E, red outline ∿∿∿∿ pieces 39 to 42

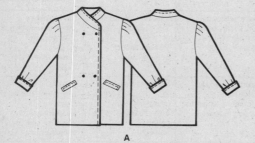

A

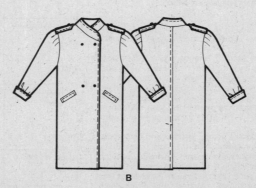

B

Total back length:
View A
Size 36/38: 88 cm (34¾")
Size 40/42: 89 cm (35")
Size 44: 89.5 cm (35¼")
Size 46: 90 cm (35½")

View B
Size 36/38: 120 cm (47¼")
Size 40/42: 121 cm (47¾")
Size 44: 121.5 cm (47⅞")
Size 46: 122 cm (48⅛")

Fabric requirements:
View A Jacket:
150 cm (59") wide plaid wool fleece coating
All sizes: 2.95 m (3⅜ yds)
140 cm (55) wide lining:
Sizes 36 to 42: 1.80 m (2 yds)
Sizes 44 and 46: 1.90 m (2⅛ yds)
View B Coat:
150 cm (59") wide wool velour:
Sizes 36 to 44: 3.10 m (3½ yds)
Size 46: 3.25 m (3⅝ yds)
140 cm (55") wide striped lining:
All sizes: 1.95 m (2¼ yds)

Notions/Haberdashery:

Views A & B

Fusible interfacing; 4 large buttons; 1 small, flat button for inside; shoulder pads.

View B

Lining remnants for pocket pouches; 2 small buttons for epaulettes.

Please note:

Views A & B

Pay careful attention to the lines and markings for the different views when tracing off pattern pieces. These are designated on pattern sheet with the view letter.

Extend pattern piece 43 to full length by adding the amount printed at arrowheads. Make sure you have enough tissue paper to trace off the entire piece to avoid having to tape sections together later on. Connect the ends of these extension lines with a straight line to make hemline that should measure as follows (make sure this is right!):

Hem width of front pattern piece:

Size 36/38 = 53.5 cm (21⅛")
Size 40/42 = 55.5 cm (21⅞")
Size 44 = 56.5 cm (22¼")
Size 46 = 57.5 cm (22¾")

Before cutting out:

Views A & B

Tape sections for front, back and sleeve pattern pieces together at the attachment lines, matching letters A as well as B. Trace off pocket pouch and welt printed on front pattern piece as separate pattern pieces. On the layout these pieces will be designated with the same number as the front.

Important: wool fleece coating and wool velour are cut out "with the nap," i.e. the pile lies flat when you stroke from the upper to the lower edge of the garment. Pin pattern pieces onto fabric as shown on layouts so that they lie in the same direction EXCEPT for sleeve and collar pieces of **View A**, which are cut on the bias. Pay careful attention to the nap direction arrows printed on pattern pieces when pinning them onto fabric.

View A

Fold fabric in half lengthwise, **right** sides together, matching the plaid exactly. Pin layers together at intervals to prevent plaid from slipping out of line. Then pin front pattern piece onto fabric and cut out. Open out remaining fabric flat, **right** side up. Pin the remaining pattern pieces onto fabric as shown on layout and cut out with the required allowances. In these already cut out pieces onto fabric, **right** sides together and matching plaid exactly, and cut out a second time. Cut out pocket welts so that the plaid matches that at pocket opening lines on front. Cut out one half of back and each collar layer, then fold fabric **right** sides together at center fold edge of pattern piece and cut out the second half.

Pay careful attention to the differing lines for right and left edges of back vent.

Cutting out:

Sizes 36 to 42:

* Front (cut twice) **A B** *
* Pocket welt (cut twice on the fold) **A B**
* Pocket pouch (cut twice) **A B** *
* Back (cut once on the fold) **A** *
* Back (cut twice) **B** *
* Collar (cut twice on the fold) **A B**
* Sleeve (cut twice) **A B** *

Sizes 44 and 46:

* Front (cut twice) **A B** *
* Pocket welt (cut twice on the fold) **A B**
* Pocket pouch (cut twice) **A B** *
* Back (cut once on the fold) **A** *
* Back (cut twice) **B** *
* Collar (cut twice on the fold) **A B**
* Sleeve (cut twice) **A B** *

Allowances:

Seams 2 cm (⅞"); hem 4 cm (1⅝"); remaining edges 1 cm (½").

Cutting layouts for all sizes

Pattern pieces numbers in parentheses pertain to sizes 44 and 46.

Views A & B

* = Cut out these pieces from lining as well. Fold front pattern piece along the line marked "extended facing" so that facing lies on the printed side of pattern piece. Trace a line along facing edge. Cut out lining fronts over to this line, i.e. minus facing width, plus 1 cm (½") allowance on this edge. Fold vent facings on back pattern piece along center back line. Cut out back lining twice, i.e. with center seam.

Extra pieces:

View B

There is no pattern piece for epaulette. This piece is drawn with tailor's chalk directly onto the fabric in the dimensions stated below and is designated on layout with the small letter **a**.

a) 4 strips on the grain for epaulettes, each 4.5 cm (1⅞") wide and 16 cm (6½") long.

Please note:

To prevent the edges of interfacing from forming unsightly ridges on the right side of fabric, iron on interfacing with a pad of velvet, terry cloth or terry velour, pile side, underneath fabric (see page 76, ill. 1). Iron strips of interfacing onto the **wrong** side of shaded areas and pieces on layout:

Views A & B

Onto the **wrong** side of front over to facing line, onto neck and armhole edges of back, onto sleeve facings, both collar layers and one half of each pocket welt.

View B

Onto the **wrong** side of 2 epaulette pieces.

Important: allow interfaced pieces to cool for at least 30 minutes before handling. Then pin pattern pieces back onto fronts and collar layers and trace seamlines and markings onto interfacing.

Construction:

See Illustrated Teaching Instructions on pages 76 and 77, ills. 1 - 23.

Views A & B

● **Welt pockets:** fold welts along their foldline, **right** sides together. Stitch both ends of each. Turn welts **right** side out, baste, press and topstitch 1 cm (½") along their seamed and fold edges. Stitch welts interfaced layer down onto the **right** side of fronts along their attachment line. Stitch lining pouch pieces into place over welts, stitching in welt attachment stitching. Stitch fabric pouch pieces onto fronts above welts, **right** sides together, so that their straight edge just touches welt. Upper stitching lines should be ½ cm (¼") shorter at both ends than lower ones (ill. 2). Slash fronts between these stitching lines, taking care NOT to cut pocket pieces. Clip diagonally to each last stitch, forming small triangles at opening ends. Pull pouch pieces through openings to the **inside** (ill. 3). Fold opening end triangles to the **inside**. Working with front on top and folded back as shown in ill. 4, stitch pouch pieces together. Begin and end directly above opening end triangles and stitch across the base of each. Hand sew welt ends onto fronts (ill. 5).

● **Sizes 44+46:** stitch bust darts. Trim dart allowances back to 1 cm (½") width, press open (see style 20, page 62, ill. 1).

● **All sizes:**
stitch shoulder and side seams, press open allowances.

Pattern overviews

Sizes 36/38 and 40/42

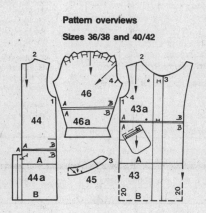

Sizes 44 and 46

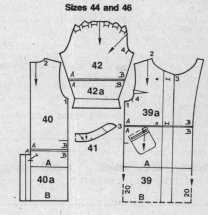

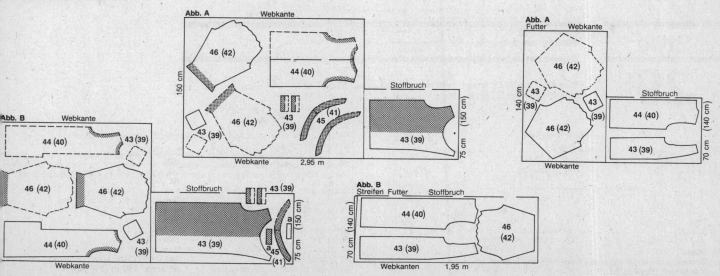

View A
- Press hem allowance to the **inside**, blindstitch into place.

View B
- Stitch center back seam down to vent mark. Topstitch seam as shown in ill. 6.
- Press hem allowance to the **inside**, blindstitch into place.
- Vent: fold vent facings to the **inside**. Topstitch left vent edge 1 cm (1/2"). From the **right** side topstitch left back along slanted line at upper end of vent, securing vent facing and underlap (ill. 7). Hand sew vent facings onto hem allowance (ill. 8).

Views A & B
- Construct collar (ill. 9). Stitch one collar layer to neck edge (ill. 10). Stitch other collar layer to neck edge of extended facings (ill. 11). Turn facings to the **inside**. Secure inner collar layer, open edged, across back neck with back stitches taken from the **right** side of coat resp. jacket exactly through collar attachment seam (ill. 12).
- Baste closing edges. Hand sew facing ends onto shoulder seam allowances (ill. 13). Topstitch 1 cm (1/2") along closing and outer collar edges. Hand sew facings onto hem allowance (ill. 14).
- Fold pleats into sleeve caps and baste (ill. 15). Stitch underarm seams in sleeves (ill. 16). Fold sleeve facings to the **inside**, press, blindstitch into place.

View B
- Epaulettes: for each epaulette stitch an interfaced to a non-interfaced piece **right** sides together along one end and both long edges. Stitch end to a point. Leave other end open for turning. Turn epaulettes **right** side out. Baste, press and topstitch 1 cm (1/2") along their seamed edges (ill. 17). Baste epaulettes onto the **right** side of coat, centered over shoulder seams, so that open end of each lies on armhole allowance.

Views A & B
- Set in sleeves (ill. 18).

- Try on coat resp. jacket. Pin shoulder pads into place, adjusting their position to best suit your figure and the garment. Then hand sew pads to sleeve attachment and should seam allowances.

- **Lining:** stitch all seams, taking into consideration that front shoulder edges will narrower that back ones. Fold pleats into caps of lining sleeves, set in sleeves. Pin linir into coat resp. jacket, **wrong** sides together. Hand sew lining to armhole allowances 20).

- **Hanger loop:** cut a 10 cm (4") long and 2 cm (7/8") wide bias strip from lining. Fold st in half lengthwise, **right** sides together. Stitch 3/4 cm (3/8") from its fold. Turn strip si out and press, stretching as much as possible. Hand sew strip onto inner collar layer center back so that its ends lie on collar allowance.
- Hand sew lining onto inner collar layer along attachment seam and onto facings dow to 5 cm (2") from hem edge (ill. 21).

View B
- Attach lining at back vent as explained in text and ill. 22.

Views A & B
- Turn up lower lining edge 1 cm (1/2"). Slip this edge upward and slipstitch onto upp edge of hem allowance (ill. 23). Turn up lower edge of sleeve lining, hand sew lining on sleeve facing.
- Work buttonholes into right closing edge as marked. Work one into left front uppermost marking as well. Sew buttons onto both fronts where marked, sewing a sma flat button onto the **inside** of RIGHT front underneath upper button to secure underla

View B
- Sew buttons onto epaulettes, 2.5 cm (1") from pointed end, securing them to should seams.

Style
28

Fur hat on page 78

Size 54 sheet C, green outline ●━━━━━● piece 84
Size 56 sheet C, green outline ∿∿∿∿∿ piece 85

Pattern overviews

84

Size 54 (head circumf. 54 cm = 21 1/4")

85

Size 56 (head circumf. 56 cm = 22 1/4")

Cutting layout for both size

1 mal

84 (85)

84 (85)

ca. 40 x 55 cr
ca. 3 qfs.

Fur requirements:
1 rabbit skin, approx. 40 x 55 cm (16" x 22") = approx. 3 sq. ft.
Fur and leather skins are sold by the square foot (30x30 cm/12"x12"). Being as the skins differ greatly in size, we state the number of skins that are required in a minimum size. This may not always correspond to the square footage figured by the merchant, for he calculates excess length of the skins as well.
Therefore, ALWAYS take along all pattern pieces required for the garment planned when purchasing fur or leather.

Notions/Haberdashery:
Fusible interfacing for support lining.

Please note
Carefully study our instructions for cutting out and sewing leather resp. fur on pages 78 and 124.

Important: interfacing is NOT applied to the leather side of fur. Rather, it is used to construct support lining that is sewn into the fur hat. Cut out interfacing from hat pattern piece down to foldline only. Before cutting out place 2 layers of interfacing COATED SIDES TOGETHER and press. Cut out support lining from these doubled layers.

Cutting out:
Size 54:
84 Hat piece (cut twice from fur)
84 Hat piece (cut once on the fold from interfacing for support lining)
Size 56:
85 Hat piece (cut twice from fur)
85 Hat piece (cut once on the fold from interfacing for support lining)

Construction:
See Illustrated Teaching Instructions on page 79, ills. 1 - 4, right.
- Support lining: stitch the darts between center front and center back first. Press op seam allowances. Then stitch center back seam and center front dart. All dart points me at center of hat. Press open seam allowances.
- Fur hat: stitch darts as in ill. 1. Stitch hat sections together as in ill. 2.
- Slip support lining over hat, **wrong** sides together, matching seams. Attach lower edg of lining with herringbone stitch to leather side of hat along marked foldline (ill. 3).
- Fold open edge of hat to the **inside** along foldline, hand sew onto support lining (ill. 4)

Allowances:
1/2 cm (1/4") on dart edges and center back edges of support lining, NO allowance on i lower edge.
NO allowance on fur pieces.

Style
29

Gloves on page 78

Size 6 sheet C, green outline ━━━━━ pieces 78 to 80
Size 6 1/2 sheet C, green outline ━━━・━━━ pieces 81 to 83

Pattern overviews

Size 6

79   78   80

Size 6 1/2

82   81   83

Fur requirements:
Rabbit fur: for both sizes 2 skins, ea. approx. 35 x 50 cm (14" x 20") = 5 sq. ft.

Before cutting out:
Cut out all pieces so that the hairs of the fur lie in the same direction, i.e. the directio indicated on pattern pieces. Make sure you cut out pieces once printed side up and onc printed side down to assure you come out with a righthand and a lefthand glove.

Cutting out:
Size 6:
78 Glove piece (cut twice)
79 Thumb (cut twice)
80 Finger gusset (cut 6 pair per glove)
Size 6 1/2:
81 Glove piece (cut twice)
82 Thumb (cut twice)
83 Finger gusset (6 pair per glove)

Important:
Before tracing off pattern pieces please read the information on page 78 pertaining to glove sizes and handling fur.

Construction:
See Illustrated Teaching Instructions on page 79, ills. 1 - 8.
● Tip: mark seam numbers onto all pieces with tiny stickers (ill. 1).
● Sew pintuck on back of each glove first. Then gather curved sections of wrist edge (ill. 2). Turn edge to the leather (right) side, sew into place (ill. 3).
● Sew finger gussets together in pairs at lower edge. Sew thumb **wrong** sides together from tip down to fitting number, sewing from the leather side (ill. 4).
● Attach thumb, making sure that you neither stretch nor ease in thumb at the curve between seam numbers 3 and 4 (ill. 5).
● Beginning between middle and index fingers and working from base to fingertip, sew finger gusset to edges of index finger (ill. 6).
● Trim upper end of gusset to match curve of fingertip. Then sew gusset to fingertip edge (ill. 7).
● Sew remaining finger gussets into place in the same manner.
● Lastly, sew side seam from the tip of little finger down to outer cuff edge (ill. 8). Tie off these threads securely, for this is a stress point when gloves are pulled on and off.

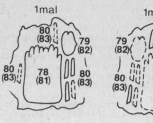
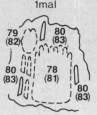

Cutting layouts for both sizes
The numbers in parentheses pertain to size 6½.

je ca. 35 x 50 cm = 2½ qfs.

Style
30

Men's leather shirt on page 81

Size 44/46 sheet D, green outline ················· pieces 76 to 85
Size 48/50 sheet E, green outline —— —— —— pieces 76 to 85
Size 52/54 sheet F, green outline ·—·—·—·—· pieces 76 to 85

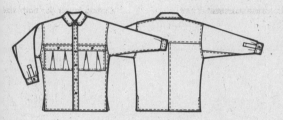

Pattern overviews

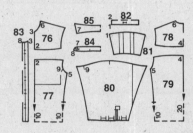

Total back length:
Size 44/46: 80 cm (31½")
Size 48/50: 82 cm (32½")
Size 52/54: 84 cm (33")

Please note:
Extend pattern pieces for front and back to full length by adding the amount printed at arrowheads. Make sure you have enough tissue paper to trace off the entire pattern piece to avoid having to tape pieces together later on. Connect ends of these extension lines with a straight line to make hemlines that should measure as follows (make sure these are right!):
Hem width of front pattern piece:
Size 44/46: 23 cm (9")
Size 48/50: 25 cm (10")
Size 52/54: 27 cm (10¾")
Hem width of back pattern piece:
Size 44/46: 25 cm (10")
Size 48/50: 27 cm (10¾")
Size 52/54: 29 cm (11½")

Leather requirements:
Suede:
Sizes 44 to 50: 40 sq. ft., i.e.
5 skins, ea. approx. 60x90 cm (24"x36") = 6 sq.ft.
2 skins, ea. approx. 50x85 cm (20"x33") = 5.5 sq.ft.
Size 52/54: 41.5 sq.ft., i.e.
4 skins, ea. approx. 60x90 cm (24"x36") = 6 sq.ft.
2 skins, ea. approx. 55x90 cm (22"x36") = 5.5 sq. ft.
1 skin approx. 65x90 cm (26"x36") = 6.5 sq.ft.
Tip: take along all pattern pieces for the garment planned when shopping for leather. Please study our instructions for handling leather on page 124.
Should you choose to make up this shirt in **synthetic suede** you will need: 140 cm (55") wide synthetic suede:
Size 44/46: 2.00 m (2¼ yds)
Sizes 48 to 54: 2.10 m (2⅜ yds)

Notions/Haberdashery:
10 buttons; leather needle.
Before cutting out:
Cut apart pattern pieces for sleeve (piece 80) and pocket (piece 81) along the marked seamlines. On the layouts these sections are designated with the number of the main pattern piece. **Important:** to make sure that you cut out righthand and lefthand pieces, tape pattern pieces once printed side up and once printed side down onto the **wrong** side of leather and cut out. Mark seamlines and markings onto leather with ballpoint pen.
Tip: before cutting out your leather garment, make it up in muslin or a cheap fabric first and then try on for fitting. Transfer any alterations from fitting garment to pattern pieces, then cut out leather.

Cutting out:
76 Front yoke (cut twice)
77 Front (cut twice)
78 Back yoke (cut once on fold)
79 Back (cut twice)
80 Sleeve sections (cut twice each)
81 Pocket sections (cut twice each)
82 Pocket band (cut twice on fold)
83 Front closing band (cut twice on fold)
84 Collar stand (cut twice on fold)
85 Collar (cut twice on fold)
Extra pieces:
a) 2 underlap strips for sleeve plackets, each 10 cm (4") long and 1 cm (½") wide.
b) 2 bands for sleeve plackets, each 12 cm (4¾") long and 5 cm (2") wide. Finished width 2.5 cm (1").
c) 2 cuffs, each 10 cm (4") wide, finished width 5 cm (2"), and for
Size 44/46 ea. 26 cm (10¼") long
Size 48/50 ea. 27 cm (10⅝") long
Size 52/54 ea. 28 cm (11") long

Construction:
See Illustrated Teaching Instructions on page 80, ills. 1 - 12.
● Stitch center back seam. Press seam allowances to one side, edgestitch and topstitch ¾ cm (⅜") into place.
● Stitch front yokes to upper edge of fronts, back yoke to upper edge of back, **right** sides together. Press seam allowances into yokes, edgestitch and topstitch ¾ cm (⅜") into place.
● Stitch shoulder seams. Press seam allowances into back, edgestitch and topstitch ¾ cm (⅜") into place.
● Stitch sections for each sleeve **right** sides together. Press seam allowances into smaller sections, edgestitch and topstitch ¾ cm (⅜") into place.
● Sleeve plackets: fold placket bands in half lengthwise, **right** sides together. Stitch one end and open long edges of each closed for 2 cm (⅞"). Clip seam allowances in close to last stitch on long edge. Trim allowances at corners diagonally. Turn bands **right** side out. Stitch the **right** side of one band layer to the **wrong** side of sleeve along attachment line. Cut sleeve along placket line, clip diagonally to last stitch for band. Place underlap strips under other placket edges (without band), edgestitch and topstitch ¾ cm (⅜") into place. Turn placket bands to the **outside**. Press seam allowances into bands. Turn under open edge of each band, edgestitch into place over band attachment seam. Continue and edgestitch upper end of band onto sleeve above upper end of placket, catching in end of placket underlap.

168 G

● Stitch sleeves to armholes, **right** sides together, matching seam numbers exactly. Press seam allowances into shirt, edgestitch and topstitch ³/₄ cm (³/₈") into place (ill. 1).
● Stitch sections for each pocket **right** sides together. Edgestitch seams (ill. 2). Fold pleats into pockets, x-onto-o. Stitch bands to upper pocket edges, **right** sides together. Press seam allowances into bands. Fold bands along foldline to the **inside** (ill. 3). Edgestitch and topstitch bands ³/₄ cm (³/₈") along fold edge and attachment seam, securing inner layer. Trim allowance on inner layer back to topstitching. Work buttonholes into bands where marked. Press allowance on side and lower pocket edges to the **inside**. Tape pockets onto fronts where marked (ill. 4), edgestitch and topstitch ³/₄ cm (³/₈") into place.
● Stitch closing bands to front closing edges, **right** sides together. Turn up hem allowance, edgestitch and topstitch ³/₄ cm (³/₈") into place (ill. 5). Fold closing bands to the **inside** along their foldline. Edgestitch and topstitch ³/₄ cm (³/₈") along both long edges of each band, securing inner layer (ill. 6).
● Stitch side seams and underarm seams in sleeves, matching ends of sleeve attachment seams and stitching side seams down to slit marks only. Clip side seam allowance on back as in ill. 7. Topstitch along these seams as in text and ill. 8, stitching slit allowances into place.
● Construct collar (ill. 9). Turn collar **right** side out, press. Edgestitch and topstitch ³/₄ cm

(³/₈") along its seamed edges. Attach stand to collar. Stitch one stand layer to neck edge as in ill. 10. Press seam allowances into stand. Pin inner stand layer into place over attachment seam. Edgestitch along all stand edges, securing inner layer (ill. 11).
● Fold cuffs in half lengthwise, **right** sides together. Stitch both ends of each. Turn cuffs **right** side out, press. Fold tucks into lower sleeve edges, x-onto-o, and pin. Stitch one cuff layer to lower edge of each sleeve, **right** sides together. Press seam allowances on cuffs. Pin inner layer of each cuff, open edged, into place over attachment seam. From the **right** side of sleeve edgestitch and topstitch ³/₄ cm (³/₈") along all cuff edges, securing inner layer of each.
● Work buttonholes into left closing band where marked (ill. 12), into cuffs 1 cm (¹/₂") from the end at placket band.
● Sew buttons onto right closing band along center front line and onto right end of collar stand, onto cuffs 1 cm (¹/₂") from ends at placket underlap.

Allowances:
Seams and hem 1.5 cm (⁵/₈"); all other edges 1 cm (¹/₂").

Cutting layouts for all sizes

The skin dimensions and square feet in parentheses are those for size 52/54.

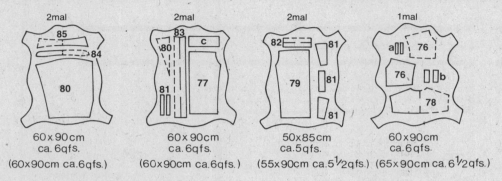

2mal
85
84
80
60 x 90 cm
ca. 6 qfs.
(60 x 90 cm ca. 6 qfs.)

2mal
83
80
c
81
77
60 x 90 cm
ca. 6 qfs.
(60 x 90 cm ca. 6 qfs.)

2mal
82
81
79
81
81
50 x 85 cm
ca. 5 qfs.
(55 x 90 cm ca. 5¹/₂ qfs.)

1mal
a
76
76
b
78
60 x 90 cm
ca. 6 qfs.
(65 x 90 cm ca. 6¹/₂ qfs.)

Neck roll pillow on page 136

Length: 1.10 m (43¹/₂"), diameter: 15 cm (6")

Fabric requirements:
140 cm (55") wide quilted fabric (the same used for bedspread on page 138): 0.55 m (³/₄ yd)

Notions/Haberdashery:
1 cylindrical foam rubber pillow form, 1.10 m (43¹/₂") long, or 3 cylindrical foam rubber pillow forms, ea. 50 cm (20") long, and 15 cm (6") in diameter; 60 cm (24") zipper; special polyester glue for foam rubber if needed.
Please note:
We have made this roll neck pillow to match the width of the bedspread on page 138. You can of course lengthen or shorten the pillow to match the width of your bed, but remember to figure more or less fabric!
Tip: If a foam rubber form is not available in this length, then combine 3 shorter ones as we have done. Cut a 10 cm (4") section off one form and glue it between the other two longer ones with special polyester glue. Or, have an upholsterer glue the sections together.

Cutting out:
1 rectangle, 110 cm (43¹/₂") wide and 50 cm (20") long
2 circles, each 15 cm (6") in diameter

Important: Don't forget to add 1.5 cm (⁵/₈") seam allowance onto outer edges of all pieces.

Construction:
Fold rectangle in half lengthwise, **right** sides together. Stitch long edges together, leaving 60 cm (24") open in center for zipper placket. Press open seam allowances. Baste zipper under placket edges so that its teeth are covered (centered application). Open zipper. Stitch zipper into place from the **right** side using a zipper presser foot. Stitch circles to rectangle ends, **right** sides together. Overcast seam allowances together. Turn pillow cover **right** side out. Insert foam rubber form into cover through open zipper.

Stockists

Ackermann-Göggingen AG, Postfach 22 11 22, D-8900 Augsburg 22; **Amann + Söhne GmbH & Co.**, Postfach 9, D-7124 Bönnigheim; **Bernina Nähmaschinen GmbH**, Oberna B.V., Industrieweg 8, NL-6871 KA Renkum; **Deka Textilfarben GmbH**, Kapellenstr. 18, D-8025 Unterhaching; **Fillawant**, Société des textiles en biais, 45a Avenue Général de Gaulle, F-68302 Saint Louis; **Gold-Zack Werke AG**, Postfach 10 01 10, D-4020 Mettmann; **Gütermann**, Gütermanns naaigaren N.V., Postbus 169, NL-Soest; **Husqvarna Nederland B. V.**, Postbus 188, NL-1110 BD Diemen; **Matamin**, Mattes & Ammann, Brühlstraße 8, D-7475 Meßstetten 7; **MEZ-Anchor-Coats**, Carp-Prym B.V., Postbus 11, NL-5700 AA Helmond; Filature et Filteries Reunies N.V., Dendermondsesteenweg 75, B-9300 Aalst; **Opti Werk GmbH +Co. KG**, Postfach 10 28 63, D-4300 Essen 1; **Pfaff**, Pfaff Benelux B. V.,

Postbus 10 24, NL-1000 BH Amsterdam; Pfaff Benelux B.V., Blokhuisstr. 47, Industriepark Noord, B-2800 Mechelen; **Prym**, Carp-Prym B. V., Postbus 11, NL-5700 AA Helmond; Simex N. V., Wazenaarstr. 14-16, B-9218 Ledeberg; **Ringelspitz**, Barthels-Feldhoff GmbH & Co., Postfach 20 01 38, D-5600 Wuppertal 2; **Frau Riether**, Postfach 60, D-7609 Hohberg; **Schnell & Vittali GmbH**, Flachglasveredelungswerk, Englerstr. 10, D-7600 Offenburg; **SDC-Singer**, EHP Sales and Marketing B.V., Postbus 1 20 40, NL-1100 AA Amsterdam; **Spitzen & Modewaren Cremer KG**, Postfach 52 04 09, D-5000 Keulen 51; **Vlieseline Freudenberg**, Ant. Schröder B.V., Postbus 8029, NL-1005 AA Amsterdam; N. V. Decon Voskenslaan 147, B-9000 Gent; **Waso-Hobby**, Eschbach 10-11, D-5650 Solingen 19; **Wiss, The Cooper Croup**, Deutschland GmbH, Postfach 13 51 D-7122 Besigheim